Fat King, Lean Beggar

ALSO BY WILLIAM C. CARROLL

The Great Feast of Language in "Love's Labour's Lost"

The Metamorphoses of Shakespearean Comedy

Fat King, Lean Beggar

Representations of Poverty in the Age of Shakespeare

WILLIAM C. CARROLL

Cornell University Press

ITHACA AND LONDON

First published 1996 by Cornell University Press.

Printed in the United States of America

⊚ The paper in this book meets the minimum requirements of the American National Standard for Information Sciences— Permanence of Paper for Printed Library Materials, ANSI Z39.48-1984.

Library of Congress Cataloging-in-Publication Data

Carroll, William C., 1945–
Fat king, lean beggar : representations of poverty in the age of Shakespeare / William C. Carroll.
p. cm.
Includes bibliographical references and index.
ISBN 0-8014-3185-9 (cloth)
1. Shakespeare, William, 1564–1616—Political and social views.
2. Literature and society—England—History—16th century.
3. Literature and society—England—History—17th century.
4. Poverty in literature. 5. Beggars in literature. 6. Poor in literature. I. Title.
PR3069.P67C37 1996
822.3'3—dc20   95-37296

For Carol and David

CONTENTS

ILLUSTRATIONS

ACKNOWLEDGMENTS

PART of chapter 1 first appeared in a review essay, "The Crisis of the Sign: Vagrancy and Authority in the English Renaissance," *Semiotica* (1995). A section of chapter 4 appeared in "Language, Politics, and Poverty in Shakespearian Drama," *Shakespeare Survey* 44 (1992); reprinted with the permission of Cambridge University Press. Another section of chapter 4 was published in " 'The Nursery of Beggary': Enclosure, Vagrancy, and Sedition in the Tudor-Stuart Period," in *Enclosure Acts: Sexuality, Property, and Culture in Early Modern England,* ed. Richard Burt and John Michael Archer, copyright © 1994 by Cornell University, used by permission of the publisher, Cornell University Press. Part of chapter 6 appeared in " 'The Base Shall Top th'Legitimate': The Bedlam Beggar and the Role of Edgar in *King Lear,*" *Shakespeare Quarterly* 38 (1987). Part of chapter 7 appeared in " 'When Beggars Die, There Are No Comets Seen': The Discourse of Poverty and the Shakespearean Beggar," *Shakespeare Jahrbuch* (Ost) 126 (1990). I am grateful to these publications for permission to reuse this material in altered form.

I have also given portions of this book as talks at various meetings of the Shakespeare Association of America and the International Shakespeare Association; at Wellesley College, Bentley College, and the University of Pisa; and at conferences in Glasgow, Graz, and Weimar. My thanks to those who listened, questioned, and encouraged the project. I also thank the extremely helpful staffs at the British Library, the Corporation of London Records Office, and the Folger Shakespeare Library for their invaluable assistance.

My project was generously supported by travel grants and fellowships from several institutions. This book began during an American Council of Learned Societies Research Fellowship, originally awarded for a slightly different topic; the time to read and think was essential in allowing me to develop my ideas in the directions that seemed most useful. A subsequent Summer Stipend Fellowship from the National Endowment for the Humanities provided the opportunity to write two chapters, and a sabbatical leave from Boston University permitted me to bring the project to a conclusion. Finally, travel grants from the National Endowment for the Humanities, the American Philosophical Society, and the Whiting Foundation made it possible to use the superb libraries and archives in London and Washington.

Many colleagues and friends over the years have provided intellectual and emotional support for this project, for which I am deeply grateful. The readers for Cornell University Press offered sharp and extremely useful reports, with many excellent suggestions for revision, as did Bernhard Kendler, executive editor of the Press. James L. Calderwood, Keir Elam, Jean Howard, Barbara Mowat, Virginia Mason Vaughan, and David Young deserve my special thanks—each of them has heard or read large parts of this book and provided provocative and stimulating commentary. Neither their extraordinarily generous professional assistance nor their friendship can be adequately acknowledged here. Three close colleagues read the entire manuscript at a late stage—and parts of it more than once—offering me the benefit of their intelligence and wisdom. John T. Matthews, Scott Cutler Shershow, and James R. Siemon challenged, encouraged, and stimulated my thinking on almost every line; the faults of this book are certainly not theirs, but many of the virtues are. Jim Siemon has been closest to the project—his assistance on this, and everything else, remains indispensable, and his own work a constant inspiration. Finally, the support of my family, Carol and David, made it all possible, and it is to them that this book is dedicated.

W. C. C.

ABBREVIATIONS AND DOCUMENTATION

QUOTATIONS from Shakespeare are from *The Complete Works of Shakespeare*, ed. David Bevington (New York: HarperCollins, 1992). Quotations from Quarto editions of the plays are from *Shakespeare's Plays in Quarto*, ed. Michael J. B. Allen and Kenneth Muir (Berkeley: University of California Press, 1981). The following abbreviations have been used in the text:

APC	*Acts of the Privy Council*, ed. J. R. Dasent (London, 1890–1964)
BCB	Bridewell Court Books, Guildhall, London
CLRO	Corporation of London Records Office, Guildhall, London
CSPD	*Calendar of State Papers Domestic*, Her Majesty's Stationery Office, London
SAL	*Calendar of the Manuscripts of the Most Honourable the Marquess of Salisbury*, Historical Manuscripts Commission, London
SCED	*Seventeenth-Century Economic Documents*, ed. Joan Thirsk and J. P. Cooper (Oxford: Clarendon Press, 1972)
TED	*Tudor Economic Documents*, ed. R. H. Tawney and Eileen Power (London: Longmans, 1924)
TRP	*Tudor Royal Proclamations*, ed. Paul L. Hughes and James F. Larkin (New Haven: Yale University Press, 1969)

References to journal titles follow the standard abbreviations used in the annual bibliography of *Shakespeare Quarterly*; otherwise, journal titles are given in full. I have silently modernized *j, i, y, s, v, u,* and contractions throughout. All dates are given new-style.

Fat King, Lean Beggar

Introduction

THIS book engages the massive and complex social problem of poverty and its representations in the Tudor-Stuart period. While my account relies on the important work of historians such as A. L. Beier, Roger B. Manning, Paul Slack, and Keith Wrightson, among many others, it also differs from that work in several ways. Above all, I seek to examine various cultural representations of the poor and to explore the frequent gaps and contradictions between what the poets, pamphleteers, governmental functionaries, dramatists, court records, and other voices of the Tudor-Stuart period represented as the truth about beggars and vagabonds. I will therefore describe some of the aesthetic, political, and socioeconomic *uses* to which different representations of the beggar were put during this period.

This project began with what at the time seemed a deceptively simple question about one particular theatrical representation of a beggar: given all the disguises possible to imagine on the Renaissance stage—where, by convention, a character could simply put on a different hat and his own father would not recognize him—why did Shakespeare choose to disguise Edgar as Poor Tom in *King Lear*? Why is he a beggar, and one from Bedlam at that? I attempt to answer that question in chapter 6, but in a sense this entire book is an answer.

I was particularly struck, at the beginning of the project, by a fairly common attitude toward Shakespeare, exemplified in E. W. Ives's conclusion that "to the historian, the remarkable thing—and a contrast to Shakespeare's sensitivity to the realities of politics and the Court—is the distance there seems to be between his plays and the socio-economic realities of Elizabeth[an] and Jacobean England." *Coriolanus*, Ives notes, "stands alone" as an exception, but in any event that play "takes very much an establishment point of view." Although a study of language and imagery might show that "Shakespeare was aware of much of this [contemporary reality]," Ives concludes, still "it gave him few explicit themes" (28). A very different view of Shakespeare's politics, and especially those of *Coriolanus,* has emerged in recent years (see, for example, Janet Adelman, " 'Anger's My Meat,' " and Annabel Patterson, *Shakespeare and the Popular Voice*), but the contextualization of Shakespeare's works has indeed frequently taken the form of accounting for them within the framework of court-centered politics. It seemed to me that Ives badly misconceived what was going on in Shakespeare's plays, and that the plays needed to be placed in different contexts; the second half of this book therefore situates several of Shakespeare's plays within the contemporary discourses of poverty.

The phrase "discourse of poverty," which will be used frequently, does not imply a monolithic, monological, or even coherent set of assumptions and viewpoints. The discourse of poverty is riddled with contradictions, and I attempt to capture some of its variety here. As a consequence, this book has to tell several different, though finally interrelated, stories in order to do justice to the subject's complexity. It offers an account of a "real" socioeconomic crisis that led to social disturbance, to official political repression, and almost, but not quite, to social upheaval. But there are also stories of discursive and political domination, by which a privileged elite preserved hierarchical order and reinforced dubious points of distinction; stories of temporary or wholly imaginary forms of resistance by which the dominated responded to domination; and stories that, openly admitting their artificiality, were performed on the London stage.[1]

Throughout this book, theatricality and the theater of Tudor-Stuart London play prominent parts. I emphasize the theater not because I believe it was central to the formation of the discourse of poverty, or because poverty was *merely* something constructed and staged—I do not think either proposition is true. But the London theater was recognized, and often denounced, as a destabilizing site of potential sedition where

---

[1] Most of the stories I will relate are about male vagrants—necessarily so, since the majority of the documents of the period refer to men; an account of the female vagrant is given in chapter 2, however. This asymmetry in source material certainly misrepresents the actual numbers at the time, for as Willen notes, "women were seen as the majority of their indigent populations" in the various surveys and censuses of the period (562). Vagrant women, moreover, were more likely to be categorized as prostitutes.

"masterless men" might gather and riots break out. Many descriptions of false beggars, too, employed theatrical language in their accounts of the beggars' fraudulence. Thus the histrionics of poverty found a natural home on the stage.

The very subjects examined here—vagrancy, marginalization, theatricality, inversion, poverty—would seem to mark this book as an instance of the New Historicism. Although I have been greatly influenced by many current (and former) New Historicists, and by cultural materialists, it will become obvious to the reader that the methods of this book at times vary considerably from each other, and from the stereotypical practices of New Historicism, such as a reliance on historical anecdote.[2] Yet, like many New Historicist projects, this book does pursue its subjects primarily through the category of "representation," starting from the position that all documents of the period do their work through signifying practices that are ideologically inflected. The figure of the beggar was constructed and invested with so many multivalent, contradictory meanings, moreover, that my own narrative necessarily pursues several different representational practices. My focus on these practices carries the further consequence that I do not pretend to offer here a full economic history of poverty, but rather an analysis of the representational embodiment of poverty in the human figures of the poor.

I will begin with a question: why are beggars so often feared by the general public? In the streets of late twentieth-century American cities, beggars may seem potential bearers of the modern plague of violence; people with money and privilege may also feel guilt, and so they project fearful qualities upon beggars, making it easier to reject them (the beggar needs money, therefore he wants my money, therefore he would take it from me). Beggars also intrude on psychological space, figuratively assaulting any conception of privacy—though since such encounters usually take place in public, the right of a privileged privacy seems difficult to sustain. Beggars also enact contradictory ideas about work: they are, on the one hand, unfortunate because they do not have jobs and, on the other hand, undeserving of sympathy because they do not have (or seek) work. Added to this mix of concerns are the other modern plagues of alcoholism and drug addiction and the deinstitutionalization of the mentally ill. The marginal figure of the beggar inevitably lends itself to projected versions of such debilitating conditions. As will be seen, the early

---

[2] See Howard (1986) for a descriptive analysis of typical New Historicist methodology.

modern discourse of poverty takes up versions of virtually all of these issues as well.[3]

Tudor-Stuart reactions to the poor and to the concept of poverty are also products of their own historical moment, during a post-Reformation transformation of the very idea of charity, and during the painful transformation of a feudal economy into early modern capitalism. In attempting to control this uncontrollable process, Tudor-Stuart writers produced an astonishingly diverse field of discourses comprising state-authorized statutes, polemics, institutions, and punishments directed toward, and usually against, the poor. The regular modification and reissuance of the Poor Laws suggest a dominant social order continually trying, and failing, to calibrate a consistent and effective response to the problem of poverty, and particularly to the phenomenon of vagrancy.

What were the principal objections to vagrants and beggars that demanded such an elaborate apparatus of state control and punishment? Two antithetical accusations lie beneath much of the discourse of poverty: on the one hand, vagrants are idle; on the other hand, they are mobile. Idleness became both a venial and an economic sin, a rebuke to those who worked, a dereliction of various written and unwritten social duties, an unacceptable choice of sloth. The Vice figure in Francis Merbury's *The Marriage between Wit and Wisdom* (c. 1571–78), who will at one point disguise himself as a poor beggar, is an embodiment of, and is in fact named, Idleness. The objection to idleness was in part philosophical but primarily religious: the Elizabethan "Homilie Against Idlenesse" preached the official view: "It is the appointment and will of GOD, that every man, during the time of this mortall and transitorie life, should give himselfe to such honest and godly exercise and labour, and every one follow his own busines, & to walke uprightly in his owne calling. Man (saith Job) is borne to labor" (Rickey and Stroupe: 249). Where idleness exists, "there the devill is ready to set in his foote, and to plant all kinde of wickednesse and sinne, to the everlasting destruction of mans soule" (251). The Puritan preacher Thomas Adams echoed this belief: "The *Idle man* is the Devils Cushion, whereupon he sits, and takes his ease" (Adams 1614: L2ᵛ), while the author of *Greevous Grones for the Poore* (1621), switching metaphors, argued that "Idlenesse maketh mens bodies the *Demeanes of the Divell:* for the bodie of an Idle person is the Divels home, viz: *Empty of Grace, swept of all Goodnesse . . .* for want of exercise, wee

---

[3] See the exchange between Dubrow and Dolan on the problems inherent in the category "early modern." I employ the term interchangeably with the more awkward "Tudor-Stuart period" (a category fraught with a different set of problems), both of them as a shorthand way of referring to the period 1500–1642 in England.

see idle people hunt and runne after evill Company" (*Greevous*. B3ᵛ). To be "idle" was thus not necessarily to be inactive, as the idle "hunt and runne" after sin. Yet the danger was not only the private sin of the individual; in these arguments, the idle hands of the Devil invariably reach into the political sphere. Idleness thus leads not to inactivity , but to the wrong kind of activity, and ultimately to rebellion. Richard Morison's *A Remedy for Sedition* (1536) is typical in its political logic: "The lacke of honest craftes, and the habundauncie of idlenes, all be it they be not the hole cause of sedicion, yet as they brede theves, murderers, and beggers, so not a litle they provoke men, or thinges like men to rebellion" (D2ᵛ). Later writers, as we shall see, did not hesitate to make an even more absolute equation between idleness and rebellion.

The second major objection to vagrants—their very vagrancy, or wandering—is thus both the antithesis and the complement to the charge of idleness. Vagrancy is objectionable per se, since there is no clear destination to wandering, but beyond that, "the first traveller was *Cain,* and he was called a vagabond runnagate on the face of the earth" (Nashe: 2.297). "A wandring Rogue," as one writer said in 1631, "is an *Individuum Vagum,* a wandring Plannet," who "might make a good description of *England,* for hee knowes all the highwayes, though not at his fingers, yet his toes-end" (Saltonstall: 38–39). Tudor and Stuart authorities, as William Lambarde suggested and as we will see in more detail later in chapter 1, would strain to give all vagrants a "mark," if not of Cain then at least the contemporary juridical equivalent. As many historians have noted, Tudor and Stuart governments repeatedly attempted to fix in place and time a (largely imaginary, it now seems) hierarchical structure of authority, epistemology, and power. The Statute of Artificers of 1563, for example, not only attempted to establish, and hence freeze, wages and professions in an eternal present, but was in effect designed to prevent mobility itself within the kingdom; this continuing pressure towards stasis was eventually enshrined in the Act of Settlement of 1662 (14 Charles II, c.12).[4] Similarly, the various Tudor sumptuary laws attempted to freeze into place the signs that established status and social identity.

---

[4] This act permitted the removal of any poor person to his or her supposed place of "origin," if it appeared that he or she might become a "charge" on the community; this act in effect merely crystallized many earlier laws that authorized the expulsion of a beggar from one town to the next, in a potentially endless chain of expulsions. As Clay notes, "the most far-reaching form of social control involved in the administration of the Poor Laws was the restrictions placed upon the freedom of the poor to move about as they liked" (1.234). In practice, of course, such laws were only selectively enforced and only partially effective. The Act of Settlement also provided for transportation to the English plantations for confirmed vagrants, and offered a bounty for those who captured

Vagrants were thus considered a physical threat as well as a philosophical one, because their very nature was to cross boundaries, to transgress categories of all kinds. Their actual wandering over the rural roads and urban streets of the kingdom is the external figure of their equally radical slippage between other conceptual and political categories. Like a "wandering Plannet," disrupting an older cosmic system of order and hierarchy, vagrants were transgressive by definition, by their very status. National and local authorities struggled throughout the period to police such free-floating signifiers.

Idleness and vagrancy predate the Tudor-Stuart period, to be sure. "Begotten on a sunny bank, where I have lain ever since" (*Dr. Faustus* 2.2.153–54), Marlowe's Sloth, like Spenser's Idleness ("Still drownd in sleepe.... From worldly cares himselfe he did esloyne, / And greatly shunned manly exercise, / From every worke he chalenged essoyne" [*Faerie Queene*, 1.4.19–20]), derives from a rich medieval iconographic tradition of the Seven Deadly Sins. But the spiritual torpor of Idleness, of which the physical inertness of lethargy is the external sign, would in the Tudor-Stuart period be further inflected in terms of economic transgression, in which the sign would be more important than the spiritual state it points to. "Johne the Commonwealth," in David Lindsay's "An Satire of the Three Estates," will

> compleine upon the idill men,
> For quhy, sir, it is Gods awin bidding,
> All Christian men to work for thair living.
> Sanct Paull, that pillar of the Kirk,
> Sayis to the wretchis that will not wirk,
> And bene to vertews [labour] laith,
> *Qui non laborat non manducet.*
> This is in Inglische toung or leit,
> 'Quha labouris nocht he sall not eit'.
> This bene against the strang beggers,
> Fidlers, pipers, and pardoners,

among others (lines 2601–11). The idle beggar, in two common metaphors of the period, is "a drone that feeds upon the labours of the bee," and "a kind of caterpillar that spoils much good fruit" (Breton: 26). The

---

them; namely, "the sum of two shillings for every rogue vagabond or sturdy beggar" (Baxter: 144).

problem seemed universal to some: "Idleness," Robert Burton remarked, "is the *malus genius* of our nation" (88).

The beggar's idleness was read and misread through a discourse that appeared near the beginning of early modern capitalism, and which lacked any adequate economic theory to explain the vast changes in progress. Thus Nicholas Breton, like many other writers, invokes the trope of the parasite, with its implicit potential subversion of the high by the low; he could not yet realize the complex and necessary links between the formation of wealth and the formation of an entire class of expendable workers. The beggar's idleness, as a result, was increasingly read as an act of will, rather than a consequence of a general economic failure, and the so-called sturdy beggar, as we will see in chapter 1, became the paradigm of the willful social parasite. Like most parasites, too, the beggar was often represented as both a carrier and an instance of "infection" and "disease," an unnatural and deviant flaw in the body politic whose "natural" state was supposedly one of health. The metaphors of parasite and infection are projections, further demonizing the beggar as another kind of plague, which serve to dissociate rather than connect economic privilege and poverty. In *Capital*, however, Marx argued that the development of the Poor Laws was a necessary product of the formation of early modern capitalism, in which the "agricultural people, first forcibly expropriated from the soil, [were] driven from their homes, turned into vagabonds, and then whipped, branded, tortured by laws grotesquely terrible, into the discipline necessary for the wage system" (808–9). Thus, in this reading, the Poor Laws were primarily a form of economic rather than strictly political control (the two can hardly be separated, admittedly), or, at best, society's attempt to mitigate, and therefore continue to permit, the new economics of exploitation which required a large labor pool, much of which would be unemployed at any given time.[5] As we will see, the commodification of surplus bodies of beggars opened the way for ambitious economic "projectors" and early schemes of forced servitude.

Vagrancy thus became simultaneously a necessity for an emerging

[5] As Innes notes, the theory of bridewell punishment—that is, correction and the provision of work—did not *depend* "on a vision of labour as the source of wealth, or of production as an inherently expansive force," but she does register the correlation in the growing "attractiveness of the bridewell idea" and the historical moment "when the labour of the poor did come to be acclaimed as the primary source of national wealth, and therefore also of national strength, and when setting as many as possible of the poor to work and thus expanding production came to figure among the chief objects of public policy" (47).

economy of exchange, and a threat to the residual hierarchical system. As Richard Halpern notes of the dispossessed classes,

> by "mirroring" the decoding effects of capital in a way that overstepped the structural limitations of late feudal production they became a precocious and nightmarishly exaggerated image of *modernity*. They were a kind of volatile fluid, coursing irregularly through the social body and visible everywhere in it, representing the possibility of a total and anarchic breakdown of the existing social mechanisms of order and control. (74)[6]

Thus the early modern discourse of poverty inscribed the beggar's body both as a potentially valuable commodity and as a site of lawlessness and subversion. Among the major strategies deployed by the dominant discourse as a way of categorizing and controlling beggars was the practice of inversion, to which I will now briefly turn.

The Fat King and the Lean Beggar

Claudius's anxious query in Act 4 of *Hamlet*—"where's Polonius?"— provokes in Hamlet a response that is at once sarcastic, exhilarating, and threatening. Hamlet offers Claudius a vision of the leveling process by which death will bring even a king low. As for Polonius's body,

> *Hamlet.* A certain convocation of politic worms are e'en at him. Your worm is your only emperor for diet. We fat all creatures else to fat us, and we fat ourselves for maggots. Your fat king and your lean beggar is but variable service—two dishes, but to one table. That's the end.
> *King.* Alas, alas!
> *Hamlet.* A man may fish with the worm that hath eat of a king, and eat of the fish that hath fed of that worm.

When Claudius, perfectly playing the straight man, asks the meaning of these epigrams, Hamlet's response again summons forth the collapse of opposites:

[6] As Halpern goes on to note, by the time of Adam Smith, it would be understood that "vagrants are simply potential laborers in search of capital; they are therefore part of the nation's economic and social life. It was only during the heyday of primitive accumulation that the vagrant classes played the role of a fully decoded body with respect to the dominant social order" (75).

Nothing but to show you how a king may go a progress through the guts of a beggar. (4.3.19–32)

Even the dissonant diction (progress/guts) reenacts the grotesqueness of this fusion. For Hamlet, as typically for the early modern period generally, the monarch, the top of the social and legal hierarchy, is understood in opposition to the figure at the bottom of all hierarchy, the socially and metaphysically null—the beggar; and the beggar is understood in opposition to the figure at the top of hierarchy—the monarch. As one writer put it in 1631, the world "may bee likened to a Scale or Praedicament of Relation, wherin the King is the *summum genus,* under whom are many subordinate degrees of men, till at last wee descend to the Begger the *Infima species,* whose misery cannot be subdivided into any lesser fortune" (Saltonstall: 17). But Hamlet also reveals how these apparent opposites are at the same time twins: "Two dishes," he notes, "but to one table." Each term of this habitually paired inversion thus requires the other in order to mount a full definition of its own identity. Earlier in the play, in response to Rosencrantz's fatuous comment—"I hold ambition of so airy and light a quality that it is but a shadow's shadow"—Hamlet mockingly answers with another linking of high and low, this time with a complete reversal of normal hierarchical status: "Then are our beggars bodies, and our monarchs and outstretched heroes the beggars' shadows" (2.2.264–65). Beggars, it seems, are merely "bodies" because they have no "ambition," while monarchs are reductively made merely "shadows"; only an ironic rhetorical inversion of "monarchs" who *do* possess bodies, and are the substance that casts shadows, can give beggars any qualities at all. But shadows require bodies, and bodies cast shadows, and the dialectic of the relation is inescapable.

The conjunction of king and beggar, with its attendant rhetoric of "bodies," "shadows," "worm[s]," and death, derives from medieval traditions; the "dance of death" trope often pairs King and Beggar, along with Old Man and Child, Wise Man and Fool,—and is found in many of Shakespeare's plays.[7] *Hamlet* is far from the only play that registers an anxiety over this fusion of opposites.[8] Consider Leontes's bitter accusation of Hermione in *The Winter's Tale.*

[7] See the plate "An Elizabethan Dance of Death" (1569?) in Farnham (292).

[8] Brown provides a useful thematic study of the opposition, concentrating on *King Lear.* Following Northrop Frye's category of the king as high mimetic hero, Brown concludes that "in terms of his severely limited power of action the beggar stands at the opposite extreme of human possibility from the King: he is a figure of pure irony, that mode in which 'we have the sense of looking down on a scene of bondage, frustration,

>   You have mistook, my lady,
> Polixenes for Leontes. O thou thing!
> Which I'll not call a creature of thy place,
> Lest barbarism, making me the precedent,
> Should a like language use to all degrees
> And mannerly distinguishment leave out
> Betwixt the prince and beggar.
>
> (2.1.82–88)

One's "place" in the "degrees" of hierarchy should be clear and fixed, then, so he will not call Hermione by her proper name; it would be "barbarism" to omit "mannerly distinguishment" between high and low. The collapse of these distinctions is unthinkable, and yet to Leontes something like it has already happened; and in thinking so, he acts in a way to make it so. Without a "place" in the hierarchy, Hermione can only be, like the beggar, a "thing" without a name.

Richard II employs similar language to register hierarchical inversion. When Bolingbroke receives the sentence of banishment, he asks his father,

> Will you permit that I shall stand condemned
> A wandering vagabond, my rights and royalties
> Plucked from my arms perforce and given away
> To upstart unthrifts?
>
> (2.3.119–22)

Thus a lord of the realm, stripped of "rights and royalties," does not merely fall, but falls as far as it is possible to fall, to the loathed, undefined, unstable status of the vagabond. In a sharp irony, Richard himself will be made to feel the same utter loss, just before his execution:

>   Sometimes am I king;
> Then treason makes me wish myself a beggar,
> And so I am. Then crushing penury
> Persuades me I was better when a king;

---

or absurdity.' " While acknowledging the "political, social, and economic terms" in which the king/beggar relation can be seen, Brown turns to a different primary focus on them as "two contrasting modes of the imagination" (375). My emphasis will be on the political, social, and economic—the various discursive representations of the beggar—not as distinct from, but as in part constitutive of the imaginative.

> Then am I kinged again, and by and by
> Think that I am unkinged by Bolingbroke,
> And straight am nothing.
>
> (5.5.32–38)

To be unkinged can only mean to be a beggar, a "nothing"—the term so often associated with beggars. The inversion allows no middle term, no social or ontological locus of identity other than the extremes. Similar examples may be gleaned from throughout Shakespeare's plays, from the epilogue to *All's Well*, where "the king's a beggar, now the play is done" (Epi.1), to the several references—in *Richard II* (5.3.80), *Romeo and Juliet* (2.1.14–15), and *Love's Labor's Lost* (1.2.105ff.; 4.1.65ff.)—to the old ballad, "A Song of a Beggar and a King," in which "the magnanimous and most illustrate King Cophetua set eye upon the pernicious and indubitate beggar Zenelophon," as Armado puts it (*Love's Labor's Lost*, 4.1.65–67), and makes her his queen. In spite of this conjunction of extreme opposites, the king of the original ballad claims, "Our wedding shall appointed be, / And every thing in its degree."[9]

This story of the king made subject to a beggar, who is raised from bottom to top to be a queen, seems to have been a favorite comic example of the meeting of hierarchical opposites, with a fantasized dismissal of such distinctions. Yet Hamlet's response to Claudius—fat king and lean beggar "but variable service—two dishes, but to one table"—also offers several different kinds of threat within its humorously epigrammatic phrasing. "A king may go a progress through the guts of a beggar," Hamlet notes, but death is only part of what Claudius must fear, for the royal "progress," one of the great theatricalized displays of monarchical power, may in the end also be leveled and reduced to carnivalesque inversion.[10] The lower bodily power of the social underclass may devour a monarch.

The king/beggar configuration enacts a variation of the trope of the "world turned upside down," a subversive gesture against institutionalized power.[11] The very existence of the beggar both confirms the king's hierarchical superiority and at the same time calls it into question. John Taylor stated the traditional position with admirable clarity.

[9] The text was printed in Thomas Percy's *Reliques of Ancient English Poetry,* from Richard Johnson's "Crown Garland of Goulden Roses" (1612).

[10] Among the many recent studies of carnival, see of course Bakhtin, and also Bristol (1985).

[11] See the important study of a somewhat later period by Hill; for the European context, see Davis.

> A Clowne to sway a Scepter is too base,
> And Princes to turne Pedlers were disgrace:
> Yet all these, if they not misplaced be,
> Are necessary, each in their degree,
> If each within their limits be contain'd,
> Peace flourisheth, and concord is maintain'd.
>
> (1641: A3)

The difficulty, of course, was that many vagrants of the period were in fact frequently "misplaced," not contained "within their limits"; the precise definitions of identity, based on "degree" and "limits," had been breaking down for many decades before Taylor wrote his poem. The proleptic irony of the poem's date—1641—only adds to the unreality of the comment. In Thomas Dekker's *The Honest Whore, Part 1*, this mode of hierarchical inversion takes its place among other forms of contemporary cultural anxiety. When the Officer tells Candido, "Y'are changde, y'are altered," the reply establishes a whole range of destabilizing practices:

> *Candido.* Changde sir, why true sir, is change strange, tis not the fashion unlesse it alter. Monarkes turne to beggers; beggers creepe into the nests of Princes, Maisters serve their prentises: Ladies their Servingmen, men turne to women.
> *Officer.* And women turne to men. (4.3.129–34)

This process of mutation is not merely the whirligig of time and fashion, however, but a signal of more profound cultural changes in process. Recent scholarly work on transvestism, for example, has demonstrated the fundamental nature of its transgressions.[12] The specter of "women on top," to use Natalie Zemon Davis's famous phrase, both caused and was caused by other anxieties attending hierarchical power.

The theater itself was understood as a primary site of such inversions and confrontations of hierarchical power. Actors—that is, "All Fencers Bearewardes common Players of Enterludes and Minstrelles wandring abroade (other then Players of Enterlude belonging to any Baron of this Realme, or any other honorable personage of greater Degree, to be auctoryzed to play under the Hand and Seale of Armes of such Baron or Personage)" (*TED:* 2.355), as the 1597 statute (39 Eliz.I, c.4) puts it—were classified in the vagrancy statutes throughout the period as vagabonds, unless under noble patronage. Beyond their literal vagrancy, their

---

[12] Among many recent studies, two stand out, by Jardine and by Howard (1988).

"wandring," the actors' ability to counterfeit royalty was often remarked both as an instance of their genius and of the danger they represented in their very histrionic powers. Their feigning of royalty was also a transgression of formal class distinctions, as Montaigne noted: "For, as enterlude plaiers, you shal now see them on the stage, play a King, an Emperor, or a Duke, but they are no sooner off the stage, but they are base rascals, vagabond abjects, and porterly hirelings, which is their naturall and orginall condition" (1.296).[13] Thomas Lupton remarked on the further irony that the beggar-player might even act the part of a beggar: "A player often changes, now he acts a Monarch, tomorrow a Beggar" (1632: 81). In some accounts, the actor seems to have no essential nature at all: "He is much like the Compters in Arithmeticke, and may stand one while for a King, another while a Begger, many times as a Mute or Cypher" (R.M.: B3).

The oppositional dynamic I have briefly described in the king/beggar relation may also be considered a specific instance of the general anthropological practice of "symbolic inversion." As Barbara Babcock has noted, this dynamic of inversion "may be broadly defined as any act of expressive behavior which inverts, contradicts, abrogates, or in some fashion presents an alternative to commonly held cultural codes, values, and norms be they linguistic, literary or artistic, religious, or social and political" (14). "Far from being a residual category of experience," she continues, symbolic inversion "is its very opposite. What is socially peripheral is often symbolically central" (32). Mikhail Bakhtin (on carnival) and Michel Foucault (on institutions) have taken similar positions quite far, although in very different directions. Foucault sees the king/prisoner relation, to take one example, as a similar kind of inversion: "In the darkest region of the political field the condemned man represents the symmetrical, inverted figure of the king" (29). So too with the insane, the sick, witches, and other marginalized groups of people: their identity derives from their necessary exclusion from central forms of power, for self-inclusion requires other-exclusion. This dynamic is not simply a modern invention, to be sure. Many scholars, such as Rosalie Colie, have described a habit of paradoxical thinking in the Renaissance, in which things are partly if not wholly defined by their opposites. Stuart Clark has observed that in this period, "a predisposition to see things in terms of binary opposition was a distinctive aspect of a prevailing mentality. What is remarkable, however, is the extraordinary pervasiveness of the lan-

---

[13] See Skura for a stimulating account of the trope of the "Player King as Beggar in Great Men's Houses" (85–148).

guage of 'contrariety,' the most extreme of the relations of opposition."
Clark associates this "mentality" with "the dominance of an inherited
metaphysic," but also "with two features peculiar to the period: a linguistic preference for standardized forms of argument and expression
based on antithesis, and a preoccupation with the extreme poles of the
religious and moral universe" (105). King James himself provides a perfect example of the habit:

> Since the Devill is the verie contrarie opposite to God, there can be no
> better way to know God, then by the contrarie; . . . by the falshood of the
> one to considder the trueth of the other, by the injustice of the one, to
> considder the Justice of the other: And by the cruelty of the one, to
> considder the mercifulnesse of the other: And so foorth in all the rest of
> the essence of God, and qualities of the Devill. (quoted in Stuart Clark:
> 117)

And any argument can be confuted, as Thomas Wilson noted in his *Log-
icke* (1567), "by inversion, that is to saie, tournying his taile cleane contrary" (Babcock: 16).

John Donne, to take a more complex example of this habit in the
specific terms of this book, asserts in a sermon (c. 1619) the equivalence
of the binary equation in logical terms but then immediately breaks it
down in religious terms: "Rich, and poor are *contrary* to one another, but
yet both *necessary* to one another; They are both necessary to one another;
but the poor man is the more necessary, because though one man might
be rich, though no man were poor, yet he could have no exercise of his
charity, he could send none of his riches to heaven, to help him there,
except there were some poor here" (2.214). So social and economic
distinction is rationalized as theological.[14] The First Citizen in *Coriolanus*
offers a more cynical version of Donne's point: "The leanness that afflicts
us [the poor], the object of our misery, is as an inventory to particularize
their [the rich] abundance" (1.1.18–20).[15] A visual emblem of this relation may be seen in some representations of the Wheel of Fortune
which place the monarch and the beggar on opposite sides of the wheel;

---

[14] To be fair to Donne, there are other comments in the sermons that suggest a spir-
itual/egalitarian leveling of the king/beggar distinction: "*Christ* was not whip'd to save
Beggars, and crown'd with Thornes to save Kings: he dyed, he suffered all, for all"
(4.276).

[15] Cf. the Bastard in Shakespeare's *King John*: "Well, whiles I am a beggar, I will rail /
And say there is no sin but to be rich; / And being rich, my virtue then shall be / To
say there is no vice but beggary" (2.1.593–97).

as in Richard II's famous comparison of the crown to two buckets in a well (*Richard II* 4.1.185–90), one *must* be down for the other to be up.[16]

Yet the limitation of inversion, as Peter Stallybrass and Allon White point out, is that it "shares with demonization the acceptance of the existing binary categories of high and low." They distinguish demonization, which proceeds from a principle of exclusion, from inversion, which "celebrated excluded elements and the lower terms of a diacritical pairing" (57). Stallybrass and White go on to describe a third dynamic, "hybridization," which "produces new combinations and strange instabilities in a given semiotic system. It therefore generates the possibility of shifting *the very terms of the system itself,* by erasing and interrogating the relationships which constitute it" (58; original emphasis). In practice, they admit, inversion, demonization and hybridization may be mixed together and difficult to distinguish. Following Stallybrass and White, and attempting to avoid the often unsatisfactory strictures of the subversion/containment paradigm, Theodore Leinwand has recently argued for a model of social intercourse for this period "based on negotiation and exchanges." Such a model "makes room for negotiation" and "acknowledges the persistence of coercive discipline but argues that disciplines themselves, not only the forces resisting them, may be eroded or curbed" (1990: 479, 480). Leinwand seeks to develop a "more literal sense" of the concept of negotiation than he finds in Stephen Greenblatt's central work, *Shakespearean Negotiations.*[17]

I understand the king/beggar relation in this historical period in a framework comparable to Leinwand's formulation: that is, it is fundamentally, though not always, constituted by symbolic inversion, in which the beggar has been systematically marginalized and demonized through official discourse. I follow as well here Stuart Clark's belief that "inversion in whatever context was thus necessarily a political act" (111). The *representation* of the beggar is of course distinct from the actual social exchange (to the extent that it can be known and described) of crime and punishment. As I will indicate in succeeding chapters, the best evidence suggests that even in the case of beggars, the full force of the law's

---

[16] See Chew (40, 44). Chew notes as well the final dumb show in George Gascoigne and Francis Kinwelmarshe's *Jocasta*, which shows Fortune riding in a chariot, with "two kings, crowned" on her right hand, and "two poor slaves meanly attired" on her left; Fortune stops the chariot, and shifts their positions, "placing the crowns on the slaves' heads and 'casting the vile clothes of the slaves upon the kings' " (41–42). "The younger rises," Edmund realizes, "when the old doth fall" (*King Lear* 3.3.25).

[17] See especially chapter 1, "The Circulation of Social Energy," in Greenblatt (1988: 1–20). All of Greenblatt's work is relevant to these comments, of course.

prescribed punishments was at times transmuted—usually, lessened—at the local level, in a process demonstrating Leinwand's model of local negotiation. Yet it is also true that in practice the destitute had little real recourse to law and the courts as a way of dealing with more powerful institutions or individuals. Rather, they were usually on the receiving end only.

This book approaches the phenomenon of the beggar in the Tudor-Stuart period from a variety of directions. The first chapter compresses much social and economic history in order to gain, first, a broad survey of "official" representations and explanations of the poor, which attempt to distinguish vagrants and beggars from the "deserving" poor. It then examines unofficial contemporary analyses of the poor, from pietistic exponents and opponents of personal and state-sponsored charity, to outlandish economic projectors, in order to show how these competing rhetorics qualify and complicate the monolithic vision encouraged by the high discourse. Unlike some marginalized figures such as witches, moreover, who were, from a modern point of view, a purely psycho-socio-economic construction, beggars were a real economic and social problem, as well as a symbolic or discursively created one.[18] The second chapter takes up one exemplary individual case in detail, that of Nicholas Genings, whose story is told in the most important of the sixteenth century's rogue books, written by Thomas Harman. Genings is perhaps the most famous single beggar of the period, represented as both a fraudulent parasite and a histrionic genius. In the third chapter, I focus on contemporary institutional responses with a description of the two chief hospitals, Bridewell and Bedlam, intended to care for the destitute of the kingdom, and their role as real and symbolic places in the drama of the period.

The second half of the book turns to dramatic inscriptions of the discourse of poverty, primarily Shakespeare's. Chapter 4 engages various dramatic representations of the beggar, particularly in the early 1590s. I begin with the urgent contemporary question of sedition and the allegedly subversive role of the poor, then discuss 2 Henry VI in this context. In chapter 5, I turn to Christopher Sly in The Taming of the Shrew and Autolycus in The Winter's Tale, linking the tradition of the merry beggar to socioeconomic forces of the period. Chapter 6, like chapter 2, focuses on an exemplary individual case, but this one is found in a play as well

---

[18] See however Stuart Clark's fine analysis of the "linguistic framework" (100) which enacted and sustained witchcraft beliefs. For other associations between beggary and witchcraft, see chapter 1 of this book.

as a rogue book—Edgar, the Bedlam beggar of *King Lear*. Chapter 7 presents a brief consideration of later plays that offer idealized representations of the beggar, such as John Fletcher and Philip Massinger's *Beggars' Bush* (1622) and Richard Brome's *A Jovial Crew* (1641); the idealization of the beggar, continuing from the earliest Tudor texts, is a counterdiscourse in which the beggar ironically turns back into a kind of monarch in his supposed freedom. Still, no matter how utopian beggars' lives were made out to be, their experience in Tudor-Stuart England was far closer to Edgar's formulation: the lean beggar is the "basest and most poorest shape / That ever penury, in contempt of man, / Brought near to beast" (*King Lear* 2.3.7–9).[19]

[19] Throughout this book, the terms "masterless man," "beggar," "rogue," "vagrant," and "vagabond" are used interchangeably, as they were in texts throughout the period. More specialized terms, such as "Dommerar" (see chapter 2), are used as early modern authors used them.

PART I

Vagrancy and Marginality

in the Tudor-Stuart Period

CHAPTER ONE

Discourses of Poverty

Falstaff. Faith, for their poverty,
I know not where they had that.
(1 Henry IV 4.2.69–70)

THE economic and social conditions of early modern England resulted in widespread hardship, dispossession, and the creation of what contemporaries believed, with considerable justification, to be an unprecedented number of beggars and vagabonds. To give a comprehensive economic history of poverty in this period would be a daunting task, well beyond the scope of this book. The brief outline that follows can only hint at the complexity of the issues involved.

The considerable growth in population, especially from the early 1560s into the 1640s, was a major factor leading to the widespread poverty of the Tudor-Stuart period.[1] D. M. Palliser notes that "by the end of Elizabeth's reign the population of England may have been as much as 35 per cent higher than it was at the start" (37). Although such growth, he also notes, stimulated the growth of the English economy, considerable hardships were also attendant on it. While these hardships did not lead to mass starvation or to internal political turmoil like that experienced on the Continent, many contemporaries registered anxiety and fear over a substantial increase in the number of vagrants and beggars in this period. Furthermore, the perceived threat of political turmoil stemming from social and economic grievances increased after 1549.

While England's population increased substantially, the growth of London's population was dramatically greater as a result of internal migra-

---

[1] See among others Clay (1.1–28), Palliser (30–59), and Wrigley and Schofield.

tion.[2] The population flow to London from the provinces was marked by all. As the anonymous author of the *Discourse of Corporations* put it in the 1580s, "the onely trade of marchantes is nowe to London, which hath eaten up all the rest of the townes and havens of England" (*TED*: 3.274). The unregulated, accelerating growth of London inevitably led to "the desperate poverty of large sections of the population and the terrible living conditions found in many districts" (Clay: 1.212). The great increase in urban poverty forced urban solutions, such as the creation of workhouses or "bridewells" (see chapter 3), and bans on the erection of new buildings, lest they encourage more people to come to London (Fisher: 175–76).

The steady growth in population was accompanied by an alarming inflation—so severe that many historians prefer the term "price revolution"—which seemed unprecedented; its consequences were often devastating for many individuals, especially the landless poor.[3] Debates about the causes of inflation—such as the relative importance of population growth or the importation of gold and silver from the New World—are beyond the scope of my present inquiry, as are considerations of other consequences of inflation, such as its impact upon the aristocracy (see Tawney; Stone 1967: 62–95). But it is clear that the most adverse effects of inflation were felt by those who were already poor if not yet destitute. Contemporary economic theory could not really account for inflation—efforts to fix wages and prices were predictably futile—but the reality of inflation was visible enough in the rising costs of such basic necessities as wheat or the rent on a small cottage, and more symbolically, in the debased coinage of the Elizabethan period.[4]

The rapid growth in population and the effects of inflation coincided with continuing changes in the patterns of landownership outside the cities—or perhaps it is more accurate to say that all these factors were causes and effects of one another. My focus, again, is not on the major effects of such shifts on other groups, such as the aristocracy, but only on the poor. The centuries-long developments that produced the enclosure of common fields, engrossment, royal disafforestation, dissolution

[2] See Ramsey (109–13), Clay (1.27, 197–213), Palliser (226–35), Wrigley and Schofield, and Finlay and Shearer, among others, on the growth of London in this period. The several essays by Fisher (105–18, 173–83, 185–98) are still valuable; the more recent collection of essays edited by Beier and Finlay is useful throughout.

[3] See Palliser (130–60), Ramsey (113–21), and Clay (1.29–52) for useful surveys of the problem.

[4] See Palliser (134–39, 142–45).

of the monasteries, and the consequent dispersal of church lands—all had generally deleterious effects on the already poor and landless, though there were positive effects for some of the more privileged.[5] As we will see in more detail in chapter 4, the widespread contemporary perception of such changes in landownership—whether one was for or against enclosure, for example—was that all of them resulted in depopulation of the countryside, creating new hordes of vagrants and beggars among those expelled from formerly common lands and forests. The result of such changes was a growing problem in rural areas, including the fear (and often the reality) of increased crime, and an even greater impetus toward internal migration to London (Slack 1974).

Changes in landownership were paralleled as well by important changes in land usage in this period; much of the contemporary debate over such changes fell under the rubric of "enclosure," which I will take up in chapter 4. But while the shift from common to enclosed lands heralded the beginnings of an agricultural revolution, it could never entirely stabilize the recurrent fluctuations in harvest yields at the mercy of weather and other uncontrollable factors: "In its most direct manifestation," Barry Supple notes, "the problem of the harvest was the problem of poverty. Relatively few people lived far away from a bare margin of subsistence" (15). A bad harvest combined with any other increase in unemployment could easily lead to a crisis: "Such a coincidence was, in fact, the principal problem of poor-law administration" (Supple: 15). Accordingly, the main crisis periods in terms of unemployment, poverty, and consequent social upheaval corresponded closely with bad harvest years.[6] The most important actions of national government during such periods of crisis, C. G. A. Clay notes, were "intervention in the grain trade and the enforcement of the Poor Law" (2.241; cf. Ramsey: 161). Intervention in the grain trade often took the form of maintaining artificially low prices of grain, and/or diverting grain from rural areas to London when the threat of urban disorder seemed greatest, as it did in the 1590s.[7] Hunger and privation never disappeared in the Tudor-Stuart period, even when harvests and other economic conditions were good; and when such conditions were bad, the poor died in the streets, and the beggars and vagabonds of the kingdom multiplied—like vermin, it was said, in "swarms."

[5] See Clay (1.67–101) for a useful summary, and chapter 4, n. 3, for other references.
[6] Cf. Clay (1.222, 2.240–44) and Palliser (182–84).
[7] See Power, Archer, and Peter Clark (1985).

"The Regiment of the Povertie"

The grim economic conditions of early modern England are inscribed in a complex cultural discourse of marginality and poverty, in which the beggar's body becomes a central site of semiotic conflict and interrogation. The origins of such poverty were of less consequence to contemporaries than the perceived need to control and contain the phenomenon through the Poor Laws.

The history of Poor Laws and laws restraining beggars and rogues, from the time of Edward III to Queen Elizabeth's day, is one of frustration and futility, of constantly changing theories of how to cut or sear this enervating social lesion in the body politic. At the Sessions of the Peace at Maidstone, on 14 June 1582, the Kentish Justice of the Peace William Lambarde reviewed this history while charging the jury that was assembled to judge the beggars, rogues, and vagabonds who had been brought before them. Lambarde urged his countrymen to employ "the uttermost force of law" in order to rid the countryside of "a many of mighty, idle, and runagate beggars wherewith we are much pestered" (Read: 168–69). Lambarde said that he himself was "very unwilling to use either cutting or searing if this sore were medicable by any salve or plaster within the box of our commission," yet the problem of such social parasites was so severe that "we have determined, first of all to whip out of our country all such of them as do not belong unto us, and then to erect a house of correction for the sturdy rogues of our own shire and therewith to provide for the relief of our own poor that be impotent either by age or infirmity" (169).

Lambarde's distinction between "sturdy" rogues and beggars—those without physical disability—and the truly "impotent" and infirm, is the standard Tudor division of the poor, offering the whip to the first and alms to the second. Lambarde's two hands of justice reflect quite clearly the statutes enacted in 1572 and 1576 (14 Eliz. I, c.5; 18 Eliz. I, c.3) which, respectively, established quite severe corporal punishments (he meant "cutting and searing" literally), but also required the establishment of bridewells, or houses of correction, throughout the realm. Lambarde's simple distinction between the sturdy and the impotent does not yet, however, allow the existence of a third type of the poor which the statute of 1576 first officially admits: the destitute who want work but cannot find it.[8]

---

[8] For an important early study of Elizabethan legislation on the poor, see Leonard. For a more recent study, see the chapter "State Policy" in Beier (1985). A useful sum-

Lambarde then paused in his comments to meditate for the jury on the entire English history of Poor Laws and laws restraining beggars and rogues. The laws—which he characterizes as if they were the personal utterance of each monarch—were too lenient in Edward III's time, he relates, but the clamp-down in the reign of Richard II had resulted in overflowing prisons and excessive public expense, and so the laws were relaxed. Henry VIII, "seeing by experience that the lenity of these former laws could not abate the number of runagate and sturdy beggars, began to draw blood of them" (Read: 170)—whipping for a first offense, the loss of an ear for a second. "And yet," Lambarde notes, "not so prevailing against them, he afterward proceeded in degrees of greater severity, ordaining that for the first fault the gristle of the ear should be cut away, that for the second fault the whole ear should be cut off, and that the third offense should be adjudged felony" (170–71). Henry's "severity" was far surpassed by Edward VI's, however, for in the statute of 1547 the ordained punishments were slavery (the term is actually used in the statute), branding, and death (1 Edw. VI, c.3).

Lambarde regretfully observes that the statute of 1547 did not endure, blaming not the king (who in fact referred to it in his journal as the "extrem law" [Davies: 538]) but the politicians for what happened three years later (3/4 Edw. VI., c.16):

> Howbeit afterward in the midst of his reign the Parliament was persuaded that the former sorts of severity did withhold men from putting the laws in due execution, and therefore it repealed all laws that had inflicted the pains of death and left that only remaining which gave whipping for the first offense and cutting of the ear for the second, which lenity of theirs,

he concludes drily, "what success it had we have seen by our own trial" (Read: 171). At last the wheel has come full circle, and Lambarde notes with approval the harsh judicial weapons which the 1572 statute enacted in the reign of "our good Queen" provided. Now it is "once more thought . . . meet to kill and cut off these rotten members that otherwise would bring peril of infection to the whole body of the realm and commonwealth" (171). Lambarde died in 1601, no doubt puzzled that there were apparently more rogues and beggars about than ever before, in

---

mary of state attempts to control the problem of the poor is found in Penry Williams (175–252). Other excellent summaries may be found in Clay (1.214–36 and 2.203–50) and Manning (1988: 157–86).

spite of over twenty years' worth of vigorous ear-borings; no doubt he lamented the lenity of the statute of 1593 (35 Eliz. I, c.7), which repealed these penalties and simply restored the whipping penalties from the time of Henry VIII. Lambarde's death ironically occurred in the year in which Parliament reenacted the two important statutes of 1597–98 (39 Eliz. I, c.3, c.4), which established the basic system of English poor relief for the next two hundred years.[9] One speaker in Thomas Dekker's *The Bel-Man of London* (1608) conveniently summarizes the range of punitive possibilities available in this period, referring to the "Statutes to *Burne* us i'th eares for *Rogues* . . . to Sindge us i'th hand for pilferers . . . to whippe us at posts for being *Beggers*; and to shackle our heeles i'th stockes for being idle vagabondes" (1963: 3.82).

William Lambarde was a learned and compassionate jurist, and I quote him here not to show that he was bloodthirsty—relatively speaking, he was not, though some contemporaries felt the provisions of the 1572 statute were "over-sharp and bloody"[10]—but because he offers such a thorough contemporary view of legal history and represents an exemplary Tudor case of personal and political contradiction regarding the poor. While professing an "unwilling" personal "disposition" to employ harsh corporal punishments, Lambarde nevertheless embraces them judicially. In 1575, moreover, Lambarde established the Collegium Pauperum Reinae Elizabeth in East Greenwich, "which lent generous sustenance to twenty poor"; he provided it more than 2,330 pounds before his death (Jordan: 142). This conjunction of sympathy and severity only begins to suggest the deeply puzzling problem the poor presented to Tudor authority. The poor "ye have always with ye," and while they must be given succor, some of them, it was universally agreed, ought to be pursued with a vengeance and punished, even cast into slavery or executed.

Before such questions of enforcement and control could be usefully addressed, however, the exact identity of the poor and the causes of their

---

[9] See Leonard's discussion (134–35) of the slight differences between the 1597 statute and the more celebrated one of 1601, 43 Eliz. I, c.2.

[10] Quoted in Leonard, p. 69. Henry Tripp, on the other hand, praised the new law because it "so charitably, wisely, and providently decreed and enacted" the whole matter of poverty (Hyperius: A3ᵛ). Edward Hext, a justice of the peace in Somerset, reported to Lord Burghley in a letter of 25 September 1596 that many vagabond thieves escaped justice altogether because the laws were felt to be too rigorous: "Most comonly the simple Cuntryman and woman, lokinge no farther then into the losse of ther owne goods, are of opinion that they wold not procure a mans death for all the goods in the world" (*TED*: 2.341).

poverty had to be identified. But here the Tudor authorities had about as little success as have those in twentieth-century America.

The Plea of the Poor

Of the genuinely poor, diseased, and destitute there was little dispute: it was a Christian duty to give them relief. The Bible had after all said "Blessed are you poor, for yours is the kingdom of God" (Luke 6:20) and commanded that we should "remember the poor" (Gal. 2:10). The Elizabethan "Homilie of Almes deeds" went into great detail to eliminate any possible argument for not giving to the poor. It asserted the best of all reasons to engage in charity to the poor: "So he that receiveth the poore and needy, and helpeth them in their affliction and distresse, doeth thereby receive & honour Christ their Master, who as he was poore and needie himselfe whilest hee lived here amongst us, to worke the mysterie of our salvation, at his departure hence he promised in his steed to send unto us those that were poore, by whose meanes his absence should bee supplied: and therefore that we would doe unto him, wee must doe unto them" (Rickey and Stroup: 155). As one writer put it in 1596, "We are all God's beggars; that God therefore may acknowledge his beggars, let us not despise ours" (Beier 1985: 109). Of the "true poore in deed," William Harrison wrote in 1577, "the word dooth bind us to make some dailie provision" (Holinshed: 1.307).

Just *how* one cared for the poor was a very different, highly contentious question. Before the Reformation, the monasteries of the kingdom provided an institutional structure by which some of the poor were relieved, mostly those in the country; the apparent inadequacies of monastic relief may be gauged by the numerous complaints, satires, and dialogues in humanist texts, both in England and on the Continent. Sir Thomas More, Erasmus, and Martin Luther were united at least in their perception that the wandering poor were a real social and spiritual problem and that the existing system had not contained them.[11] Moreover, monastic mendicants themselves, from a Protestant point of view, only exacerbated the problem, and begging priests were as unwanted a presence in the English discourse as any other beggar.

---

[11] Luther in fact had some embarrassing personal experiences in such matters: "I have myself of late years been cheated and befooled by such tramps and liars more than I wish to confess" (65).

The dissolution of the monasteries in the reign of Henry VIII resulted in, among other things, even greater numbers of vagrants on the roads of the kingdom, while the Protestant emphasis on faith rather than good works may have provided less incentive for individual acts of charitable relief. The history of the English Poor Laws after the monastic dissolution, according to one historical argument, reflects a gradual enlightenment, culminating in an organized national taxation providing relief for the needy; little by little, the state recognized an obligation to provide for the helpless. Margo Todd has argued that the charitable instincts of the Christian humanist tradition, and the Puritan movement in particular, helped lead to the statutes of relief (118–75).[12] Perhaps the most famous and moving religious appeal was Bishop Ridley's letter to William Cecil in 1552, supporting an attempt to take over the palace of Bridewell as a house of correction:

> I must be a suitor unto you in our good Master Christ's cause; I beseech you be good to him. The matter is, Sir, alass! he hath lain too long abroad (as you do know) without lodging in the streets of London, both hungry, naked and cold. . . . I do take you for one that feareth God, and would that Christ should lie no more abroad in the streets. (*TED*: 2.312)

A number of pietistic sermons and pamphlets in this period continued to urge fellow Christians to give alms to the poor in individual, private acts of charity; as their titles suggest—Henry Arthington, *Provision for the poore, now in penurie. Out of the Store-House of Gods plentie* (1597); John Downame, *The Plea of the Poore, or A Treatise of Beneficence and Almes-Deeds: teaching how these Christian duties are rightly to be performed, and perswading to the frequent doing of them* (1616)—true generosity is the essence of the Christian spirit. "It is plaine," Robert Allen argued in 1600, "that all stand bound to give" (G2ʳ). The benefit received by the soul who gave exceeded, for some Protestants, the benefit conferred on those who received charity. Reflecting one contemporary concern, Donne asked, "How shall you know whether he that askes [for alms] be truly poor or no?" In an important sense, the true status of the recipient of charity did not matter: "my mistaking the man," Donne went on, "shall never make God mis-

---

[12] Beier is skeptical: "The case for a distinct Protestant or Puritan position remains therefore unproven" (1983: 14–15). Breen has convincingly argued that within the Protestant tradition there is no essential difference between Puritan and Anglican attitudes toward work and wealth in the period 1600–40. For a later discussion of the so-called Puritan work ethic, see Seaver.

take my meaning" (8.277). The locus of charity moved, to some extent, from institutions to the individual heart, not as a "good work," but as a freely given gesture of charity.

Not every individual heart was so moved, obviously, for the history of poor relief also reveals an inexorable movement toward compulsory rather than voluntary donation. Christian charity was not willingly bestowed by some citizens, as Philip Stubbes observed in 1583. "God commaundeth in his law," wrote Stubbes, that "there be no miserable poore man, nor begger amongst us, but that every one be provided for and maintained of that abundance which God hath blessed us withal." Yet, "we thinke it a great matter if we geve them an old ragged coate, dublet, or a paire of hosen, or els a penny or two, wheras not withstanding we flow in abundance of all things. Than we thinke we are halfe way to heaven, and we need to do no more" (59).

As Thomas Adams lamented three decades later, "It is the nature of the wicked to have no care of the poore. . . . Your gallant thinkes not the distressed, the blinde, the lame to be part of his care: it concernes him not: true, and therefore heaven concernes him not" (1613: D2ᵛ). One farmer, asserting virtually a modern possessiveness, in 1597 refused to pay a poor tax, claiming, "my goodes are my nowne . . . they nor the queene nor the Councelle have to doe with my goodes, I will doe what I liste with them" (Leonard: 125). There was a considerable religious debate on the whole question of the spiritual as well as material efficacy of charity in this period.[13] From another point of view, however, the move toward a state-originated compulsory poor tax also exposes the structural function of charity in economic terms: to ease the pressures of poverty and unemployment created by an emergent capitalism.

The Fear of the Poor

One historical narrative thus accounts for the development of the Tudor Poor Laws as a reflection of Christian, specifically Protestant, concepts of charity, free will, and duty, with Bishop Ridley's letter as an exemplary text. Yet quite different explanations, contradicting the one just described, have also been offered. One counterdiscourse is summarized in the classic, acerbic analysis by R. H. Tawney: "As far as the ablebodied are concerned the Poor Law is in origin a measure of social police. Relief is thrown in as a makeweight, because by the end of the

---

[13] See Todd, passim. Archer (163–82) provides an excellent review of the question.

sixteenth century our statesmen have discovered that when economic
pressure reaches a certain point they cannot control men without it. The
whip has no terrors for the man who must look for work or starve" (272).
Tawney does concede, though, that the state was sufficiently enlightened
"to recognize that even among vagrants there is a class which is more
sinned against than sinning" (273). An even more cynical view of Tudor
altruism is offered by J. Thomas Kelly, who bluntly claims that "the intent
behind Tudor social legislation demanded control of the masses and *did
not* stem from Christian or humanitarian motivation" (134; my emphasis). How this negative can be proven is unclear.

Yet no system of relief or control of poverty, whatever the alleged motives behind it, was particularly effective during the Tudor period. Philip
Stubbes complained of the shortage of adequate facilities and offered
this apocalyptic vision of the streets of London in 1583:

> The poore lie in the streats uppon pallets of straw, and well if they have
> that to, or els in the mire and dirt, . . . having neither house to put in
> their heads, covering to keep them from the cold, nor yet to hide their
> shame withall, penny to buy them sustenance, nor any thing els, but are
> permitted to die in the streats like dogges, or beasts, without anie mercie
> or compassion shewed to them at all. (59–60)

Writing in 1587, John Howes offered a comparably bleak vision of London, complaining that the governors of Bridewell were failing their duty.

> They see in the streates a number of poore, aged and lame in greate
> miserie, but that they can not remedie. They see in the streates a nomber
> of poore children lie under stalles all the yere longe. They see divers
> poore woemen delivered of of [sic] childe in the streates, churches and
> cadges, and no provision for them. They have sene allso a greate nomber
> of poore men, which have died this sommer of the sicknes in the streats
> for wante of reliefe, and no place provided for them. These things are
> to[o] to[o] apparant in the eyes of the people, that heaven and earthe
> cryeth vengeance, and suerly god can not but be angrie with us, that will
> suffer our Christian Bretheren to die in the streates for wante of reliefe.

The speaker here, "Dignitie," rightly concludes that "it is a badde kinde
of governemente to see them die in the streates" and an abuse which
forgets "the words of Christ, where it is saide: I was naked and ye clothed
me not, I was hungry and yee gave me no meate. And therefore hell and
damnacion is prepared for yee." The reply to "Dignitie" by "Dutie" is

striking, and suggests how hopeless the problem seemed at the time: "For the poore which lie in the streates or die in the streates, it is answered before: London cannott reliefe inglande" (*TED*: 3.441–42).

Analyzing less dramatic archival sources, A. L. Beier has recently shown that the situation in London in the period 1550–1600 was as desperate as Stubbes and Howes had claimed. "For those out of work and homeless," Elizabethan London "was positively lethal," writes Beier (1985: 46). In a persuasive analysis of the available evidence, Ian Archer has recently offered a slightly less melodramatic picture than Beier does ("Most Londoners faced impoverishment rather than death"), though he demonstrates the "strong case for asserting the reality of a *perceived crisis*" (13).[14] The humiliation of the poor did not always end with their deaths: in his *Supplicacion for the Beggers* (c. 1546), Simon Fish describes how the naked corpse of a poor man, brought to church for burial, was not attended to for lack of a "duty," and so "they caused the dead corps to be caried into the strete againe, and there to remaine till the poore people, which dwelled in the place where the poore creature died, had begged so moch as the pristes call their d[e]we" (86).

It is difficult even to say how many vagrants there were, as contemporary estimates vary enormously. There were said to be 1,000 beggars in London in 1517 and 12,000 by 1594 (Aydelotte: 4). John Manningham in 1602 quoted a figure of 30,000 "idle persons and maisterles men" in London (113); this extraordinarily high estimate, in an urban population estimated at 200,000 in 1600, seems all the more fanciful when compared with national estimates. William Harrison claimed in 1577 that the figure amounted "unto above 10000 persons," and that "there is not one yeare commonlie, wherein three hundred or four hundred of them are not devoured and eaten up by the gallowes in one place and other" (Holinshed: 1.309, 313). One reliable observer, the Somerset Justice of the Peace Edward Hext, estimated in 1596 that "of these sort of wandringe Idell people there ar three or fower hundred in a shere [shire]" (*TED*: 2.345). The Norwich census of 1570—one of the most trustworthy documents of the period—reported that there were as many as 2,300 beggars in Norwich alone (*TED*: 2.316). A recent estimate by a modern historian offers national figures of approximately 15,000 wandering homeless in 1572, and 25,000 in the 1630s (Beier 1985: 16). Whatever the actual numbers, contemporary observers, from pamphleteers to the

---

[14] Archer is discussing the "crisis" of the 1590s (9–14), generally considered the most unsettled and difficult decade of the century. See also Peter Clark (1985). Rappaport stresses the social stability all through this period, but he is not entirely convincing.

Privy Council, *felt* that the problem of beggars was real, acute, and rapidly growing. As early as the 1530s, Thomas Starkey had written that "this is sure, that in no cuntrey of Christundome, for the nombur of pepul, you schal find so many beggaris as be here in Englond, and mo[re] now then have bin before time" (89).

Yet the reports of foreign visitors rarely mention beggars at all; one exception is the Duke of Stettin-Pomerania, who in 1602 remarked that it was a pleasure to visit the Exchange, "for one is not molested or accosted by beggars, who are elsewhere so frequently met with in places of this kind. For in all England they do not suffer any beggars, except they be few in number and outside the gates" (Bulow 1892: 11–13). It is difficult to reconcile such observations with the enormous number of complaints, observations, proclamations, and analyses of the English themselves. The year before Stettin-Pomerania visited London, for example, John Chamberlain wrote to Dudley Carleton (14 November 1601) that at Lady Ramsey's funeral, "the number of beggars" who appeared "at Leaden hall" to claim her six-penny dole "was so excessive and unreasonable that seventeen of them were thronged and trampled to death in the place and divers sore hurt and bruised" (McClure: 1.135). Leadenhall and the Exchange were only a few blocks apart.

Certainly the problem of the poor *was* real, of enormous scope, complex, and highly resistant to any solution. The situation was clearly desperate for many people, even in good harvest years, as is evident in this chilling account of the plight of the Norwich poor in 1570 (by no means a bad harvest year):

> Those [beggars] that daielie wente abowt pretendinge to satisfye their hunger, were not onelye contented to take at mens doores that suffized them, but being overgorged they caste foorthe the reste into the streete, so that they might be followed by the sight therof in pottage, breade, meate, and drinke which they spoiled verie voluptuouslye.

"These crewes," the report continues, refused offers of lodging, and even clothing,

> though the colde strooke so deepe into them, that what with diseases and wante of shiftenge their Flesh was eaton with vermine and corrupte diseases grewe upon them so faste and so grevouslye as they were paste remedye, and so much charges (by this meanes) bestowed upon one that wold have suffized a great sorte came all to waste and consummacion.
> (*TED*: 2.317)

The mixture of sympathy, disgust, and anger in this description is easily understood; beggars are a claim on charity, a test of conscience, and an affront to human sensibilities. The Norwich authorities accepted the responsibility to care for them, but were angry at them for their proclivity to waste and their lack of enlightened self-interest.

If a sense of charitable obligation was the major positive force leading Tudor society to care for its poor, certainly an even greater, negative force was fear. Wandering beggars were routinely linked with all kinds of minor and major crimes, from petty theft to murder. The beggar was and always has been a convenient outsider on whom much could be blamed—sometimes rightfully, but often falsely.[15] To *be* a beggar at all was itself a crime defined by statute, for vagrancy was, as Beier notes, "perhaps the classic crime of status" (1985: xxii).

If local authorities feared personal crime among the beggars, national authorities feared state crime, or sedition, far more. It has been argued that "the sixteenth century," in R. H. Tawney's famous aphorism, "lives in terror of the tramp" (268). An enormous number of official acts and proclamations agreed that, as a letter from the Privy Council in 1571 said, "there is no greater disorder nor no greater root of theftes murders, pickinge stealinge debate and sedicion then is in these Vagabonds and that riseth of them" (Aydelotte: 157). The desperation engendered by Tudor economic failures was simple and powerful, as Richard Morison noted: "Men wille steale, thoughe they be hanged, excepte they may live without steling" (E3ᵛ). Edward Hext, writing "in this time of dearthe"— during the calamitous harvest failures in the mid-1590s—tells of a group of eighty desperate men who hijacked a cartload of cheese, and of others "(and I feare me imboldened by the wandringe people) that stick not to say boldlye they must not starve, they will not starve." Some agitators, he reports, have even suggested to the local destitute that "the ritche men have gotten all into ther hands and will starve the poore" (*TED*:

---

[15] For a brief discussion of the real and imaginary connections between beggars and crime, see Beier (1985: 123–39). Penry Williams notes, "At most times the menace of the sturdy beggar was probably much less great than those in authority feared" (213), and he observes that the rogue books of Harman and Dekker (discussed in more detail in chapter 2) were "brilliant pieces of romantic journalism" which were "perhaps based on a modest reality" (213). Sharpe concludes, "The first impression to strike anyone turning from the statutes and the rogue literature to court archives is that the vagrant emerges as a much tamer phenomenon from the second than from the first. The large bands of vagrants, generally speaking, are absent; there is little evidence of a 'fraternity of vagabonds'; and the justices examining vagabonds seem not to have been in any way concerned about such matters. Most of those apprehended do not seem to have been the professional rogues legislated against in parliament, but were usually unremarkable representatives of the lower, and hence more vulnerable, strata of society" (100).

2.341). Confusing cause with effect, Hext goes on here to claim that "the Infinite numbers of the Idle wandringe people and robbers of the land are the chefest cause of the dearthe" (*TED*: 2.341–42), because they do not work and only consume.[16] The wandering poor were thus inscribed in the discourse of poverty as a potentially threatening political force, yet even though London in the 1580s and 1590s was particularly unsettled, still the authorities prevented any full-scale rebellion or class warfare in this period.[17]

There seems to have been no clear focus to the seditious impulses that surfaced among the country's wandering beggars. Although there were some organized risings, most protests were individual and isolated. What many observers found most unsettling was the reputed insolence of these masterless men. In his 1596 letter, for example, Hext was especially concerned that the "wanderinge Idell people" have bred fear in justices and other inferior authorities so that "no man dares to call them into question." At one recent sessions, he reports,

> a tall man, verye sturdy and auncient traveller, was Comitted by a Justice and browght to the Sessions and had Judgment to be whipped, he presently att the barre, in the face and hearinge of the whole benche, sware a great othe that if he weare whipped it shold be the dearest whipping to some that ever was; it strake suche a feare in him that Comitted him as he prayed he might [be] deferred untill the assises, wher he was delivered without anye whipping or other harme, And the Justice glad he had so pacified his wrath. (*TED*: 2.345)

The result of such impudence, Hext concludes, is that "they lawghe in ther sleves att the lenity of the lawe and the timerousnesse of thexecutioners of it" (*TED*: 2.345–46).

It was rare for any form of social protest to touch Queen Elizabeth directly. In Thomas Heywood's *If You Know Not Me, You Know Nobody* (Part 1, c. 1604), in fact, she is represented as personally relieving the desperate poor (instead of ordering their summary execution, as she once did in 1595 [Manning: 210]), who worship her beneficence and the grace of her charity. Here, though not yet queen, her care and regal qualities

---

[16] Starkey's earlier comment is typical: "As touching the multitude of beggaris, hit arguth no poverty, but rather much idulness and il pollicy; for hit is their owne cause and necligence that they so begge" (89–90).

[17] See the analysis of the authorities' success in Penry Williams (328–50) and Archer (1–17), as well as Manning's account of the London riots which did take place (1988: 187–219).

are nostalgically evident: "I spend my labours to relieve the poor. / Go, Gage; distribute these to those that need" (Thomas Heywood: 1.220). It must have seemed quite shocking, then, when "her Majestie in her Cooch," one evening in January 1582, "nere Islington, taking of the aier, her Highnes was environed with a nosmber of Rooges" (*TED*: 2.335). We learn no more of what happened at that confrontation, in this letter from William Fleetwood, Recorder of London, to Lord Burghley, but the shock of it galvanized Fleetwood and his colleagues into a general roundup of vagrants in London conducted with an evangelical zeal. The queen's carriage was surrounded on a Thursday evening; that same night, Fleetwood sent out warrants. On Friday morning he went out himself and took 74 rogues, and sent them to Bridewell; on Saturday, he examined them and ordered their punishment. Within eight days of the incident, more than 235 vagrants were brought in and punished, a very good week's work for the industrious and appropriately named Fleetwood. After dinner one evening, Fleetwood went to St. Paul's again and noted with considerable satisfaction that there "and in other places as well within the liberties as elswhere, . . . I founde not one rooge stirring" (*TED*: 2.336).

The example involving Fleetwood is colorful but somewhat misleading, since relatively few records of overtly seditious acts by wandering beggars exist, and even fewer records of any form of organized social protest. Even where there were enclosure riots, as Penry Williams has noted, "the peasants acted, not as men determined to overturn the social hierarchy, as the government generally thought, nor as men driven into unreasoning mob action by hunger and despair, as they were sometimes described at the time and later" (335). Rather they seemed to act by what E. P. Thompson has called "the moral economy of the crowd," defending a traditional, hierarchically sanctioned set of stable economic relationships.[18] In his important study of popular protest in Kent, Peter Clark has reached a similar conclusion: "Most popular disturbances 1558–1640 were distinctive for their customary, deferential character, exemplified by the citation of authorities, the claim to be acting in the Prince's name, and the absence of personal violence." The typical disorder, he concludes, "was small-scale, localised and customary, confirming rather than challenging the hierarchic structures and central norms of parish society."[19] The masterless men of the kingdom never produced a revolution,

[18] For a recent reassessment of Thompson, see Stevenson.
[19] Actual events, Peter Clark concludes, were "a far cry from the many-headed, class monster conjured up by official propagandists inspired by political concern to divide gentry and peasantry, and by royal memories of 1381 and 1549" (1976: 380–81).

but as chapter 4 will show, vagabonds, sedition, and the theater were closely associated.

The inescapable conclusion is that Tudor authorities feared vagrants far out of proportion to their actual menace. While it is true that a charitable impulse does motivate much of the Poor Law legislation, there was undoubtedly an equally strong motive of social control at work.[20] The beggar was tarred with every brush—Catholic or Anabaptist, criminal or rebel, gypsy or Irish—and inflated into a repulsive bogeyman haunting the state. Bacon referred to beggars and masterless men as "a burthen, an eye sore, a scandal, and a seed of peril and tumult in a state" (11.252). Looking back in 1651, Hobbes felt that, next to civil war, the greatest danger to England was "that dissolute condition of masterless men" (Beier 1985: 6). In an association of one marginalized group with another that seems, in retrospect, completely inevitable, beggars and witches were also often linked. One Puritan writer in 1617 warned that "many times Witches go under this habite [of the poor]."[21]

Beggars were described in some accounts as wandering, idle, disordered, anarchistic, or masterless—the complete inversion of the stable, fixed, ordered realm of the masters, and preeminently, the monarch. Although they occasionally move about in large groups, even gangs of forty to sixty, the vast majority wander alone or in twos or threes.[22] They are random, atomized figures on the social landscape. It might seem that the beggars' marginal existence would render them innocuous in the eyes of the authorities, since they were individually so helpless and impotent: as Paul Slack has noted, the vagrants "were individuals with few household or kinship ties, and they had often fled from masters, husbands, or wives" (1974: 377). But as we might expect, this marginality becomes the foremost charge *against* them: they are a threat precisely because of their antihierarchical status.[23] Under the statutes, furthermore, even some of those who did work in certain professions were

[20] As Beier notes, "Attacks upon the established order in religion and politics were as scarce among vagrants as in the criminal population generally" (1985: 139); see also his comments (155–56) on the motives behind the national searches of 1569–72 and 1631–39. For a close examination of Tudor control of the cloth market and economic planning in general, see Stone (1947).

[21] Quoted in Macfarlane, who also notes that "literary authorities agreed that witches often seemed poor, and it was a characteristic feature of their behaviour to beg" (151).

[22] In his letter detailing the 1582 incident with the queen, Fleetwood described one sweep "from whence I received a shool of xl [40] rooggs, men and women, and above" (*TED*: 2.335). See Beier's discussion of the evidence for and against the belief in an organized "underworld" (1985: 123–27).

[23] See the interesting essay "Masterless Men" by Hill (32–45), which treats a later period than I do. Hill observes of the vagabonds, "Such men were almost by definition

defined as vagrants by the law—peddlers and tinkers became illegal occupations under the 1572 and 1597 acts as, of course, did the profession of actor if not under special license. The Tudor authorities thus *increased* by statutory definition the number of vagrants beyond those who were unable or unwilling to work, ironically expanding the threat it claimed to wish to extinguish.[24] Thomas Adams remarked on this irony in a sermon of 1613: "Indeed our lawes have taken order for their restraint; wheresoever the fault is, they are rather multiplied; as if they had been sowen at the making of the statute, and now (as from a harvest) they arise ten for one" (1613: D4ᵛ).

When the literary or political imagination writes about these beggars, however, they are described not as isolated figures, but as highly organized and carefully gradated in their status and power among their colleagues. Writers such as John Awdeley, Thomas Harman, Thomas Dekker, and Robert Greene treat the beggars as if they were organized members of a national underworld of rigidly structured and wildly successful criminals. They are imagined to have their own traditions and customs, their own business plans and quarterly staff meetings. Beggars even have their own language, variously known as "canting" or "Peddler's French." Beggars' cant is first set out in detail in England in a special section of Thomas Harman's *Caveat* (1568; see chapter 2).[25] The hierarchical list of rogue types—first highly developed by Awdeley and Harman and widely imitated thereafter—is a standard feature of this literature, with the various types of beggars classified by skill, experience,

---

ideologically unmotivated: they could steal and plunder, but were incapable of concerted revolt" (33).

[24] One Wiltshire musician arrested in 1605, "who was 'sometimes a weaver, sometimes a surgeon, sometimes a minstrel, sometimes a dyer, and now a bullard' [i.e., one who keeps a bull], . . . was accused of having 'no trade to live by' " (Beier 1985: 88).

[25] Some of the cant terms are used in Awdeley's *Fraternity* (1561), but Harman is the first in English to offer an elaborate glossary of their "pelting speche" (82–87), as well as samples of dialogue between an Upright Man and a Rogue. Later writers copied, amplified, and corrected Harman's list. Some documentary evidence from court transcripts and interrogations demonstrates that beggars' cant was actually used by peddlers and vagabonds throughout the Tudor-Stuart period. Fleetwood, as one example, recorded in 1585 the use of such terms as "foiste," "nippe," "lift," and others at a school of pickpockets in London (*TED*: 2.339). Beier rejects the notion that beggars' cant constituted an "antilanguage," in Halliday's term, and argues instead that it was a jargon, primarily semantic in nature (Beier 1995), not "an alternative ideology" (Beier 1985: 126). I want to argue, however, that beggars' cant is at least one of the markers of a counterdiscourse and hence of an alternative politics—partly projected from above, partly generated from below. I am grateful to Professor Beier for allowing me to see a manuscript of his 1995 essay—which provides an excellent history of cant up to the late seventeenth century.

and power, in a kind of Great Chain of Thieving. The rogue, John Webster remarked, "paies his custome as truly to his graund Rogue, as tribute is paid to the great Turke" (4.41). Criminal vagrants are thus seen to be essentially just another craft-guild in their organization. Their canting, according to Jonathan Haynes, is itself "the language of a 'mystery,' " a specialized craft usually taught in a guild (105).

In *The Bel-Man of London* (1608), taking the socializing impulse even further, Thomas Dekker claims to have secretly witnessed one of the "Quarter-dinners" of the country's rogues: "They hold these sollemne meetings in foure several seasons of the yeare at least, and in several places to avoid discovery" (1963: 3.82). Moreover, there are said to be "degrees of *Superiority* and *Inferiority*" in their society. One after-dinner speaker offers a speech in praise of beggars and beggary, suggesting an idealistic romanticizing totally at odds with the historical records. At the end of the evening, every rogue is, like Willy Loman, given a territory to cover and quotas to meet.

In Dekker's version—and his must, for my purposes here, stand for several similar accounts, such as Samuel Rid's in *Martin Mark-All, Beadle of Bridewell* (1608)—the "Ragged Regiment" of rogues is just like any other group. Their status is as it were only *defined*: *"Villaines* they are by birth, *Varlets* by education, *Knaves* by profession, *Beggers* by the Statute, & *Rogues* by Act of Parliament" (1963: 3.82). Dekker's description suggests to some extent that the beggars are beggars because the prevailing social order says they are, and while Dekker only summons moralistic clichés ("They are the idle *Drones* of a Countrie, the *Caterpillers* of a Common wealth, and the *Aegyptian* lice of a *Kingdome*," 82) when he tells us who they are, he makes them finally little different from the mainstream of society when he represents them at their banquet. Thus one paradox of their representation: on the one hand, beggars are disordered, chaotic, without self-discipline, utterly alien and opposite to the hard-working proper citizenry; but on the other hand, they are said to make plans, form conspiracies, are hierarchically organized, and act and sound very much like the proper citizenry. The Great Chain of Thieving turns out to be a version of the Great Chain of Being superimposed on a fundamentally chaotic and unrelated group of individuals. The dominant discourse thus projects upon the vagrants and beggars a replication of the social structures which in fact define, exclude, and contain them.

Aside from the literary interest in this form of projection, it is easy to see how this fantasy served the political interests of the state: by vastly magnifying a real but dispersed social threat into a grand conspiracy, harsher and more extreme forms of punishment might be justified. Yet the greater the degree of order projected upon the beggars, the greater their resemblance to ordinary society became, and the extremities of inversion begin to collapse. In his *Notable Discovery of Coosnage* (1591), Robert Greene describes the oxymoronic "lawes of villanie," which were rigid and formal enough to have satisfied a Lambarde. The distinction between Webster's "graund Rogue" and the monarch may be only semantic. In Fletcher and Massinger's *Beggars' Bush* (c. 1613–22), there is actually an "election" of the "King of Beggars," which is about as paradoxical a political and social position as one can imagine in this period.

There are several discrepancies between the reality and the representation of beggars in early modern England, then. The estimated number of beggars varies widely; the political threat offered by so many masterless men and women, moreover, is reckoned as grave by most authorities, and yet there is very little evidence of any organized political action by them. Nor does the actual isolation of the vagrant, to take a final example, accord with the many lively descriptions of a "fraternity of vagabonds" (the title of a famous rogue book). Surely one explanation for the apparent discrepancies is that the Tudor authorities *were* successful in containing the threat offered by the wandering idle, and that the inflated estimates of their numbers and their potential subversiveness served the state's interest by establishing grounds for harsh and repressive statutory control. The few true revolts, like the Oxfordshire Rising in 1596 and the genuine attempts on Queen Elizabeth's life, may have made the more melodramatic claims about the beggars seem plausible.

The Sturdy Beggar and Penal Semiotics

The existence of large numbers of genuine wandering beggars and masterless men and women was rightly understood as potentially a major threat to the very foundation of Tudor culture, yet within this mass of the truly destitute was thought to be an even greater menace, the so-called sturdy beggar—the man or woman fully capable of work but refusing to seek or accept it. A sturdy beggar was by definition a paradox of deceit: this was not a real beggar stricken by disease or mischance, but a man or woman whose body was whole and unmarked who "counterfeits" (in the favorite term of the period) disease and mutilation in order to escape detection, evade work, and prey upon our sympathies.

The authorities who so assiduously provided for the truly infirm at the same time pursued the sturdy beggar with relentless energy. Many official documents of the period as well as the popular literature of the day elevated sturdy beggars to near demonic proportions, inflating their numbers, exaggerating their powers of disguise and deception, and dramatically overstating the seditious threat they represented. Local historical documents, such as court and assize records, however, reveal that in most cases the truth has been highly inflated and in some cases simply invented. It seems evident, in retrospect, that the *genuine* phenomenon of the sturdy beggar—for there certainly were such people—was systematically demonized by the prevailing discourse. As with other forms of deviant behavior during this period, preeminently witchcraft, the alleged threat to authority was used to legitimate authority; the need to control the threat is employed to justify the authoritarian repression already in place.

Why the sturdy beggar prompted such harsh official and private persecution remains a difficult question. In part this vengeful attitude must derive from a failure of contemporary economic theory to understand the causes and nature of unemployment; still, with the establishment of the bridewells, which were to provide work at state expense, this gap in theory (though certainly not in practice) seems closed. Anyone still without work could therefore be declared incorrigibly and willfully idle, beyond reformation. Other complex economic and social causes thus remained invisible. The demonization and suppression of the sturdy beggar may in part be understood then as a means of defining and legitimating the dominant culture's discursive power.

The terminology of the actor is frequently used in describing the more brazenly effective sturdy beggars, who are invariably described as sophisticated "counterfeitors" who could feign helplessness, disease, and mutilation. Complaints about fraudulent beggars are already plentiful in the early 1500s, as in Robert Copland's *The Highway to the Spital-House* (c. 1536, see Fig. 1), which describes beggars who

> By day on stilts or stooping on crutches
>   And so dissimule as false loitering flowches,
> With bloody clouts all about their leg,
>   And plasters on their skin when they go beg,
> Some counterfeit lepry, and other some
>   Put soap in their mouth to make it scum,
> And fall down as Saint Cornelys' evil.
>   These deceits they use worse than any devil;
> And when they be in their own company,
>   They be as whole as either you or I.

(Judges: 7)

Figure 1. Robert Copland, *The hyeway to the Spyttell hous*, 1536(?). By permission of the British Library, C.57.b.30.

Copland goes on to describe other types of counterfeiting—of soldiers, of mariners, of scholars from Oxford and Cambridge, and of pardoners, among others. Every rogue book from Copland on attributes superlative histrionic powers to the sturdy beggar. Official acts and proclamations invariably stress the need to distinguish carefully between the real and the fraudulent. In a typical warning, the Privy Council alerted the London Aldermen in 1569 that in searching out rogues and vagabonds, "diverse vagrant personnes will be founde who will counterfait them selfes as impotent beggars" (Aydelotte: 153). As a result of these concerns, the various organs of local and national government waged what can fairly be described as a war of signs against the country's vagrants and criminals before the audience of the general populace. The figure of the counterfeiting beggar, as we will see, exposed the signifiers of social status as something constructed rather than "natural." As a result, the ideology of order and authority engaged in various futile efforts to recuperate a purity of signification.

During the sixteenth century the authorities devised several ways, all equally ineffective in the end, by which to distinguish "true" beggars from sturdy beggars so that the "true" poor could be cared for, and the others properly punished. First, the truly poor or diseased were to be officially certified and given some mark or conspicuous sign to indicate their status as approved beggars. In 1517, the Court of Aldermen ordered officials in London to distribute specially made tokens to licensed beggars (about 500 were given out):

> That is to say a paier of beedes rounde with tharmes of london in the middis, to be striken with a stampe in metall of pure white tinne, and . . . to be sette upon their right shulders of ther Gownes openly to be seene, which persones having the seid tokens upon theim shalbe sufferd to begge and aske almes. (Aydelotte: 140–41)

Similar measures were attempted throughout the period—from York in 1515 (Beier 1985: 154) and Lincoln in 1543 (Leonard: 41) to Salisbury in 1638; in Salisbury even children were to wear badges and blue caps "whereby they might be known the children of the workhouse and distinguished from all other children" (Slack 1972: 192). In one ironic variation on this theme in Elizabethan Essex, all those poor people who received clothing under the terms of Henry Smith's will "were to be given 'upper garments on the right arm of which shall be a badge with the letters H. S.'" (Wrightson: 182).

Badging licensed beggars was ordered for the entire country in the

1563 statute (5 Eliz. I, c.3); when poor relief later became nationally mandatory, there was even greater reason for the authorities to attempt to mark the licensed beggars with badges. Some observers noted, however, that badging could be an odious cultural sign. John Howes remarked in 1587 that "the shame of this badge will make somme kepe in and not to goe abroade" (*TED*: 3.426), and thus not receive the alms they were entitled to, but the response was made that by such measures "the cittie will be well cleansed of beggers, Roges and idell people" (*TED*: 3.427). This utopian vision of a "cleansed" city never came to pass, for neither local nor national efforts at badging seem to have met with success. Fraudulent badges were simply counterfeited, and in any event badging could never eliminate the causes of vagabondage or significantly reduce the numbers of unlicensed and illegal beggars.

The next step beyond badging licensed beggars was to turn the semiotic arrow in the other direction and mark the unlicensed beggars. Since anything disposable was an unacceptable sign, the beggar's own body would receive the mark of signification. The statute of 1547 (considered so harsh as a whole that it was repealed six years later) authorized the branding of convicted vagrants, who were "to be marked with an hot iron in the breast the mark of V" (C. H. Williams: 1030).[26] Branding was revived in the Act of 1604 (1 James I, c.7): incorrigible rogues were to be "branded in the left shoulder with a hot burning iron of the breadth of an English shilling, with a great Roman 'R' upon the iron." The size of the sign of dispossession is thus ironically measured by the width of a coin, the very absence of which helps define the beggar to begin with. The brand was to be "so thoroughly burned and set on upon the skin and flesh, that the letter 'R' be seen and remain for a perpetual mark upon such rogue during his or her life" (Beier 1985: 159–60).

If a branding iron was not legally authorized or handy, a whip would be sufficient to inscribe the desired sign. Henry VIII's proclamation against vagabonds in 1531, for example, provided that any beggar or vagabond found guilty will be "stripped naked, from the privey partes of their bodies upwarde (men and women of great age or seke, and women with childe onely excepte) and being so naked, to be bounden, and sharpely beaten and skourged." If a beggar is arrested again within a short time, he risks the same punishment again unless, being stripped naked before the law, "if it may evidently appere unto them by the tokens on his body, that he hath ben al redy skourged or beaten, they

---

[26] Bellamy questions whether this penalty of the 1547 statute was ever enforced (1973: 182).

shall than suffer him to depart without other harme, with a billet signed by them, mencioninge where, and at what time he was beaten" (Aydelotte: 143–44). The difficulty with this semiotic scheme was that the signs faded and the incorrigible could go on; reading the signs also required an inquisitorial procedure. Permanent markings were therefore superior; the more easily visible the better.

So the harsh 1572 act provided an ingenious alternative to branding; as Harrison notes (and Lambarde applauded), anyone convicted of being a vagabond suffered "verie sharpe" punishment which produced a new and more easily visible permanent "token" on the body. In addition to the standard whipping, the offender was to be "burned through the gristle of the right eare, with an hot iron of the compasse of an inch about, as a manifestation of his wicked life, and due punishment received for the same" (Holinshed: 1.310). A second offense meant the other ear, a third the punishment of death. Thus the semiotic mutilation of the vagrant's body became both the "manifestation of," *and* the "due punishment received for," his "wicked life"—that is, his class status—in an eerie anticipation of Franz Kafka's short story "In the Penal Colony." In the vicious bodily economy of "marking," those sturdy beggars who had counterfeited broken limbs or horrible mutilation to move pity in the onlookers might well have found the "tokens" of authority permanently marked over their own false signs of impoverishment and suffering; the state could make real what had only been feigned, writing the true text of pain over the counterfeit one.

In the statute of 1572, the government of Elizabeth thus seems to have achieved a profound moment in what Michel Foucault has termed "penal semiotics," when the actual punishment for vagrancy has become its external physical sign, a bodily wound which is not life-threatening but which can never be separated from what it signifies (98). It establishes what Foucault says is most required in "the theatre of punishments, a relation that is immediately intelligible to the senses and on which a simple calculation may be based: a sort of reasonable aesthetic of punishment" (106). While this punishment eliminates the constant need to uncover and "read" the sturdy beggar's body so as to reveal his fraudulence, it also ensures that the vagrant can *never* escape his or her status, and thus preserves the very condition that it purports to control and suppress.

The major effect of this semiotic program is therefore not on the guilty beggar, for whom one brand or mark is much like another, nor on the judicial authorities, who can always order a beggar stripped and examined. Rather, this penalty, like all punishment, is, as Foucault says, "directed above all at others, at all the potentially guilty. So these obstacle-signs . . . must therefore circulate rapidly and widely; they must be accepted and redistributed by all; they must shape the discourse that each individual has with others and by which crime is forbidden to all by all" (108). In leaving its mark on the body of the guilty, the state establishes that that body is the king's property; the monarch ironically reasserts possession of his or her dispossessed inversion—the beggar.

Nevertheless, it cannot be said that even this innovation had a noticeable effect on the general problem of vagrancy or on the specific phenomenon of the sturdy beggar. Moreover, the inequities in the policy of marking did not go unnoticed: in *Kind-Hartes Dreame* (c. 1592), Henry Chettle observed that "the Rogue that liveth idly is restrained, the fidler and plaier that is maisterlese is in the same predicament, both these by the law are burned in the eare, and shall men more odious scape unpunished[?]" (18).

These attempts at a permanent denotation reveal the recurring official concern with counterfeiting. If civil authorities could not distinguish the vagrants *qua* vagrants whom they wished to control, they had an even more difficult time in distinguishing some counterfeiting vagrants from the proper citizenry—at least, there were many claims that some vagabonds had mastered the codes of civil society, infiltrating the very hierarchy from which they supposedly chose to be (and were) excluded. John Awdeley reported in 1561 that some vagabonds "will go commonly well appareled, without any weapon, and in place where they meete together, as at their hosteries or other places, they will beare the port of right good gentlemen, & some are the more trusted." Others, he reports, take their place at the very center of London's social world, dressing and acting in such a way that no semiotic analysis can distinguish them from anyone else: "Scarcely a man shall discerne, they go so gorgeously, sometime with waiting men, and sometime without. Their trade is to walke in such places, where as gentlemen & other worshipfull Citizens do resorte, as at Poules, or at Christes Hospital, & somtime at ye Royal exchaunge" (7–8). (Perhaps this is why the Duke of Stettin-Pomerania did not notice any beggars at the Exchange.)

After remarking on those who "sometime counterfeit the possession of all sorts of diseases," Harrison describes vagabonds' imitations of other vocations: "Diverse times in their apparell also they will be like serving men or laborers; oftentimes they can playe the mariners, and seeke for ships which they never lost" (Holinshed: 1.309). Hext claimed that they had even infiltrated the legal system, as he explains why so few of them were taken in a recent operation: "They have intelligens of all things intended against them, for ther be of them that wilbe present at every assise, Sessions, and assembly of Justices, and will so clothe them selves for that time as anye shold deame him to be an honest husbondman, So as nothinge is spoken, donne, or intended to be donne but they knowe it" (*TED:* 2.345).

If marginality itself is understood as a role, if rogues and beggars can choose to become like "serving men or laborers," "mariners" or the "honest husbondman," wearing "hansome cleane linnen," going "so gorgeously . . . with waiting men," bearing themselves like "right good gentlemen," then the sturdy beggar may be semiotically indistinguishable from the rest of society, no matter what schemes of punishment and marking the state attempts. The more sturdy beggars were exiled toward the margins of society, ironically, the greater the threat they seemed to pose for the center.

These supposedly remarkable powers of simulation are occasionally borne out by documentary evidence, but in many cases they are fantasies of projection, a downward displacement of a general crisis of the sign.[27] These sturdy beggars thus enact Jean Baudrillard's distinction between dissimulation and simulation: "To dissimulate," he notes, "is to feign not to have what one has. To simulate is to feign to have what one hasn't. One implies a presence, the other an absence." Thus the beggars' feigning of wounds and sores to gain sympathy is an annoying social fact, but dealing with such dissimulation is primarily a matter of gaining control of the signifying systems. "Thus," as Baudrillard concludes, "feigning or dissimulating leaves the reality principle intact: the difference is always clear, it is only masked." But the beggars' assumption of the clothing, speech, and role of the middling sort represents something far more threatening, since "simulation threatens the difference between 'true' and 'false,' between 'real' and 'imaginary' " (5). The nature of representation itself thus comes under interrogation, and the arbitrariness of the sign is exposed.

The more strenuously civil authorities attempted to control the means and methods of social signification, it seems, the more slippage there was. The semiotic penal program undertaken by Tudor authorities was always one of reaction, invariably lagging a step or two behind the quicker wiles of vagrant counterfeitors in a continuing war of signs and, more generally, lagging far behind overwhelming and at the time inex-

---

[27] See Barry Taylor for a stimulating account of this crisis (exemplified in his readings of Hooker, Gascoigne, Puttenham, Castiglione, and Jonson).

plicable social and economic forces. Governmentally required passports and badges were simply forged when needed. Even bodily mutilations were subject to invention and dissimulation (discussed later in greater detail). The failure of punitive marking—ear-borings, inscribed letters, lashings—as a means of social control was substantial, if not total. As such, this failure replicates the subversion of semiotic intention demonstrated in state attempts to manage other punitive spectacles, especially that of the public execution.[28] As Foucault argued, and Thomas Laqueur has recently confirmed in the case of England, the instability of this penal spectacle derived from the necessity of a crowd to observe it and the inability of the state to govern response, because the presence of large crowds inevitably turned the occasion into a "momentary saturnalia . . . in which rules were inverted, authority mocked and criminals transformed into heroes" (Foucault: 60–61); the "natural genre of [the] execution [scene]," Laqueur echoes, "is carnival," and hence subversion (340). Upon such occasions, Foucault noted, the "terror of the public execution" itself "created centres of illegality" (63).[29] In the case of judicial markings of beggars' bodies, the actors themselves either refused to cooperate, or rewrote the scripts altogether, thus demonstrating a sophisticated, ultimately subversive, understanding of the cultural codes of punishment.

There seems little, in these accounts, that such beggars cannot do: they can forge official documents, feign disease and mutilation, obliterate distinctions between true and false, and, if the occasion demands, even "playe" the role of middle-class citizen. Their histrionic powers would seem to outdistance those simultaneously on display in the public theaters on the south bank of the Thames. Rarely has any culture fashioned so wily and powerful an enemy out of such degraded and pathetic materials.

[28] See Breight's two essays, detailing how the Tudor and Stuart governments used treason charges and the public execution as a matter of policy.

[29] Show trials, as modern states are always still discovering, rarely show what they are intended to show. When Thomas Platter, a Swiss traveler, visited London in 1599, he remarked, as virtually all visitors did, on the grisly spectacle of some thirty impaled heads of executed traitors stuck on tall stakes on top of London Bridge, swaying in the breeze to greet all those who crossed into the City—an admonitory spectacle of perfect semiotic clarity, one might think. And yet, Platter noted, the dead traitors' "descendants are accustomed to boast of this, themselves even pointing out to one their ancestors' heads on this same bridge, believing that they will be esteemed the more because their antecedents were of such high descent that they could even covet the crown, but being too weak to attain it were executed for rebels." The ironic moral was clear: "Thus they make an honour for themselves of what was set up to be a disgrace and an example" (155).

Figure 2. Alexander Barclay, *The Shyp of Folys*, 1509. By permission of the British Library, G.11593.

The Theater of Pain

At one end of the range of cultural attitudes toward beggars lies the idea of the beggar as pure actor, then. In *The Ship of Fools* (1509; see Fig. 2), Alexander Barclay describes the typical beggar of this sort, who though "stronge and full of lustines / And yonge inoughe to labour for their fode," nevertheless

> Givith their bodies fully to slewthfulnes
> The beggers craft thinkinge to them moost good
> Some ray their legges and armis over with blood

> With levis and plasters though they be hole and sounde
> Some halt as cripils, their legge falsely up bounde.
>
> (Barclay: 303).

This is conventional enough, but Barclay's next type offers a far more horrific vision:

> Some other beggers falsly for the nonis
> Disfigure their children god wot unhappely
> Manglinge their facis, and brekinge their bonis
> To stere the people to pety that passe by
> There stande they begginge with tedious shout and cry
> There owne bodies tourninge to a strange fassion
> To move suche as passe to pite and compassion.
>
> (304)

Luther described comparable mutilations by one type of beggar, people "who treat their children badly in order that they may become lame—and who would be sorry if they should grow straight-legged—for thereby they are more able to cheat people with their lying words" (129). Ambrose Parey paints similar scenes of horror in France: some who are not satisfied with their own self-mutilations, he says, "have stollen children, have broken or dislocated their armes and legges, have cut out their tongues, have depressed the chest, or whole breast, that with these, as their owne children, begging up and downe the country, they may get the more reliefe" (994).[30]

Our horror at the practices Barclay, Luther, and Parey describe is not anachronistically modern, for the shattered bones and mangled faces of children were designed expressly to provoke a similar reaction at the time, to move pity and compassion in the onlooker. The older beggars can willingly turn their own bodies "to a strange fassion," as Barclay has it, but their children are not yet adepts in the histrionics of disfigurement and so must be disfigured by others to achieve the same status as the counterfeits. Montaigne warned, too, that when children

> counterfeit to be blind with one eye, crompt-backe, squint-eyed, or lame, and such other deformities of the body; for besides that the body thus tender may easily receive some ill custome, I know not how, it seemeth that fortune is glad to take us at our word; And I have heard diverse

---

[30] Parey registers beggars' deceits in a section of his work significantly titled "Of Monsters and Prodigies" (Book 25, 992–96).

examples of some, who have fallen sicke in very deede, because they have purposed to faine sicknes. (2.415)

Donne (in 1625) ironically described such practices as a "Calling." "For Parents bring up their children to it, nay they doe almost take prentises to it, some expert beggers teach others what they shall say, how they shall looke, how they shall lie, how they shall cry" (6.304).

Spectacles of suffering such as Barclay and Donne describe became part of the traditional scene of "enforced charity," to borrow Edgar's oxymoron in *King Lear*. Countless similar scenes—though usually minus the torture of the children—can be found in the literature of the period. A century later, in William Rowley's *A New Wonder, A Woman Never Vext* (c. 1610), the uncle and father of Robert Foster propose an identical plan.

> *Stephen.* Why, I'll be for thee, boy;
>   I'll break this leg, and bind it up again,
>   To pull out pity from a stony breast,
>   Rather than thou shalt want.
> *Old Foster.* Ay, do; let him sear up his arm, and scarf
>   it up
> With two yards of rope.
>
>   (1.1)

In Massinger's *The Picture* (c. 1629), the distraught servant Hilario thinks "Ile weepe my eyes out, and bee blind of purpose / To move compassion" (2.1.170–71). When the sturdy beggar smears himself with blood and excrement, he reenacts the cultural sign of degradation and marginality—the beggar not simply as body, but as broken body, the need to conceal wholeness balanced by the equally strong desire to reveal or perform disintegration and marginality.

No matter how conventional such scenes became, they still carried a persuasive power. Consider, for example, the effect that a comparable scene is imagined to have on the onlooker more than a century after Barclay, in John Downame's *The Plea of the Poore* (1616). Downame is giving reasons, in almost Dickensian detail, why men should visit the poor in their own houses:

> It would be a notable means to make us more compassionate, when as we should see their small provision, hungrie fare, thinne cloathes, and hard lodging: the children crying for hunger, and the parents out crying

them because they have no foode to give them; some lying in straw for want of beddes, others drinking water in stead of drinke, and a third sort neere starved with hunger for want of bread, or escaping that, quaking and shivering with cold for lacke of fire.

Such miseries "move a christian hart" simply in hearing of them, Downame notes, but "how much more would it stir them up to compassion if they saw them, for things seene more feelingly affect us, then those which we conceive by report of others (56–57)." The beggar must be *seen*, above all, in order to work powerfully on us; he must represent himself as both an image of poverty and as a concrete instance of it. His body is his only prop: he makes "his Rags and Soares, the *Orators* of his *necessity*" (Lupton 1634: 118). Read properly, such scenes of poverty and degradation

> make us lay the afflictions of others to heart, partaking with them in their sorrowes by a sympathy and fellowfeeling: and this compassion working upon our hearts, will not let our hands be idle, but will inlarge their bountie and make them more readily and liberally to contribute towards the reliefe of the poores necessities. (Downame: 56–57)

Downame's sentimentality seems perfectly modern, and naive, in its conception of the sympathetic heart, moved by "fellowfeeling," stirred to direct action to relieve the poor. Yet this assumption of a sympathetic and compassionate audience stands behind every scene of begging. The theater of deprivation contains only a single scene, endlessly replicated in different costumes and "strange fassion[s]"; the audience for this scene is always the same, ever different. Other writers, however, perhaps the majority, wished to avoid seeing these beggars altogether, for disgust and fear rather than sympathy more generally ruled. In *The Regiment of the Povertie* (1572), Andreas Hyperius insists that "those monstrous bodies or deformed with sundrie diseases, bloude, matter, wounds, and lothsome filthinesse, shall not be sette in sighte to terrifie and dismay women great with childe, or any other, which are soone troubled with the sighte of such gastly and sodayne shewes" (D3). Yet Donne, for one, urged his flock not to turn away from such "gastly . . . shewes."

> Thou seest a needy person, and thou turnest away thine eye; but it is the Prince of Darknesse that casts this mist upon thee; Thou stoppest thy nose at his sores, but they are thine own incompassionate bowels that stinke within thee; Thou tellest him, he troubles thee, and thinkest thou

hast chidden him into a silence; but he whispers still to God, and he shall trouble thee worse at last, when he shall tell thee, in the mouth of Jesus Christ, *I was hungry and ye fed me not.* (3.137)

The spectacles of pain and deprivation of London street theater must have been shocking indeed, and contemporary writers reached again and again to figurative language borrowed from the theater in order to describe both the performative aspect of the beggars' act and of their punishments, and the emotional impact on the urban audience. In *Worke for Armorours* (1609), Dekker offers a remarkable vision which equates the public punishment of the poor with another theatricalized public spectacle, bear-baiting.

For the *Beares,* or the *Buls* fighting with the dogs was a lively representation (me thought) of poore men going to lawe with the rich and mightie. . . . At length a blinde *Beare* was tied to the stake, and instead of baiting him with dogges, a company of creatures that had the shapes of men, & faces of christians (being either Colliers, Carters, or watermen) tooke the office of Beadles upon them, and whipt monsieur *Hunkes,* till the blood ran downe his old shoulders: It was some sport to see Innocence triumph over Tyranny, by beholding those unnecessary tormentors go away with scratchd hands, or torne legs from a poore Beast arm'd onely by nature to defend himselfe against *Violence:* yet methought this whipping of the blinde *Beare,* moved as much pittie in my breast towards him, as the leading of poore starved wretches to the whipping posts in *London* (when they had more neede to be releeved with foode) ought to move the hearts of Cittizens, though it be the fashion now to laugh at the punishment. (1963: 4.98–99)

Dekker's fascination with the violence in both scenes—with those who administer it—does not undermine his sympathy for the victims; his irony and sarcasm throughout this allegory of the battle between Poverty and Money are finally subversive ("Innocence . . . over Tyranny"), and never more so than in his final line, after a truce has been declared between the two warring social elements: "The rich men feast one another (as they were wont) and the poore were kept poore still in pollicy, because they should doe no more hurt" (4.166).

The only power the poor have is the power to "hurt," then, by means of the threat they represent to the social order, but the only "Violence" we are shown in this passage is that directed against the poor at "the whipping posts in London." The theatricalizing of the spectacle of punishment however does not succeed as Downame, for example, might expect—it "ought to move the hearts of Cittizens," Dekker agrees—but instead it is now the "fashion . . . to laugh at the punishment." What this remark reveals about the citizenry of London is that some of them, at least, had far stronger stomachs for spectacles of suffering and violence than many modern readers, and that in general they apparently had little sympathy for the victim, bear or beggar. Yet Dekker's comment also reveals the enormous contradictory range of reaction to the same cultural event: from sympathy to disgust to laughter. He knows what "ought" to move the human heart, but actual social interpretation leads in contrary directions. When human beings are equated with bears, moving the heart becomes even more difficult.

The Beggar's Body as Commodity

Theatricalized in some texts, the beggar's body was openly commodified in others; this swelling pool of surplus labor—calculated at a steady 20 percent, with seasonal variations as high as 50 percent (McMullan: 29)—represented both a threat to public order and an opportunity for emergent capitalist entrepreneurs. As one index of this movement, the Act of 1576 had ordered the national establishment of houses of correction, modeled on London's Bridewell Hospital; work was to be provided the poor, and training offered where needed. The ostensible motivations behind such establishments (see chapter 3) were first, the banishment of idleness, thought to be among the central causes of beggary; second, in an advance of economic theory, the indigent could be taught a useful, self-supporting trade. Yet a further consequence of this movement toward the encouragement of work, however, was that a calculation of profit and loss could now be measured on the beggar's body.

Renaissance "projectors" had little difficulty in suggesting far more imaginative, not to say lunatic, uses of these surplus bodies than merely beating hemp in Bridewell. Rather than being eaten, as Swift's modest proposer envisioned for his poor, the English vagabonds could be put to presumably lucrative work, as set forth for example in a 1580 scheme by Robert Hitchcock, *A Politic Plat for the honour of the Prince, the great profit of the public State, relief of the poor, preservation of the rich, reformation of rogues and idle persons, and the wealth of thousands that know not how to live.* Hitchcock begins his *Plat* with a survey rather like William Lambarde's review of the history of vagrant legislation, which concludes, in contrast to many of his contemporaries, that the law alone cannot provide the necessary cure. "Yet, nevertheless, all these laws, so circumspectly made, could not, nor cannot banish that pestilent canker out of this common weal by any degree; but that the same increaseth daily more and more: to the great hurt and impoverishing of this realm" (141). Hitchcock's cure is simply for the state to provide work: "The lusty vagabonds and idle persons (the roots, buds, and seeds of idleness) shall at all hands and in all places be set on work, and labour willingly, and thereby prove good subjects, and profitable members of this common weal" (141).

Hitchcock frequently stresses the "profitable" nature of his plan—one of his aims on the title page is after all the "preservation of the rich"—and he goes on to suggest, through an elaborately unreal calculus, how much wealth the realm loses because of this problem, and how much might be gained even beyond what could be saved. Hitchcock proposes that an entire national fishing fleet be equipped and staffed with vagabonds: he calculates the amount of herring that could be caught, how much it would sell for, what the costs of such a fleet would be; he describes the ports where the ships would lie, and when and where to catch the herring. Each of the thousands of ships would have "one skilful Master to govern it, twelve mariners or fishermen, and twelve of the strong lusty beggars or poor men taken up through this land" (142). When he quotes a hypothetical opinion on this plan—"It were good to give a subsidy for this purpose to ship these kind of people in this sort; for if they should never return, and so avoided, the land were happy: for it is but the riddance of a number of idle and evil disposed people"—Hitchcock responds not with a humanitarian but an economic reply: do not banish them, because we can make a fortune through their labor (167).

Apart from its untenable economic theory, Hitchcock's *Plat* is of interest here because of its assumptions about the causes and cures of vagrancy. For Hitchcock, economic self-interest is the central human motivation. The problem of the poor ought to be relieved, in the first place, because they are

> perhaps apt to assist rebellion, or to join with whomsoever dare invade this noble Island, if any such attempt should be made. Then are they meet guides to bring the soldiers or men of war to the rich men's wealth. For they can point with their finger, "There it is!" "Yonder it is!" "Here it is!" "And he hath it!" and, "She hath it that will do us much good!" and so procure martyrdom with murder to many wealthy persons, for their wealth.

It therefore behooves "the wise and wealthy men of this land" to seek relief for the poor, so that through work they can "relieve themselves of their great need and want" (159).

Hitchcock imagines that everyone on the margin can be brought into the center by a process of enlightened self-interest. "Having some good trade to live upon," he argues, "there is no doubt but that they will prove good and profitable subjects; and be careful to see this common wealth flourish; and will spend their lives and blood to defend the same, and their little wealth, their liberties, their wives, and children. For having nothing, they are desperate; but having some little goods, they will die before they lose it" (159).

Hitchcock estimates that every man will each year earn "20 £ clear, and for ever to continue" (160). This substantial income will allow these beggars "to live in estimation amongst men, whereas before they were hated, whipped, almost starved, poor and naked, imprisoned, and in danger daily to be marked with a burning iron for a rogue, and to be hanged for a vagabond." In Hitchcock's scheme, "When they shall find these dangers to be avoided by their travail, and thereby an increase of wealth to ensue: they will be glad to continue this good and profitable vocation, and shun the other" (160). Hitchcock's assumptions about human nature, and social and economic reality, are transparent enough that they require little comment; the existence of Nicholas Genings alone, as we will see in the next chapter, undermines most of them. For Hitchcock, though, there are few or no distinctions among the causes or motives of the beggars; they remain for him a faceless mass—both a social threat and an untapped economic commodity.

A second, even more ambitious projector with a plan was one Thomas Stanley; his scheme appears in *Stanleyes Remedy: Or, the Way how to reform wandring Beggers, Theeves, high-way Robbers and Pick-pockets. Or, An Abstract of his Discoverie: Wherein is shewed, that Sodomes Sin of Idlenesse is the Poverty and Misery of this Kingdome* (printed 1646 but written during the early years of James's reign). Stanley had firsthand experience as a man of the roads, being himself "somtimes an Inns of Court Gentleman, afterwards by lewd company became a highway Robber in Queen *Elizabeth's* reign, having his life pardoned" (A1ᵛ). Stanley wrote King James that some authorities believe that "there are not so few as 80000 idle Vagrants in this Land" (A2ᵛ), costing the kingdom at least 1,000 pounds a day. Stanley offers as his own analysis the less apocalyptic number of 19,450 vagrants (at least two in each of the 9,725 parishes in England), if anything a low figure. Stanley reckons that these vagrants waste 3d. a day each, totaling 243£.2s.6d. a day, or almost 90,000 pounds year. "This great sum of money is spent idly, besides the great sums of money the Vagrants, and Idlers get by begging, stealing, and other misdemeanours, and the Common-wealth loseth that now, which might bee well saved by their labours, if they were set to work" (A2).

Stanley claims that "it is evident to all men, that Beggerie and Theeverie did never more abound within this your Realme of England, and the cause of this miserie is Idlenesse" (A4). James is urged to set all the vagrants to work in "houses of Instruction or Correction"—hardly a new idea, given the Act of 1576. For those who will not work, he goes on, "but are resolved to live a refractorie life, they may be sent either to sea (to rid the land of them) or sold to the English Plantations, to see whether God will turne their hearts and amend their lives, that they may not come to a shamefull end, but rather hope they may return to their Countrey againe with joy" (A3).

Transportation or actual slavery can thus be rationalized as a form of instruction or correction. Stanley justifies his proposal by observing that beggars may be branded and thus marked "with such a note of infamie, as they may be assured no man will set them on work." Justice is served, then, but "the point of Charitie" remains undone, "which is [to] provide houses and convenient places to set the poore to work, which ought to be done in equitie and justice, as well as the other" (A3ᵛ). Stanley sounds quite modern when he notes the unfairness of the current law and the contradictions in the various forms of punishment—the branding which prevents future work, or the remanding of vagrants to their birthplaces or to where they last dwelled, when some never dwelled anywhere, and few knew where they had been born.

Stanley concludes his brief essay by drawing closer to the reality of the beggars, even representing their voices, if not their names, in one of the most plangent of the poor appeals in this period.

> I have heard the Rogues and Beggars curse the Magistrates unto their faces, for providing such a Law to whip and brand them, and not provide houses of labour for them ... for tell the begging Souldier, and the wandring and sturdy Beggar, that they are able to work for their living, and bid them go to work, they will presently answer you, they would work if they could get it. (A4)

Like Hitchcock, Stanley is a realist in his diagnosis of the social disease, but an optimist in his belief in a cure ("for surely many would go voluntarily to the work-houses to work, if such houses were provided for them," A4). The workhouses that did exist in James's time, such as Bridewell, had long since become notorious as prisons and sites of punishment rather than reformation; Stanley knew this quite well.

Stanley's enlightened analysis can be eloquent indeed—"the right end and intent of punishing of Rogues, is but the destruction of vices, and saving of men" (A4)—and he speaks with the voice of personal experience. It seems all the more ironic, then, when we learn that a group headed by Stanley was actually given control of Bridewell in 1602, with disastrous results. The governors of Bridewell apparently succumbed to the temptation offered by Stanley: to surrender control of the hospital into private hands and pay a substantial fee, but presumably save substantial amounts of money and aggravation. On 16 January 1602, tenders were offered to the Lord Mayor and Aldermen "by Stanley and others, for setting four hundred poore on worke in Bridewell" (Bowen 1798: 26).[31] On 29 March 1602, with consultations completed, "an indenture was made between the governors and *Thomas Stanley*, of London, gentleman," and three other men, "who agree to undertake the charge, oversight, and guiding of the *idle* and *evil disposed persons* in Bridewell, as ministers and fit instruments under the lord mayor of London and governors, for the terme of ten years, receiving £ 300 per annum" (27). On 20 April 1602, Stanley and his group "took upon them the charge of all the prisoners [note the use of this term] in the house, except the Spaniards" (Bowen 1798: 27). The "ten years" agreement actually lasted fewer than seven months, for on 16 October 1602, Stanley's group "surrender[ed] the indenture of leese granted to them, with all their right, title, and interest" (27).

What occurred during those seven months ought to make us pause before swallowing all the humanitarian and utopian rhetoric of the period. Although Stanley's group were "bounde" to keep "five hundred vagrants at worke," they in fact "had not anye time above one hundred of all sorte." Moreover, the hospital had been turned into a brothel complete with gourmet amenities:

[31] Beier incorrectly dates Stanley's takeover of Bridewell as 1605 (1985: 151, 167), which is actually the date of the entry in the CLRO *Journals* 26/336b-338a; the entry in the CLRO *Remembrancia* (2.254) is essentially identical to the *Journal* version. The *Journal* entry refers to these events as taking place during the time of "John Garrard then Lo: Maior"—Garrard was Lord Mayor in 1601-2 (Stow: 2.186)—and the governors of Bridewell again "all debated [Stanley's misrule] in the time of the mayoralty of Robert Lee" (CLRO *Journals* 26/338a)—who succeeded Garrard in 1602-3. These dates are corroborated by the Bridewell Hospital records; see the BCB entries for 29 July, 4 August, 11 September, and 16 October 1602 ("Extracts": 12.37-40).

such lewde women as were commited unto them for their wicked life, and should have beene kept hard at worke, and had the diet of the house, weare suffered to intertaine any that would resorte unto them in as great loosenes as they would have done abroad in their lewd houses, and there were feasted with varietie of wines, and delicate meates.

It might be argued that Stanley did not so much abandon his economic premises as shift to a different labor pool. With so few actual "prisoners," moreover, Stanley had the space and the financial resources to set up yet another thriving enterprise parallel to the brothel, to wit, "a common tapphouse of stronge beere which they had there sett upp to the greate scandall of the said hospitall." Once revealed, Stanley and his colleagues surrendered the lease and were "found indebted (over and above the yearely allowance of the house)." Here is where one really has to admire Stanley's nerve, for he immediately "made earnest suite" to the Aldermen that if they would advance yet more money, "and discharge that debte," then Stanley "and the rest stood ingaged as aforesaid."[32] This offer was, needless to say, not taken up.

The "great misgovernment" of Stanley has its comical as well as its tragic side—other records document the misery of those imprisoned in Bridewell—but it is just one of many purely economic schemes designed not merely to solve a pressing social problem, but to take advantage of a cheap labor pool. We have already seen how Robert Hitchcock dismisses the notion of simple transportation of vagrants because he believes they will be needed for the crews of his herring fleet. Although the possibility of the forced transportation of vagrants had been discussed for some time (Hitchcock wrote in 1580), particularly in various texts in Richard Hakluyt's *Voyages,* the first statutory authority was the Act of 1597 (39 Eliz. I, c.4), which provided that the most dangerous or incorrigible rogues and vagrants "may lawfully . . . be banished out of this Realme . . . unto such partes beyond the Seas" (*TED:* 2.357).[33] With this legal backing, the first deportations of vagabonds began in the next decade. Ridding the kingdom of an undesirable and noisome social element was a sufficient motivation, to be sure, but the action dramatically accelerated when the advantages of acquiring cheap labor in the new colonies were realized. Stanley noted the two possibilities: those who refuse to work could "be sent either to sea (to rid the land of them) or sold to the English Plantations." Simple banishment soon became indentured ser-

---

[32] All quotations in this paragraph from CLRO *Journals* 26/337b.

[33] For a brief summary of the practice of vagrant transportation, see Beier (1985: 162–64). A useful account of this practice is given by Smith (especially 136–51).

vitude; slavery became a form of punishment; and a drop in the supply of available bodies eventually led to nothing less than the kidnapping of vagrant children off the streets of London.[34]

The forced transportation of beggars and vagabonds to Virginia is a relatively small event in comparison to the far greater magnitude of slavery and indentured servitude in New World colonies, but it serves as the logical completion of the cultural process by which the beggar's body became a commodity. Eventually the language of charitable intention was evoked to justify the deportation of vagabonds into indentured servitude, and it may well have been true that even the very low odds of survival of the voyage and the life in Virginia were better than those of survival on the streets of London. The colonization of Virgina seemed to many at the time to promise economic, social, and spiritual gains all at once.[35] Remarking on the seemingly intractable phenomenon of the surplus poor, Sir Edwin Sandys told Parliament in 1621 that previous social remedies had merely moved the poor around, from country to city and vice versa. In Sandys's remarkably disingenuous analysis, "the cause of this [flood of vagrants] I suppose is the Monopolies, wherby all haveinge not libertie of trade all the poore can not be imployed. . . . And in other countries more populous ther be no beggars." The solution of course was to send the unemployed poor to Virginia: "Never was ther a fairer gate opened to a nation to disburden it selfe nor better meanes by reason of the abundance of people to advance such a plantation" (Notestein: 5.114).

The spiritual side of the argument was developed by Sandys's acquaintance and colleague, John Donne, who had sought to be appointed secretary to the company in 1608–9 (Bald: 162). In 1622, the now successful Dr. Donne, Dean of St. Paul's, had been made an honorary member of the Virginia Company on 22 May, and on 13 November Donne had preached a sermon (his first to be published) to the assembled Virginia Company, in which he pressed upon them their main, spiritual mission:

[34] In examining the implications of the 1547 "slavery" act, Davies reminds us "that slavery itself was not so very different, in theory or in practice, from the compulsory apprenticeship of the young (or indeed, of compulsory service for the rest of the community, except those of private means) of Elizabethan social legislation" (543). Davies argues that while "slavery as a formal concept" in the law was unacceptable, the equivalent can frequently be found under different names; Henry VIII, for example, had ordered in 1545 that vagrants and masterless men should serve "in these his wars in certain galleys, and other like vessels" (*TRP*. 1.352). Davies also argues that the slavery provisions of the 1547 act were never actually enforced.

[35] For a recent review of the rise and fall of the Virginia Company, in the framework of the company merchants and colonial development, see Brenner (93–102).

"Onely let your principall ende, bee the propagation of the *glorious Gos-pell*' and the glory of God (4.271). Still, the colony might have other "great uses" of a socioeconomic nature, as Donne went on to note.

> It shall redeeme many a wretch from the Jawes of death, from the hands of the Executioner, upon whom, perchaunce a small fault, or perchance a first fault, or perchance a fault heartily and sincerely repented, per-chance no fault, but malice, had otherwise cast a present, and ignomin-ious death. It shall sweep your streets, and wash your dores, from idle persons, and the children of idle persons, and imploy them: and truely, if the whole Countrey were but such a *Bridewell*, to force idle persons to work, it had a good use. But it is already, not onely a *Spleene*, to draine the ill humors of the body, but a *Liver*, to breed good bloud. (4.272)

This vision of the potentially utopian effects of the Virginia plantation rests on different discursive rhetorics—the colony as redeemer, moral and economic cleanser, bodily purifier of the humors—and, in a telling analogy, briefly imagines the entire plantation as a "Bridewell."

The most offensive employment of these arguments occurred in the period 1618–22, when vagrant children were singled out as especially desirable to be sent to Virginia and were simply taken.[36] The Common Council began to negotiate with the Virginia Company in 1618, and the first group of ninety-nine children—some of whom "may have been as young as 8 years old" (Canny: 26)— were shipped off to Virginia by the following spring. Finding the children was simple: the Lord Mayor in-structed the city constables to "walk the streets within their several pre-cincts, and forthwith apprehend all such vagrant children, both boys and girls, as they shall find in the streets and in the markets or wandering in the night to be apprehended by the watch, and then to commit to Bride-well, there to remain until further order be given."[37] The process was repeated again in 1619–20, but with the added outrage that those par-ents "overcharged and burdened with poor children" who did not agree to surrender some of their children "were to be told that they would not receive any further poor relief from the parish" (Robert C. Johnson: 142).

---

[36] See Smith (147–51). The fullest treatment of this episode in the history is found in Robert C. Johnson; see also Canny. The names and BCB entries for each child are given by Robert Hume.

[37] CLRO *Journals* 30/382; quoted from Robert C. Johnson (139). Each child, Johnson notes, "after having served as an apprentice, would be given fifty acres of land, the boy when he was twenty-four years of age and the girl on her twenty-first birthday or day of marriage, whichever occurred first" (139).

The difficult conditions of life in Virginia must have become known in London, for a number of children in this second group, who were being held in Bridewell, refused to go; under the law, they could not yet be forcibly compelled (what it took to get children to agree to go can only be guessed at). That omission soon changed when Sir Edwin Sandys appealed to the king's secretary on behalf of the Virginia Company, on 28 January 1620. Sandys noted that the Virginia Company had contracted for one hundred children out of the "superfluous multitude" in London:

> Now it falleth out that among those Children, sundry being ill disposed, and fitter for any remote place then for this Citie, declare their unwillingnes to goe to Virginia: of whom the Citie is especially desirous to be disburdened, and in Virginia under severe Masters they may be brought to goodnes. But this Citie wanting authority to deliver, and the Virginia Company to transport theis persons against their wills: the burden is layd upon me ... to procure higher authority for the warranting thereof. (Kingsbury: 3.259)

The mixture of motives here again is typical: of social utility ("the Citie ... disburdened"), of charitable reformation ("brought to goodnes"), and, everywhere, of economic self-interest. Sandys's wish was soon granted, for on 31 January the Privy Council granted the necessary authority and also authorized that if any of the children should be found "obstinate to resist or otherwise to disobey," they should be imprisoned, punished, and shipped to Virginia (*APC*. 37.118). So much for the children's revolt. They were shipped out in February, many of them on a ship ironically named *Duty* (Robert C. Johnson: 144). The City's actions were praised by the Privy Council: "The citty deserveth thankes and commendacions for redeemeing so many poore soules from misery and ruine and putting them in a condicion of use and service to the State" (*APC*. 37.118).

After the Indian massacre of colonists in 1622, the Court of Aldermen agreed to send forth yet another group of one hundred vagrants, who turned out to be the last such group provided by the City of London. Robert C. Johnson offers several inconclusive speculations on why the Virginia Company lost the support of the City of London, but the fact is that Sir Edwin Sandys then asked Parliament to order that "the poor that cannot be set on work may be sent to Virginia." His argument turned on all the familiar reasons. Parliament was dissolved before it could act, however, and soon after Parliament met again in 1624, the colony passed from private to royal control. In the end, this interlude of forced vagrant transportation seems to have had little or no impact on the problems in London. As one writer observed in 1621, in a listing of all the ways in which a beggar might die or vanish,

> this Rotting sore [of beggars] hath runne farre of late, if wee consider how many of these people the Warres hath swallowed up: How many of them are shipped to that famous Plantation of *Virginia & Sommer Islands*: How many the Judgement of the Law hath turnd over: How many of them greevous diseases have ended their dayes: How many have perished in the fields: And how the realm is yet pittifully pestered with them. (*Greevous*. C1ᵛ)

As a token played in the process of imperialist expansion, then, the vagrants of London made little impact on the Virginia Colony, and their absence in London was not marked at all.[38]

As a source of surplus, involuntary labor, however, the beggar continued to prove a potentially valuable commodity over a long period of time. Military impressment would in the end consume vastly greater numbers of the surplus poor than the New World colonies would. In 1578 Barnabe Riche complained of London military recruiters that "either they scour their prisons of thieves or their streets of rogues and vagabonds" (Beier 1985: 94).[39] A constable in Ben Jonson's *Eastward Hoe* describes Flash and Quicksilver as "a couple of Maisterlesse men . . . prest for the Low-countries," who should be carried "to Bridewell . . . [from which] they may be shipt away" (4.2.188–91). In a particularly vicious cycle, beggars would be rounded up to become soldiers and sent overseas to battle; those who survived and returned home as unemployed soldiers would be condemned as vagrants and rounded up again for further service. Shakespeare's Falstaff shows the way in misusing "the King's press," replacing the best recruits with "slaves as ragged as Lazarus in the painted cloth . . . discarded unjust servingmen, younger sons to younger brothers, revolted tapsters, and hostlers trade-fallen, the cankers of a calm world and a long peace." Few even have shirts, but like any vagabond "they'll find linen enough on every hedge." When Westmoreland remarks that "they

---

[38] Vagrant transportation in support of colonization efforts in Ireland began even earlier, but the overall impact on the vagrant population was similarly small.

[39] A typical order by the Privy Council: on 17 December 1591, the Lord Mayor and Alderman are to take up within the city and liberties "to the nombre of one hundred loose and masterles men (of whom and especiallie of such as are returned from the service in France there are at this time great nombers) to be sent forthwith to Ostend" for further military service (*APC*. 22.129).

are exceeding poor and bare, too beggarly," Falstaff responds with cheerful indifference, "Faith, for their poverty, I know not where they had that" (*1 Henry IV* 4.2.12–70). Falstaff pretends to mistake the Lord Chief Justice's servant calling his name in Part 2: "What, a young knave, and begging? Is there not wars? Is there not employment?" (*2 Henry IV* 1.2.71–72).

The Beggars' Holiday

For all their differences, the representations of both pietists and projectors reflect a common economic reality of poverty and vagrancy, while at the same time a very different group of writers romanticized and idealized the beggar's life, turning every social and economic negative into a positive. The tradition of the merry beggar dates at least from the late fifteenth century and has always been contemporaneous with the more realistic texts I have been examining, indeed at times a recurring element *within* these same texts.[40] Even Hyperius, at the very end of such a sympathetic tract as *The Regiment of the Povertie*, observes that "a spare and sober supper, is yet a supper: and the poore mans parsimonye or frugalitie is much more healthfull, than the riche mans excesses" (K6). The anonymous author of *The Run-awayes Answer* (1625), to take a later example, defines a "Runne-away" as he who will not learn a trade, but

> turnes Roague, runnes into the Countrey a *Padding*, keepes company with *Gipseys*, and strowling Pedlers, fatting himselfe with the lazy bread of Sommer, tumbling (during that Season) in a Hay-cock with his *Dell*, and in Winter, lying snug in a Brickkill with his *Doxy*. (1)

This vision of blowsy plenitude, with its Edenic "lazy bread of Sommer" virtually falling into one's hands and its natural eroticism, spiced with a bit of beggar's cant, is of course a species of pastoral; imagining a vagrant "lying snug" in the winter—if anything, better off than most other people—is a comfortable evasion of the social reality. The key distinction, Dekker notes in *The Honest Whore, Part 1*, is that "although their bodies beg, their soules are kings" (5.2.504–5). In showing how similar kinds of "romance" become a feature of the rogue tradition, John Timpane notes that the social assumption behind such visions as *The Run-awayes Answer*—"that because they wander, rogues are free of social restric-

---

[40] Timpane's is the best description of this tradition.

tion—becomes translated into the realm of fantasy . . . this fantasy assumes that he who is free of social culture must be happy'' (34).[41]

Perhaps the most elaborately conceived idealization of beggars—certainly among the deepest fantasies of the period—is John Taylor's lengthy poem, *The Praise, Antiquity, and commodity of Beggery, Beggers, and Begging* (1621; see fig. 3) For Taylor, the beggar is first of all a primitive, Adamic figure, "Old *Adams* sonne," in fact, "and heire unto his sins"; as Adam "did possesse / The world, there's not a Begger that hath lesse" (1621: B). Of the four elements, Taylor says, "every Begger hath in plenteous store, / And every mighty Monarch hath no more" (B), a possession which however one cannot eat or use to clothe oneself. The whole cosmos, Taylor rhapsodizes, conspires to make life pleasant for the vagrant, as the Great Chain of Being becomes a kind of genial servant.

> Thus all degrees and states, whate're they are,
> With beggers happinesse cannot compare:
> Heav'n is the roofe that Canopies his head,
> The cloudes his Curtaines, and the earth his bed,
> The Sunne his fire, the Starre's his candle light,
> The Moone his Lampe that guides him in the night.
> When scorching *Sol* makes other mortals sweat,
> Each tree doth shade a begger from his heat:
> When nipping Winter makes the Cow to quake,
> A begger will a Barne for harbour take,
> When Tree and Steeples are o're-turn'd with winde,
> A begger will a hedge for shelter finde.

"He lives in such a safe and happy state," Taylor concludes, "That he is neither hated, nor doth hate. / None beares him malice, rancour, or despight" (B2). This conspiracy of pleasurable attention would have been a considerable surprise to the destitute of the kingdom, who were if anything increasing in number in the 1620s and 1630s; the statutes of the kingdom alone contradict everything in this statement.

Later, in a sequence of Marvellian visions of personified natural fecundity, Taylor shows how the garden of the world helps feed the beggar

---

[41] Timpane is here discussing Henry Melwall's *Fulgens and Lucres*, but his point seems generally true to me. There were certainly occasional reports of vagrants living comfortably in the country, such as Henrie Davies in Staffordshire, in 1591, who boasted "boeth at Enston and at Geaton that in fishinge in the waters he coulde be worthi his x *s.* or noble adaie." Davies reported a whole series of fish-stealing episodes; he eventually "posted a surety of £100 that he would leave the county within the next ten days" (Manning 1988: 304).

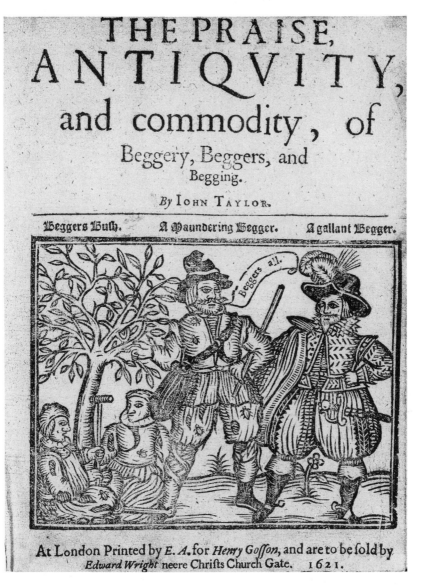

Figure 3. John Taylor, *The Praise, Antiquity, and commodity, of Beggery, Beggers, and Begging,* 1621. Reproduced by permission of The Huntington Library, San Marino, California, RB 30622.

(each hedge "attends his appetite where e're he goes"), how "his musicke waytes on him in every bush" in the form of a harmonious choir
of birds, and how the "Earth embrodered" sates his senses of sight and
smell, from the "Carnation, Crimson, Damaske, spotles White, / And
every colour that may please the sight" to "The odoriferous Mint, the
Eglantine, / The Woodbine, Primrose, and the Cowslip fine" (C^v). In a
bizarre echo of the discussion between Polixenes and Perdita in Act 4 of
Shakespeare's *The Winter's Tale*, Taylor culminates his apostrophe by
claiming that "begg'ry is an Art that lives by Nature," for the beggar

> neglects all Trades, all Occupations,
> All functions, Mysteries, Artes, and Corporations.
> Hee's his owne Law, and doth even what he list,
> And is a perfit right *Gimnosophist.*
> A Philosophicall *Pithagoras,*
> That without care his life away doth passe.
>
> (C2^{r-v})

The apotheosis of this line of fantasy may be found in Taylor's assertion,
at the end of his poem, that not only is the beggar free from the punishments of humankind, but the beggar is exempted from divine punishment as well. "Old *Adams* sonne," we heard in the second line of the
poem, is "heire unto his sins," but by the end of the poem Taylor asserts
that

> though (for sinne) when mankind first began,
> A curse was laid on all the race of man,
> That of his labours he should live and eate,
> And get his bread by travell and by sweate:
> But if that any from this curse be free,
> A begger must he be, and none but he.
>
> (D3)

This extraordinary idealization of the beggar's life is a species of denial
so absolute as to insist upon an inverted reading: it suggests just how
desperate the beggars' situation must have been at the time. Nevertheless, even in Taylor's fantasy, Tyburn, the site of execution, makes a brief
appearance (D3), and it can be said that the entire work is a rhetorical
response to an antithetical position; the logical machinery is so inexorable that even lice are said to be "unto the begger Natures gifts" (C3^v).
  Social reality intrudes most conspicuously, and most contradictorily, in

the narration of an interpolated story—"a merry tale" (C1ᵛ–C2ʳ)—that appears near the end of the poem. Taylor tells of a "Rich hard miserable Lord" who

> ignobly did oppresse
> His Tenants, raising Rents to such excesse:
> That they their states not able to maintaine,
> They turn'd starke beggers in a yeare or twaine.

No matter how bad conditions were, though, the lord kept a "well furnish'd Table" in his house: "Great store of Beggers dayly at his Gate, / Which he did feed, and much Compassionate" (C2).[42] The contradictions in this description of a compassionate but ignoble lord climax in Taylor's aside: "(For 'tis within the power of mighty men / To make five hundred Beggers, and feed Ten)." And when the lord asks his fool what should be done with these beggars, the answer does not please him:

> I thinke it best we straight wayes hang them all.
> That were great pitty, then the Lord reply'd,
> For them and me our Saviour equall di'd:
> Th'are Christians (although beggers) therefore yet
> Hanging's uncharitable, and unfit.

The fool's reply is as cynical and mocking a voice as one is likely to hear anywhere at this time:

> Tush (said the Foole) they are but beggers thoe,
> And thou canst spare them, therefore let them goe:
> If thou wilt doe, as thou hast done before,
> Thou canst in one yeare make as many more.
>
> (C2)

The clash between the sensibility expressed by the Foole and the pastoral idealizations which dominate the main body of the poem is extreme, and the dissonance is left unresolved by the final ecstatic dispensation from original sin. "He that can picke nothing from this tale" of the ignoble lord, Taylor says, "then let him with the begger drinke small Ale" (C2). The contradictions remain, no resolution appears. Taylor acknowledges

---

[42] Stow tells how "at the Lord [Thomas] *Cromwels* gate in London, more than two hundred persons [were] served twise every day with bread, meate and drinke sufficient" (1.89).

but finally suppresses the counterdiscourse to his own, and contents himself if not the reader with the observation that "thus is a Begger a strange kind of creature" (C2). One could hardly disagree at this point.

It may be useful here briefly to compare Taylor's poem with another work printed in the same year, 1621, the year also of perhaps greatest activity in the forced transportation of vagrant children: *Greevous Grones for the Poore*. The dedication by "M.S." (presumably Michaell Sparke) "To the Right Honourable, Right Worshipfull, and worthy Company of the Virginian and Sommer-Iland Plantations" seems at odds with the values expressed in the main text. The company, M.S. says, should be patrons of this work because of their "continued and dayly exercise in the relapse of mean and decayed persons, by transporting of them to a Land, where they have Corne which they sowed not, Vines which they planted not, and plenty which some of them deserved not" (A3ᵛ). The "charity" of the company is worthy of the highest praise, he says.

The text of *Greevous Grones*, however, moves in another direction. After offering the usual distinction between the "impotent" and "the idle Rogues," the author offers a vision of bodily suffering that conflicts with every line of Taylor's poem:

> Great is the misery that the Carkasses of the poore sustaine; as extreame hunger, pinching colde, pittiful nakednesse, great disdaine, strange surfeits, greevous sores, deadly diseases, and painefull deaths: but greater and much more lamentable, is the daungerous distresse of their silly soules. For, they are the slaves of *Sathan*. (Bᵛ)

Noting that of the various statutes designed to relieve the poor, "Negligence hath overthrowne that Famous Worke," the author calls on his reader: "But come, come, deere Christians, let everie man now bee more mooved with pittie" (B2). Throughout the work, the author rehearses the physical and spiritual suffering of the poor in vivid figures of speech, including a two-page-long allegorical figure of the human body infected with the sore of poverty (Cʳ⁻ᵛ). The indictment of the current social situation is precise: "Though the number of the poore do dailie encrease, all things yet worketh for the worst in their behalfe. For, there hath beene no Collection for them, no not these seven yeares, in many Parishes of this Land, especiallie in Countrie townes" (C3ᵛ). Later he articulates "three kindes of Oppressions" of the poor, including the "taking in to the Lords hands of Coppy-hold Lands" (Dᵛ), the "surchargyng of Commons, so that the poore cannot have any benefit of them" (Dᵛ), and finally "Incroachment," "the purchasing of Land unto Land, untill rich men get whole Townes into their hands" (D2). This work ends with a warning—really a threat—to the rich in a long story about a "devouring Pike" which greedily swallowed up bugs; one of these was a baited hook, and then the Fisherman fried the Pike on hot coals and ate it.

The chronological coincidence of the publication of Taylor's poem, the publication of *Greevous Grones*, and the highpoint of forced transportation of vagrant children, and even a rebellion within Bridewell, with the worst economic crisis since the 1590s reflects a discourse of economic conditions, social commentary, and cultural interpretation that is riddled with contradiction.[43] Even within individual works, as we have seen, angles of perception can change suddenly. As for the poor themselves, "for whom hard fare, colde lodging, thinne cloathes, and sore labour is onely allotted" (Chettle: 46), they "daily do harken when the world should amend with them," writes one author, but "they are indifferent in what sort, so that their state were relieved" (Hitchcock: 159).

[43] See Clay (1.222). Reviewing the depression years, 1620–24, Supple remarks that "1622 was the bottom of the economic trough: England seemed to be on the verge of ruin" (56).

CHAPTER TWO

Thomas Harman and *The Caveat*
for Commen Cursetors

Iᴛ would be difficult to imagine another Tudor vagrant who fulfilled his culture's fantasies and stereotypes as perfectly as did a man known as Nicholas Genings (the public alias of Nicholas Blunt). Genings's story is one of extravagant feigning and bizarre incident, told by Thomas Harman in *A Caveat or Warening for Commen Cursetors Vulgarely Called Vagabones* (1566, 1568, 1573).[1] Harman's was the most complete of the many rogue books written in the sixteenth century; though not the first, his book was

---

[1] There were apparently four editions of the *Caveat* (many authorities, such as Kinney [296], identify only three). The first, Q1, was apparently printed in 1566: Robert Burton dated it 11 November 1566 in a manuscript note in his own copy of Dekker's *The Bel-Man of London* (Aydelotte: 123), and this edition was entered in the Stationers' Register on 8 January 1567; Harman saw Nicholas Genings "Apon Alhollenday [i.e., All Saint's Day, 1 November] . . . Anno domini 1566, or my booke was halfe printed" (51). Two further editions were printed in 1568. The second, Q2, is dated "Anno Domini 1567, the eight of January" (i.e., 8 January 1568) on its back page; its title page reads only "Anno Domini. M.D.LXVII." Its title reads: "A Caveat for Commen Cursetors." The Houghton and Bodleian copies are of Q2. The third edition, Q3, is dated on its title page only as "Anno Domini. M.D.LXVII" and "Anno Domini. 1567," yet it has to be later than Q2 for several reasons. First, Q3's title is "A Caveat or Warening, for Commen Cursetors"; second, Q3 contains the famous "double" picture (more on this later), which Q2 lacks; and third, the long list of names of notorious rogues (G1ᵛ–G3ʳ) is alphabetized in Q3 but not in Q2. The Folger, Huntington and Huth (British Museum) copies are of Q3. The fourth edition, Q4, was printed in 1573; it contains additional material which will be discussed later. Viles and Furnivall's edition, which I quote here since it is relatively accessible, follows the Huth version, with some quotation from the 1573 edition. (The Huth copy lacks H1 and a substitute page has been added; H1ʳ, however, erroneously includes a paragraph on Nicholas Genings which is found only in Q2.) Some of the differences among these editions will be discussed later in the text.

perhaps the best known and its listing of the different types of rogues was widely plagiarized.[2] As we will see in Harman's treatment of Genings and other vagrant types, including female vagrants, the working principle of the *Caveat*—of all the rogue pamphlets, for that matter—is one of mirroring and inversion. A sixteenth-century equivalent to the supermarket tabloids of today, the rogue pamphlets represent beggars and vagrants as the irremediably Other, yet these vagrants can only be "seen" on an ideological grid that has been projected by, and thus deeply resembles, the dominant culture. In defining the margin, the center (as always) also defines itself.

Nicholas Genings was a sturdy beggar of the type Harman and others called the "Counterfet Cranke"; John Awdeley did not use the name but described the type, while the author of the *Liber Vagatorum* (c. 1509) used different terms to describe the same deceits (see Fig. 4).[3] "The Cranke in their [beggars'] language," Harman notes, "is the falling evill" (51), or epilepsy; they "depely dissemble the falling sicknes."[4] Their feigned disease—the condition of falling—is thus an apt figure for their real condition as the fallen of society, the outcasts on the margin. Counterfeit Cranks are masters of deceit, Harman says, who prefer to "go halfe naked, and looke most pitiously," and reject any clothes that are given to

---

[2] Harman's work was simply plagiarized in the anonymous *The Groundworke of Conny-catching* (1592) and Dekker's *The Bel-Man of London* (1608), which became one of the most popular of all the rogue books; Dekker reworked similar materials from Harman, among others, in *Lanthorne and Candle-light or the Bell-mans second Nights walke* (1608), *O per se O* (1612), and *Villanies Discovered* (1616). Dekker's plagiarisms from Harman were exposed by Samuel Rid in *Martin Mark-all, Beadle of Bridewell* (1608). Harman was also extensively plagiarized by Richard Head in *The English Rogue* (1665–74). Harman is explicitly cited as an authority by William Harrison in his "Description of Britaine" (1586), and Harman's rogue types are repeated there as well. Mark Koch has argued that "the social and economic impetus towards the desanctification of the beggar [following the dissolution of the monasteries] found its greatest secular expression" in the rogue pamphlets (95).

[3] In Martin Luther's edition, translated as *Der Betler Orden* (1510), the term for a Counterfeit Crank is a *Grantner* (Luther: 87–93). *Klenckners* (75–79), *Seffers* (119), and *Schweigers* (121) all practiced comparable physical deceits.

[4] The story of a young boy named Robert Shakysbery (the name is not invented!) is typical. Brought before the Court of Aldermen a second time in 1548 (he had deceived them the first time he had been arrested in 1547), he was finally exposed: "Item, it is agreid that Robt. Shakysbery who falsely counterfeitheth the disease of the palsey and here loitereth and continueth begging contrary to the order here taken 15 December ult shall according to the same order be whipped to morowe throughout the markett places of the Citie att a carrel [i.e., cart-tail] and be then expelled out of the same Citie" (CLRO: *Repertories* 11/394b).

Figure 4. Liber vagatorum. Der betler orden, 1510(?). By permission of the British Library, C.53.bb.9(4).

them. Among their various theatrical props, they "never go without a peece of white sope about them, which, if they see cause or present gaine, they will prively convey the same into their mouth, and so worke the same there, that they will fome as it were a Boore, and marvelously for a time torment them selves; and thus deceive they the common people, and gaine much" (51).[5]

The case of Nicholas Genings is remarkable in part because of the complex relations between the narrator Harman and the narrated Genings. Thomas Harman, like William Lambarde a Kentish justice of the peace, encountered Genings while in London overseeing the printing of the first edition of the very book we are reading—a book recounting Harman's many encounters with rogues and beggars. Suddenly in mid-printing, this new beggar appears on All Saint's Day, 1 November 1566. When "my booke was halfe printed," Harman saw a ragged beggar early in the morning from the window of his lodging in Whitefriars. The beggar was "lamentably lamentinge and pitefully crying to be releved, declared to divers their his painfull and miserable disease" (51). Suspecting fraud, Harman confronts his

> ugly and irksome attire, his lothsome and horible countinance . . . he was naked from the wast upward, saving he had a old Jerken of leather patched, and that was lo[o]se about him, that all his bodye laye out bare; a filthy foule cloth he ware on his head, being cut for the purpose, having a narowe place to put out his face, with a b[e]aver made to trusse up his beard, and a string that tied the same downe close aboute his necke; with an olde felt hat which he still caried in his hande to receave the charitye and devotion of the people, for that woulde he hold out from him; having his face, from the eyes downe ward, all smerd with freshe bloud, as thoughe he had new falen, and bin tormented with his painefull panges,—his Jerken beinge all be rayde with durte and mire, and his hatte and hosen also, as thoughe hee hadde wallowed in the mire: sewerly the sighte was monstrous and terreble. (51–52)

[5] Cf. Luther: "These are the beggars who say in the farmhouses: 'Oh, dear friend, look at me, I am afflicted with the falling sickness. . . . *Item*, some fall down before the churches, or in other places with a piece of soap in their mouths, whereby the foam rises as big as a fist, and they prick their nostrils with a straw, causing them to bleed, as though they had the falling-sickness. *Note*: this is utter knavery. These are villanous vagrants that infest all countries" (Luther: 87–89). Ambrose Parey observed the same phenomenon in sixteenth-century France: "Such as falling downe counterfeit the falling sicknesse, bind straitly both their Wrests with plates of iron, tumble and rowle themselves in the mire, sprinkle and defile their heads and faces with beasts blood, and shake their limbes and whole body. Lastly by putting sope into their mouths, they foame at the mouth like those that have the falling sicknesse" (995).

In its length and specificity, this remarkable topography of the beggar's body reveals Harman's admiration of Genings's histrionic powers as much as any condemnation of him. Harman's aim in telling these rogues' stories, he said, was to "understande their depe dissimulation" (20), and Genings's case begins with a reading of the body—or rather, of the lie that is his body, because Harman's major goal throughout his book will be to discover the truth of the beggar's body.

When questioned, Genings offers Harman a standard but still effective beggar's tale of woe and mischance:

> I was borne at Leicestar, my name is Nicholas Genings, and I have had this falling sicknes viii. yeares, and I can get no remedy for the same; for I have it by kinde, my father had it and my friendes before me; and I have bine these two yeares here about London. (52)

Beyond the fantasy of infectious as well as hereditary epilepsy, two further details stand out in Genings's story, both of which lead to his downfall. First, he claims to have slept in excrement and blood—"I fell downe on the backeside here in the fowle lane harde by the waterside; and there I laye all most all night, and have bled all most all the bloude owte in my bodye" (52). But his refusal to wash up when offered the chance further arouses Harman's suspicions. Second, Genings claims to have been "a yeare and a halfe in bethelem," that is, in Bedlam Hospital.[6] When Harman tests this assertion by asking the name of the Keeper of Bedlam, Genings answers with what must be the first recorded instance of the weakest pseudonym in English culture: "John Smith" (52–53). Perhaps Harman is merely having his fun with the reader here. When this story is proven false, two boys are engaged to tail Genings through his day.

Genings is observed at one point in an alley: "There hee renewed his face againe with freshe bloud, which he caried about him in a bladder, and dawbed on freshe dirte upon his Jerken, hat, and hoson" (53). At the end of a long day of successful begging, Genings is confronted, and a constable seizes him and brings him to a victualing house where he is searched. The various purses hidden about his body add up to a one-day total of 13s.3½d.—an enormous sum, perhaps twenty times the average daily wage of a laborer.[7]

---

[6] Genings thus appropriates part of the type known as the "Abraham Man," the counterfeit madman described by Harman (47–48); we will examine the most famous of them, Poor Tom in *King Lear* , in chapter 6.

[7] A laborer's daily wage was estimated to have been 6d. a day by Aydelotte (33), and reiterated by Pound (31). Pound quotes a Norwich Court Book dated 12 September 1562

The moment of Genings's final revelation however is now at hand, and predictable: "Then they stript him starke naked, and as many as sawe him said they never sawe hansommer man, with a yellowe flexen beard, and faire skinned, withoute anye spot or greffe" (55). Like the judges who order a beggar stripped to see if there is any mark of branding or prior whippings, they strip Genings in a search for the *absence* of any mark or sign—which *is* the sign of Genings's deceit.

Unaccountably believing that Genings was secured simply because he was naked, his "faire skinned" body wrapped only in an old cloak, his captors go off on another errand. Genings is, as usual, underestimated. He settles in, orders a pot of beer, "dranke of[f] a quarte at a draft, and called for another, and so the thirde, that one had bene sufficient for any resonable man, the Drinke was so stronge" (55). Just as we wonder how Harman knows that, he tells us that "I my selfe, the next morninge, tasted thereof" (55). Genings still had his wits about him, however, for after the several drinks he asks the alewife if "hee might goe out on the backeside to make water, and to exonerate his paunche" (55). She does not fear his escape because he is naked, and yet "when hee was out, he cast awaye the cloke, and, as naked as ever he was borne, he ran away over the fields to his own house, as hee afterwards said" (56).[8] His "faire skinned" body, "withoute anye spot," flashes buck naked over the fields, his hypocrisy perfectly revealed by his normality.

The career of Genings to this point is spectacular enough, but there is more. Two further metamorphoses of the beggar are described (the source of knowledge for these descriptions is not entirely clear in Harman's text). First, Genings is said to have

> craftely clothed him selfe in mariners apparel, and associated him self
> with an other of his companions: they having both mariners apparel, went
> abroad to aske charity of the people, faining they hadde loste their shippe
> with all their goods by casualty on the seas, wherewith they gained much.
> (56)

The destitute mariner is another of the traditional beggar's roles.[9] Indeed, in the chapter just before the story of Genings, Harman had

---

which states that "one Mother Arden [not the Bard's mother-in-law, of course] who used daly to go a begging the strettes," was found upon examination to have accumulated more than 44 pounds, a small fortune (100).

  [8] This is the phrasing of the 1573 edition; the Huth version reads, "he ran away, that he could never be hard of again." I discuss the significance of these changes later.

  [9] Robert Copland, *The Highway to the Spital-House*: "These be they that daily walks and

described "a Freshe Water Mariner or Whipjacke," whose chief characteristic, both Awdeley and Harman agree, is his possession of a "counterfeit license . . . a large and formall writinge" indicating permission to beg; sometimes, Harman says in a tone of wonder, such beggars even "counterfet the seale of the Admiraltie" (48).

In yet another costume change, Genings—"fearinge to be mistrusted"—"apparelled himselfe very well with a faire black freese cote, a new paire of white hose, a fine felt hat on his head, a shert of flaunders worke esteemed to be worth xvi. shillings" (56). Here Harman's admiration—perhaps even his envy of that sixteen-shilling shirt (five times more expensive than the average shirt [Cook: 233])—is immense; Genings's sartorial choices are "faire," "new," "fine."

A second, even more revealing encounter with Genings occurs two months after the first, "upon newe yeares day," when he is seen by chance, once again in Whitefriars. Dressed to the nines in his new finery, the ever-inventive Genings offers yet another classic beggar's story:

> "Forsoth," saith he, "my name is Nicolas Genings, and I came from Lecester to seeke work, and I am a hat-maker by my occupation, and all my money is spent, and if I coulde get money to paye for my lodging this night, I would seke work to morowe amongst the hatters." (56)

As before, Genings is quickly exposed and arrested, and he again runs away, though this time he is caught by Harman's fleet-footed printer, who "overtoke him at fleete bridge, and with strong hand caried him to the counter, and safely delivered him" (57).[10] Genings again tells a story that is quickly proven a lie and he is again "stript starke naked" (57) to stand before the law.

Genings is taken to Bridewell, where "his ougly attire [is] put upon him before the maisters thereof" (now the exposed beggar, in a semiotic reversal, is clothed in order to signal his guilt). The authorities

> wondered greatly at his dissimulation: for which offence he stode upon the pillery in Cheapside, both in his ougly and handsome attire.

---

jets, / In their hose trussed round to their doublets, / And say, 'Good masters, of your charity, / Help us poor men that come from the sea!' " (Judges: 8). Cf. John Awdeley: "A Whipjacke . . . doth use to beg like a Mariner" (4).

[10] In Q2 and Q3, however, the printer is not mentioned as having been present. The story is told in brief at the end of Q2; the verbs are in the passive tense (Genings "was founde begging," "committed unto a offecer"). The printer mentioned in Q4 is referred to in Q2 simply as "a nother": "one lighter of fote then the other over toke him" (87). The printer therefore does not exist as a participant in the earlier rendition of the second encounter with Genings.

And after that went in the mill while his ougly picture was a drawing; and then was whipped at a cartes taile through London, and his displayd banner caried before him unto his own dore, and so backe to Bridewell again, and there remained for a time, and at length let at libertie, on that condicion he would prove an honest man, and labour truly to get his living. And his picture remaineth in Bridewell for a moniment. (57)

Genings's punishment has a strong sense of poetic and semiotic justice about it: this master feigner must be publicly exposed in both his costumes, the "ougly and handsome attire." Moreover, Genings's mastery of artifice redounds against him when the authorities order a picture drawn of him, carried above him as he was whipped through London, which was eventually mounted in Bridewell as a "moniment." But a monument to what? To Genings's wit and imagination? to his capture and fall? or simply to the phenomenon of his doubleness? Harman does not say.

Harman's book eventually offered three illustrations of Genings, none of which seems to be the same as the one carried above him. The appearance of these pictures in the various editions of the *Caveat* says much about Genings's apparent popularity.[11] The first of these, found in the second and third editions but not the fourth, is a woodcut of a man placed in pillory with three guards attending (see Fig. 5). His hat seems to have just fallen off, suspended in mid-air. His body can be seen from the waist down, and his pants, boots, and the part of his jerkin visible all accord with Harman's earlier description. The accompanying verse says (in Q2): "This is the figure of the counterfet Cranke, that is spoken of in this boke of Roges, called Nicholas Blunt other wise Nicholas Genings. His tale is in the xvii. lefe of this booke, which doth showe unto all that reades it, woundrous suttell and crafty deseit donne of and by him" (90). In Q3, however, this descriptive paragraph is omitted and replaced by a stanza of verse:

This counterfet Cranke, nowe vew and beholde,
   Placed in pillory, as all maye well se:
This was he, as you have hard the tale tolde,
   before recorded with great suttilte,
   Ibused manye with his inpiete,

[11] Q2 and Q3 were, according to Harman, "in printinge" when the New Year's encounter occurred, and only a brief paragraph account of it (quoted in a footnote) could be placed at the end of the text.

Figure 5. Thomas Harman, *A Caveat for common cursetors vulgarely called vagabones,* 1567/8 (Q2). By permission of the Houghton Library, Harvard University.

> his lothsome attire, in most ugly manner,
> was through London caried with displayd banner.

(90)

Clearly Harman wished to cash in on the notoriety of the Genings case, but scarcely had time to insert the news of the second encounter in the second or third editions; it is even possible that the woodcut figure in pillory—who could be any rogue, like the one going to the gallows earlier—was not originally intended to be Genings. In any event, for the third edition Harman has had time to add the verse stanza and to add a new detail of his punishment—that he was carried through London with the displayed banner depicting himself—to the paragraph already in the text.

In the third edition, moreover, Harman placed a second woodcut di-

Figure 6. Thomas Harman, *A Caveat or Warening for Commen Cursetors Vulgarely Called Vagabones*, 1567/8 (Q3). By permission of the Folger Shakespeare Library.

rectly in the main text of the book, in the chapter relating to Genings (Fig. 6). This woodcut is justly famous: it shows Genings as *two* people, standing side by side as mirrored images. On the left is "A upright man Nicolas Blunt," who is extremely well-dressed, prosperous, with a well-trimmed beard, a smart hat, and a sturdy walking stick or cane. A man of position and accomplishment, in short. On the right is "The counterfet Cranke Nicolas Genynges," who is dressed in rags, the mud/blood visible on his face, almost precisely according to Harman's description of him in the text. He stands in a position of mock servility, one arm across his chest as if a bow is just beginning or ending, the

other arm stretched out, holding a rough hat to "receave the charitye
and devotion of the people" (52). The two figures merge in the middle, where the walking stick of "Blunt" seems to pass through the
hand, but behind the hat, of "Genings." Beneath the picture is the following verse:

> These two pictures, lively set out,
>   One bodye and soule, god send him more grace.
>   This mounstrous desemblar, a Cranke all about.
> Uncomly coveting, of eche to imbrace,
>   Money or wares, as he made his race.
> And sometime a marinar, and a sarvinge man,
>   Or els an artificer, as he would faine than.
> Such shiftes he used, beinge well tryed,
>   A bandoninge labour, till he was espied.
> Conding punishment, for his dissimulation,
>   He sewerly received with much declination.

Genings's career earns another promotion here—now he is not only formally titled an Upright Man[12] but is also said to have been a "sarvinge
man, / Or els an artificer" as well. Genings seems to have been just about
everything and anything.

A third new picture of Genings was then added to the text of Q4 where
his escape is described—the words "as naked as ever he was born" in
fact stand right next to it (Fig. 7). Here the naked Genings is shown
running through the fields, leafy trees in the background, a well-worn
path under his feet. Genings's body is in half-profile, one striding leg
discreetly crossed over to shield the privates from view. The face is the
same as that of the Upright Man, the "flexen beard" prominent.[13] Certainly he is a "hansommer man" than many. This woodcut represents
one of the true highlights of Genings's career, and it indicates as well

---

[12] In the hierarchical ranking of rogues, according to Harman, the Upright Man is
second only to the "Ruffler" in terms of power and authority. Harman's long account
of particular incidents and characters of Upright Men (31–35) is succinctly anticipated
in Awdeley's account of the Upright Man, who "is of so much authority, that meeting
with any of his profession, he may cal them to accompt, & commaund a share or snap
unto him selfe, of al that they have gained by their trade in one moneth. And if he doo
them wrong, they have no remedy against him, no though he beate them, as he useth
commonly to do. He may also commaund any of their women, which they cal Doxies, to
serve his turne. He hath ye chiefe place at any market walke, & other assembles, & is not
of any to be controled" (4).

[13] Both this and the Blunt/Genings "double" picture are copied in *The Groundworke
of Conny-catching* (1592).

Figure 7. Thomas Harman, *A Caveat or Warening for Commen Cursetors Vulgarely Called Vagabones,* 1573 (Q4). Reproduced by permission of The Huntington Library, San Marino, California, 61292.

Harman's continuing interest in the semiotics of Genings's body: his various disguises, and the unusual, even enviable normality beneath these "shifts" and deceits.

By the time of the 1573 edition, Genings had become famous, and Harman takes advantage of it, adding two full pages of new text telling of the second encounter as well as the third woodcut.[14] The title page now also reflects Genings's notoriety: this edition is "Augmented and enlarged by the first Author hereof. Whereunto is added the tale of the second taking of the counterfet Crank, &c." The title page of the anonymous plagiarism, *The Groundworke of Conny-catching* (1592), also featured Genings—a full twenty-five years after his first appearance: "The Groundworke of Conny-catching; the manner of their Pedlers-French and the meanes to understande the same, with the cunning slights of the Counterfeit Cranke." In the various accounts, Genings plays many roles; foremost is the Counterfeit Crank, his marquee-name, but he is also an Upright Man, a Mariner or Whipjack, a hat-maker, a serving man, a

---

[14] Much of the other art work is also improved. The woodcut with a figure in pillory, found in Q2 and Q3, is deleted along with its verse stanza; a picture of the "fetters or shackels" is also deleted, though the verse accompanying it remains. A picture of a rogue, wearing only a loincloth, with his arms tied over a beam, being lashed by two men, is added to Q4.

rogue,[15] an artificer, a parody of himself, and finally "a moniment" in Bridewell. Whether his stage is the pillory in Cheapside, the streets of Whitefriars, or the cells of Bridewell, Genings is one of the minor celebrities of his age. If he had not existed, it might have been necessary for Harman to invent him.

We may justifiably wonder if, in the press to develop Genings's notoriety, Harman did not indeed invent part of the story. There is much to be suspicious of: Harman's detailed descriptions of actions and objects which he had not been present to see; the curious mediation of the printer (who better to employ in amplifying a story than the man actually printing it?); the absence of the printer from the 1568 account of the second encounter, and his major presence in the 1573 version; the fatidic dates—All Saints' Day and New Year's Day—on which the two encounters take place; the repetitions of events in the two encounters; and the iconological development of Genings, from being forced to represent himself on the pillory in both "ougly and handsome attire," to the authorities' representation of him through "his ougly picture" carried before him through the streets, to Harman's woodcut portraits of him.

Although Harman may have invented some of Genings's story, he clearly did not invent Genings himself or his punishment. Harman's *Caveat* is one of the few such rogue books for which a minimal test of historical accuracy is possible.[16] The existence of Genings/Blunt can be verified from a court document of 13 January 1567—that is, contemporaneous with the second encounter with Genings.[17] The Court of Aldermen dealt with a man known not as "Genings" but only as "Blunt,"[18] who had

> divers and sundry times heretoforre used and counterfeited him selfe to

[15] The list at the end of the *Caveat* (see n. 16 below) groups the vagabonds into three categories—"Upright Men," "Roges," and "Palliards." In this listing "Nicholas Blunt *alias* Nicholas Gennings, a counterfet Cranke" (Harman: 81) appears under the list of "Roges."

[16] For one thing, Harman prints at the end of it a list of more than two hundred names of "the moste notorious rogues and wickedst walkers that are livinge nowe at this present . . . [in] Essex, Middlesex, Sussex, Surrey, and Kent" (78–82). Aydelotte has correlated records from various of these areas and found the names of fourteen of Harman's rogues arrested or punished as vagabonds in the early 1570s, and four others in the period 1589–90 (none of them Genings). It seems likely that several of these are more than mere coincidence.

[17] The existence of this document was brought to my attention by a brief note in Beier (1985: 117–18). The document is in the CLRO, *Repertories* 16/149a; this transcription is my own.

[18] In the text of Harman's version, the Crank is always referred to as Genings, and he

be A diseased person with the grevous disease of the faling sicknes And hath also of A set purpose disfiguring his body with dire lothsome spottes and other filthines in his face and other partes of his body to the only intent to be thereby the rather permitted to begge and to delude as he hath already of A long tim don the good and charitable people.

Blunt's punishment was the same as that described for Genings in Harman's *Caveat*: he was to be "tied naked" at a cart's-tail and "wipped throughout all the coemmon market places of this Citie having A picture of his own personage deformed in manner and form . . . as he was wont to use the same carried bifore hym upon A long pole and then to be recomitted to Bridwell." The correlation of detail is obviously too great to be a coincidence. I have also discovered that a "Nicholas Jennings" was arrested and set free on bond in Dartford, Kent, on 20 March 1564 (Cockburn 1979: 234). (Kent was, coincidentally, Harman's home.)

What fascinates Harman the most about these beggars is "their double demeaner in eche degree" (91), as he puts it in the final stanza of his book. His every effort is to expose that doubleness, indeed to eradicate it—and one means of eradicating feigned disease or mutilation is to create real disease and mutilation, to write the true text of pain over the counterfeit one. The primary point of contention, moreover, is the beggar's body, and Harman's *Caveat* registers a complex corporeal semiotics from its very title page (Fig. 8), which includes enough detail in its woodcut so that the reader can already see the marks on the bodies of two beggars being whipped through the streets at cart's-tail. The entire book is in one sense an effort to expose and then mark the bodies of *all* beggars in a parallel way. Harman may be said to be a very early but an expert practitioner of what Foucault has termed "the political technology of the body" (26), in which power relations hold authority over the body: "They invest it, mark it, train it, torture it, force it to carry out tasks, to perform ceremonies, to emit signs" (25). Genings himself, of course, seemed equally the master of such signs.

The general history of the Tudor obsession with the sturdy beggar, and the case of Genings in particular, seems an illustration of Foucault's observation. Certainly one of the central objections against the sturdy

---

twice identifies himself as Genings (52, 56), but in the listing of the country's rogues he is "Nicholas Blunt *alias* Nicholas Gennings" (81), and in the brief paragraph added at the end of Q2 and Q3, he is "Nicholas Blunte, who called him selfe Nicholan [sic] Gennins, a counterefet Cranke" (87). The pillory picture also has him as "Nicholas Blunt other wise Nicholas Gennings" (90), and the famous "double" picture labels the Upright Man "Nicolas Blunt" (50).

Figure 8. Thomas Harman, *A Caveat or Warening for Commen Cursetors Vulgarely Called Vagabones,* 1567/8 (Q3). By permission of the Folger Shakespeare Library.

beggar is that he subverts or even invalidates the prevailing ideology of work: his able body resists participation in economic production, *choosing* instead the role of parasite. The Counterfeit Crank takes this subversive logic even further, for he not only refuses to work but also feigns the bodily incapacity to work, as if he could simply through his own will remove his body from the social economy. Hence the peculiar zeal with which his *normality* is hunted out and exposed, and the importance of revealing the integrity of his body publicly. Harman thus serves as an instrument of social power, working in part, as he says in his dedicatory epistle, so that these sturdy beggars may be "set to labour for their liv-inge" (21) and brought into a hierarchical economic relationship. As we have seen, the beggar's body was understood by many to be simply a commodity demanding exploitation. Judicial lashings are thus the state's reinscription of the beggar's bodily identity within the economy.

The phenomenon of the beggars' doubleness has several implica-tions for Harman. First, that they are superb actors, exemplary in-stances of the histrionic imagination subverted to base uses. One reason Harman spends so much time on their costumes, makeup, and acting styles is that his audience wants to know, as he does, how such marginality can be achieved through sheer performance. A second im-plication of their doubleness is that if they are not really beggars, then they must simply be social deviants; this is one of the reasons that Har-man spends so much time in exposing the *normality* of their bodies. In insisting on the beggars' normality, and thus their equivalence with the ordinary citizenry, Harman wishes to use this mirroring as a way to dis-tinguish more sharply between himself and the other, to make their corrupted wills seem more evident, and (presumably) different from his own. Harman's special interest in Genings/Blunt thus stems from his revealed doubleness—the famous picture shows the beggar *and* the prosperous-looking Blunt: "two pictures," but only "One bodye and soule," two dishes to one table. The marginal seems to be only the in-verted reflection of the center, then: it is not a true margin but only a representation of one.

Yet in the end it seems that there really are *two* souls in Genings's one body. For in addition to the several "public" roles Genings plays, there is a private, bourgeois Genings to be found—that is, the appro-priately named Blunt—a self that Genings has buried deeply, and whose existence Harman reveals only casually. After some effort, we learn, the authorities have found out Blunt's "habitation, dwelling in maister Hilles rentes, havinge a pretye house, well stuffed, with a faire joine table, and a faire cubbard garnished with peuter, having an old

auncient woman to his wife" (57). This denouement, at first surprising
and ironic, seems in retrospect to have been inevitable. Genings's fundamental doubleness, we see, mirrors the doubleness of Harman himself: Genings is to Blunt as Genings is to Harman. Harman's voyeurism
finds its perfect subject in the inventions of Genings, whose life seems
to fulfill every fantasy about beggars that the culture has ever produced. Although Genings is the economic parasite feeding on the host
of society, their relationship seems reversed in terms of the imagination, for Harman needs Genings, and in Harman's several accounts,
Genings grows ever larger and more resourceful. Harman's admiration
of Genings's clothing (his sixteen-shilling shirt) is more than matched
by this appreciation of his home and his possessions, because Harman
sees that he and Genings (or Blunt) are at heart the same. It takes one
bourgeois to properly admire the "well stuffed" home of another.
Both of them moreover have, as a touchstone middle-class possession, a
collection of pewter, for Harman had proudly told the reader earlier of
his own "doson of pewter dishes, well marked, and stamped with the
connizance of my armes" (35).

Genings chooses marginality as his theater, disease and degradation as
his costume; he does this apparently for the sake of a life of modest
possession, family, and comfort. His choice helps reveal the self-
deceptions of a Harman, who from his own position of comfort and
security at the center of society, passes judgment on those on the margins
and coerces the subjection of their bodies. What Genings's career suggests is that the center and the margins are not so different. While in
London, moreover, Harman lived at Whitefriars, "within the cloister, in
a little yard or coorte, where aboutes laye two or thre great Ladies, being
without the liberties of London." Seeking his prey here, Genings "hoped
for the greater gaine" (51), because the city authorities had no jurisdiction in these former monastic districts. In the Liberties of London, as
Steven Mullaney has recently demonstrated, "the spectacle of the outcast
and the marginal traditionally held sway" (26).[19] Into this wealthy en-
clave, so unlike those Liberties outside of London, the beggar stepped
literally "under" Harman's lodging (51).[20] When Genings is followed
through the city to his home, he does not head north, to Harman's
surprise, but south: "He went to the water side . . . and was sette over the

[19] Mullaney is primarily concerned with the Liberties surrounding London rather than
those within it.

[20] John Stow described "many faire houses builded [in Whitefriars], lodgings for Noble
men and others" (2.47).

Water into Saincte Georges feldes, contrarye to my expectatian; for I had thought he woulde have gonne into Holborne or to Saint Gilles in the felde" (54). Crossing the river by boat was not inexpensive—perhaps three pence by the 1590s (Cook: 195)—but Genings, we recall, had by now taken in plenty of money. Genings eventually "crossed over the feld-des towardes Newington" (54), far from the city, where he is captured for the first time.[21] Genings has thus crossed over more than one social and geographical boundary during his movements this All Saints' Day, showing himself an adept of the margins, whether they are the isolated jurisdictional enclaves within and without the city or those self-conscious representations of the social outcast.

Even in Newington, then, Genings apparently established a life of relative comfort which mirrors that of the honest citizens of Kent for whose protection Harman is writing this book. In perhaps the ultimate irony of the entire story, Harman took the money confiscated from Genings at his first arrest, and "tooke order with the chiefe of the parish that [it] ... might the next daye be equally distributed, by their good discrecions, to the povertie of the same parishe, and so it was done" (56). By the time of the 1573 edition, Harman realizes he has been had, though, for Genings, he now knows, "had both house and wife in the same parishe" (56) in which the alms were distributed, and so "this crafty Cranke had part him selfe" (56). Harman thus unwittingly served as little more than a medium for the circular exchange of Genings's money, since part of the confiscated money was returned to the same pocket from which it had been seized.

In the end, the authorities not only had Genings whipped through the streets with "his ougly picture" carried before him, but before returning him to Bridewell they made him in effect retrace the journey of All Saints' Day, finally going with his iconic banner "unto his own dore" (57). Home, after all, is where the art is.

A foundation of fact underlies Harman's work to some degree, but Harman's literary impulses also help structure the form of the *Caveat*. Apart from his expressed moral purpose—"that the whole body of the Realme may se and understand their [beggars'] leud life and pernitious practisses, that all maye spedelye helpe to amend that is amisse" (28)—

---

[21] The parish church in Newington was "distant one mile from London bridge" (Stow: 2.52). Newington was well known as a low-life haunt. In the 1582 roundup of vagrants, Fleetwood conducted a sweep through "Southwarke, Lambeth, and Newington" (*TED*: 2.335) with good results.

Harman's chief aim seems to be literary, to provide a colorful and interesting story of an actual beggar to illustrate each individual type, thus
commodifying the story for bourgeois consumption. After defining a type
of rogue, the text usually shifts to a first-person narration of an actual
encounter with a rogue. The authenticity of these encounters derives
from the concrete and credible details about himself offered by this in-
quisitive former country justice of the peace. He is the type of man, for
example, who will feed deserving beggars (20, 66), and when he confis-
cates the ill-gotten gains of a Genings, Harman will see that they are
"equally distributed . . . to the povertie of the same parishe" (56). He
had some personal experience with thieving beggars himself, for "a great
cawdron of copper" (34) of his was once stolen, and he tells of neighbors
whose houses were "broken up in the night" (21).

The underlying structure of the illustrative narratives is simple: a rogue
of some sort appears before Harman himself (occasionally it is a neighbor's experience being related), and Harman quickly assumes an inquisitorial role, occasionally lapsing into moralistic haranguing.[22] After
Harman's interrogation—the "exposition"—most of his stories then describe a specific encounter or event involving the type of rogue in question, with his exposure and punishment a desired, and frequently
achieved, end. In its most typical form, as in the Genings case, the narrative concludes with a confession of repentance and the punishment of
the rogue. In Genings's case, it sounds particularly unconvincing and
formulaic. Harman's printer confronts Genings in his cell, "and rebuked
him for his beastly behaviour, and told him of his false faining, willed
him to confesse it, and ask forgivenes: he perceived him to know his
depe dissimulation, relented, and confessed all his disceit" (57).[23]

After his whipping and public display, we are told, Genings is eventually released from Bridewell "on that condicion he would prove an honest man, and labour truly to get his living" (57). Surely this is the most
remarkable fantasy in the entire story of Genings! It flies in the face of
everything we have heard about Genings himself, and all that we know
about the real condition of urban beggars in the period. Genings's
abrupt repentance—he of the quick lie and even quicker feet—and the

[22] "I axed him wher he was borne, and where he dwelt last" (66); "then I asked of
him where he was borne, what is name was, how longe he had this disease" (52); "once
with muche threatninge and faire promises, I required to knowe of one companye who
made their licence" (49). Curtis and Hale concisely trace the rogue pamphlets' reliance
on the "exemplum" from Copland to Greene (114).

[23] The Court of Aldermen reported only that the real-life Blunt was convicted "aswell
by good and Sufficent witness as by his own proper confession" (CLRO: *Repertories* 16/
149a).

formulaic piety here are the most unrealistic moments in the entire story, suggesting a narrative desire to establish status as merely subject to will.

Harman penetrates and exposes the mysteries of the beggars with a self-obsessed zeal which seems unrelated to the more abstract moral designs he has described. These beggars bring, if nothing else, an element of eccentric interest and even danger into Harman's prosaic bourgeois life. Harman's suppressed identification with the beggars only goes so far, however: for the real misery behind the beggary, Harman, as C. S. Lewis once remarked, "shows no more pity than a stone" (296).

If masterless men were considered threatening, then masterless women must have seemed equally if not more so: such wandering women were "errant" in several senses. Because she had escaped from (or been rejected by) the hierarchical structures of social and domestic order, such a woman, particularly one on the road, must have seemed at once threatening and vulnerable. A woman without a master, moreover, must be asserting mastery herself and was therefore assumed to be sexually errant as well. Yet the reality must have been that such women were overwhelmingly the victims of virtually every encounter with men.[24]

It is impossible to say accurately how many vagrant women there were or what percentage of them were abandoned mothers or prostitutes.[25] The evidence that does exist, however, strongly suggests that their sexual status was the central defining category for vagrant women in patriarchal discourse, whether unmarried pregnant girls, prostitutes, or seduced widows. One assumes poverty in vagrants, of course, but the repeated conjunction of poverty with some sexual/domestic catastrophe is significant. Carol Wiener notes that a woman "was likely to be seen as one of the worthy poor simply because she lacked a man" (41). The large majority of vagrant women appear to have been on the road because of some abandonment or victimization. The further abuses to which they would be subject are obvious. G. R. Quaife's documentation reveals extensive sexual misconduct and exploitation (and not just among vagrants). "Violence," he reports, "was very much part of the sexual scene.... Sexual attacks on the wife of an enemy, on a girl encountered on the highway, or, worse for drink, accosted in an inn were very much part of

[24] In "The Female Vagrant in Early Seventeenth-Century England," Mikalachki analyzes the often desperate situation of some female vagrants in the 1620s. Willen surveys the predominance of women in relief roles, and their predominance, ironically, as workers in relief institutions. Her study is urban-based and generally not concerned with women on the road, as the rogue pamphlets generally are.

[25] See Griffiths for an analysis of prostitution in London, as well as Quaife.

seventeenth-century life" (172). Proving a rape charge, even for a young girl living with her family in a village, was exceedingly difficult because of substantial loopholes in the law and popular belief systems.[26]

All this is to demonstrate the obvious: young or old, pregnant or prostitute, vagrant women in this period had little legal protection and were frequently doubly victimized once on the road. Yet when female vagrants were represented in works of popular culture, such as Harman's pamphlet, the nature or extent of the victimization was usually invisible. Rather, their sexuality was understood to be aggressive, disorderly, and a social threat, as if *all* vagrant women were prostitutes. However, it should be noted that vagrants as a group, male and female alike, were invariably thought to be sexually unrestrained. Their generalized social disorderliness was routinely translated into explicit kinds of sexual misconduct. In *The Highway to the Spital-House*, Robert Copland describes those who come begging for relief as "Lechers, fornicators and advouterers, / Incests, harlots, bawds, and bolsterers, / Apple-squires, enticers, and ravishers" (Judges: 19), and the women, in particular, as "the sisterhood of drabs, sluts and callets" (24). Even a sympathetic, pietistic author like John Downame could write that vagrants were "a promiscuous generation, who are all of kin, and yet know no kindred, no house or home, no law but their sensual lust" (38). A more sensationalistic writer like Thomas Dekker is even more lurid. In *The Bel-Man of London* (1608), he claims that "in all Shires have they such Innes as these; and in all of them and these recited, shall you find sometimes 40. *Uprightmen* together ingendring beggers with their *Morts*. No sinne but is here committed without shame. Adultery is common amongst them, Incest but laughed at, Sodomy made a jest" (Dekker 1963: 3.111). In *Lanthorne and Candle-light* (also 1608), Dekker says that gypsies lie with their "queanes" in barns, "as Swine do together in Hogsties" (1963: 3.263).

---

[26] "Rape was a wide term," according to Youings, "covering not only forcible intercourse (though it was popularly believed that pregnancy could not result unless a woman was willing), but also that particular hazard of the woman of property, abduction" (366). In his review of the nature and incidence of crime in the period 1559–1625, Cockburn concludes that "rape was probably poorly reported" (1977: 58), perhaps because, as Quaife observes, "proof of rape was very difficult" (65). "To have any hope of proving ravishment," a woman "had to complain at the time of offence, to inform reliable people as soon as possible afterwards, must not conceive with child and must not have put herself in a position where the attacker could claim she had slept with him previously. If the woman could be proved a concubine (in this context a mistress or *de facto* wife) she had no rights. She, like a *de jure* wife, had to submit to the sexual advances of her male partner whenever and however he wished. However, if it could be proved that she was harlot (a woman who accepted material rewards for her sexual favours) then she was in a much better position to prove rape" (Quaife: 173).

Like the other male authors of rogue pamphlets, Harman understood his audience's desires to hear stories of the wiles and deceits of errant women, of vagrants, prostitutes, petty thieves, and cheats, no matter what the truth of their social and economic position. He begins this section of his book with a list of the hierarchy of female vagrants (parallel to though shorter than the list of male vagrants), which includes such familiar types as the Walking Mort, Doxy, and Dell. Harman reveals himself to be particularly moralistic, inquisitorial, and even voyeuristic, when interrogating women. In one famous passage, in the case of "A Walking Mort" (an unmarried female beggar), Harman berates the woman in moralistic terms, and she replies, "God helpe . . . how should I live? none will take me into service; but I labour in harvest time honestly" (68). This passage says much about the beggars' plight in the early Elizabethan period; Paul Slack ends his important essay by quoting it (1974: 378). What is equally striking, it seems to me, is Harman's cruel retort (which Slack does not quote) to her claim to labor honestly in harvest time: "I thinke but a while with honestie" (68). The sentimentality of the moment is cynically hammered back.

Harman has an insinuating way with the women—he cajoles the Walking Mort into telling one of the longest stories in the book—but his patronizing friendliness only lightly covers over a voyeuristic moralism. He constantly inquires into and remarks on the rogues' sexual habits— of the Abraham Men, he tells us, "all wemen that wander bee at their commaundemente" (47); of the Autem Mort (a married female beggar), "they be as chaste as a Cowe I have, that goeth to Bull every moone, with what Bull she careth not" (67). When he inquires into the life story of a Doxy ("these Doxes be broken and spoiled of their maidenhead by the upright men, and then they have their name of Doxes, and not afore," 73), he is interested primarily in the men she has known. A Doxy, after all, he tells us, "is commen and indifferent for any that will use her, as *homo* is a common name to all men" (73). Harman discovers that this Doxy—"surelye a pleasant harlot, and not so pleasant as witty"—has "passed her time lewdlye eighttene yeares in walkinge aboute" (74) and so should prove a goldmine of information. "Before I woulde grope her minde," Harman goes on obliviously, "I made her both to eate and drinke well; that done, I made her faithfull promise to geve her some money, if she would open and discover to me such questions as I woulde demaunde of her, and never to bee wraye her, neither to disclose her name" (74). Unlike her other customers, Harman is perfectly ready to pay for the pleasure of aural sex, so to speak.

Harman is particularly interested in all the Upright Men and Rogues she knows, but it turns out that the great majority of them are dead, most by hanging. This prompts one of the more revealing moments in the *Caveat*. The internal contradictions in Harman's feelings are exposed here, when the humanity of the woman's remarks and feelings are directly represented by Harman the narrator, but then pitted against the moralistic self-righteousness of Harman the character in his own narration. She tells him she was sorry to lose all these men she has known,

> "for some of them were good loving men. For I lackt not when they had it, and they wanted not when I had it, and divers of them I never did forsake, untill the Gallowes departed us." "O, mercifull God!" quoth I, and began to blesse me. "Why blesse ye?" quoth she. "Alas! good gentleman, every one muste have a livinge." Other matters I talked of; but this nowe maye suffice to shewe the Reader, as it weare in a glasse, the bolde beastly life of these Doxes. (75)

Well, yes, but the "glasse" keeps showing Harman's reflection, as well, and his prurient interest in these stories. Harman's obsessive interest in the innermost details of the beggars' lives—male and female alike—occasionally seems unbalanced or contradictory. He concludes his moralizing on Doxies with a generalization about their incorrigibility. What follows contains a nonsequitur surrealistic enough to bring any reader to a halt:

> I have hadde good pro[o]fe [of Doxies' incorrigibility] thereof. There is one, a notorious harlot, of this affinitye, called Besse Bottomelye; she hath but one hande, and she hath murthered two children at the least. (75)

The fact of her bodily mutilation thus somehow proves her viciousness. The odd circumstantiality of this detail is counterbalanced by the perfunctoriness of the anecdote—does she kill her own children or murder randomly?—and by the generic quality and the ironic pun in her first and last names, respectively. Harman's dream hath a Bottomelye.

The Doxies and Morts easily yield their stories to Harman; if necessary, he'll even pay for them. But Harman never penetrates their deeper secrets, and he condemns them even as he is repeatedly drawn toward the magnet of their sexuality. In one defining moment, he imagines a kind of primal scene in the story of the Upright Man, in which such men join with their Morts and Doxies in a carnivalesque vision set in those infamous inns and barns. Their transgressions may at first seem innocent to the modern reader: "Their talking tongues talke at large. They bowle and bowse one to another, and for the time bousing belly chere." But soon their loose festivity turns to clandestine sexual encounter, and Harman knows exactly what it reminds him of:

> And after there ruysting recreation, if there be not ro[o]me inough in the house, they have cleane strawe in some barne or backehouse nere adjoining, where they couch comly together, and it were dogge and biche, and he that is hardiest maye have his choise. (32)

Like swine in hogsties, like cows to bulls or a bitch to a dog, vagrant women are all errant women, sexually available and therefore desirable, but sexually aggressive and voracious, like animals, and therefore contemptible. The *Caveat*, along with the other rogue pamphlets, reworks and inverts the facts of victimization among vagrant women, demonizing the sexual victims into sexually knowing and aggressive criminals. And yet they are, ironically, often still dependent on men. The male vagrants known as Palliards, Harman writes,

> have their Morts with them, which they cal wives; and if he goe to one house, to aske his almes, his wife shall goe to a nother: for what they get (as bread, cheese, malte, and woll) they sell the same for redy money; for so they get more and if they went together. Although they be thus devided in the daie, yet they mete jompe at night. If they chaunce to come to some gentilmans house standinge a lone, and be demaunded whether they be man and wife, and if he perceave that any doubteth thereof, he sheweth them a Testimonial with the ministers name and others of the same parishe (naminge a parishe in some shere fare distant from the place where he sheweth the same). This writing he carieth to salve that sore. (44)

This counterfeit version of marriage is a mockery intended to "salve that sore," to satisfy social desires for sexual legitimation, but as Harman elsewhere notes, "I put you out of doubt that not one amongst a hundreth of them are maried, for they take lechery for no sinne, but naturall fellowship and good liking love" (60).

In his establishment of a vagrants' hierarchy of order and degree, and in his vision of female dependency, Harman has projected upon the female beggars a replication of the social structures that in fact define, exclude, and contain them; their libidinal license inverts Harman's bourgeois restraint, and so exposes his own desires. Women who are vagrant precisely because they have no husbands or have been abandoned by them are matched up with the more powerful male vagrants in parodies of marriage. The male sexual fantasy of the rogue pamphlets domesticates and subjugates these women all over again, representing a society in which the bonds of marriage only appear to exist, and male sexual responsibility is not required. In this dream, women are a measurable commodity to be passed around among men; they are both desired and despised. If the Upright Man comes to a barn where vagrant women lie for the night, "he hath his choise, and crepeth in close by his Doxe," but the mere Rogue, two steps down on the hierarchical scale, only "hath his leavings" (77). Harman thus offers a Hobbesian vision of masculine power: "He that is hardiest maye have his choise" (32). But choice, as ever, is in the eye of the beholder.

The cases of Genings and the female vagrants show that Harman is more than willing to be personally involved, even prepared to intervene in their histories. His encounter with the "Dommerar" in his chapter 12, however, best shows just how far Harman is willing to go in order to penetrate the beggars' secrets and make their bodies speak to him. In this case, we find a complex mixture of curiosity, self-righteousness, physical cruelty, and charitable impulse which is in many ways typical of the whole Tudor attitude toward "sturdy beggars." Dommerars, Harman tells us,

> are leud and most subtill people: the most part of these are Walch men, and will never speake, unlesse they have extreame punishment, but will gape, and with a marvelous force will hold downe their toungs doubled, groning for your charity, and holding up their handes full pitiously, so that with their deepe dissimulation they get very much. (57)[27]

If there is one thing Harman wills all these beggars to do, it is to speak to him, to uncover their deceptions, confess their deceits—at the least, to tell their stories, which he may then place in a moralistic frame. But the Dommerar's silence is by definition *his* story, and Harman evidently

[27] The Bridewell Court Books offer contemporary examples of the type: a woman named "Janse Philips *alias* Pele" on 28 June 1560 was charged with having "caused a boy named Edward Pewter of the age of xiiii years to feign himself deffe and dumb"; the boy was sent to the pillory with the woman, where he was forced "to speak to the people and to show his tongue" ("Extracts": 80). William Dorall, a former apprentice, was brought to Bridewell on 29 December 1561 for "feigning himself to be born dumb" and given a similar punishment ("Extracts": 82). Parey describes similar counterfeiting in

finds this intolerable. The Dommerar is, moreover, a Welshman, from the wild outskirts of the kingdom, and thus by definition rude and uncivilized.

In this case, the Dommerar is undone by his own writing—his counterfeit license is perceived when the ever-vigilant Harman "founde one of the seales like unto a seale that I had aboute me, which seale I bought besides Charing crosse, that I was out of doubte it was none of those Gentlemens seales that had subscribed" (58). Once again, we wonder at Harman's prior possession of a tool or trick of the trade—what was he doing with it? He confronts this particular Dommerar with the assistance of a "Surgien . . . cunning in his science," who promises, "you shall se a miracle wrought anon. For I once . . . made a dumme man to speake" (58). The surgeon forces open the Dommerar's mouth, "and we could see but halfe a tounge." Harman is just warming to the task now:

> I required the Surgien to put his finger in his mouth, and to pull out his toung, and so he did, not withstanding he held strongly a prety while; at the length he pluckt out the same, to the great admiration of many that stode by. Yet when we sawe his tounge, hee would neither speake nor yet could heare. (58)

This recalcitrance is clearly unacceptable to Harman, whose every action in these stories is to prove that the bodies of these beggars are *normal*—that they are not different from his own. No effort will be spared in order to prove this point, and Harman helpfully suggests to the surgeon that he "knit two of his [the Dommerar's] fingers to gether, and thrust a sticke betwene them, and rubbe the same up and downe a litle while, and for my life hee speaketh by and by" (58). This casually sanctioned torture revives one of the grim ironies of the period: to prove that the beggar's body is *not* disfigured, it must be *made* disfigured.

The surgeon has a better idea, however, which Harman describes with admiration. The surgeon, he says, had the Dommerar taken into a house, "and tied a halter aboute the wrestes of his handes, and hoised him up over a beame, and there did let him hang a good while: at the length, for very paine he required for Gods sake to let him down. So he that was both deafe and dume coulde in short time both heare and speake" (58–59).

France: "Such as feigne themselves dumbe, draw backe and double their tongues in their mouthes" (995).

What follows is that typically odd Tudor conjunction of charity and chastisement, of sympathy and sadism, as the two kinds of beggars, true and false, are directly juxtaposed. Harman relates,

> Then I tooke that money I could find in his pursse, and distributed the same to the poore people dwelling there, which was xv. pence halfepeny, being all that we coulde finde. That done, and this merry miracle madly made, I sent them with my servaunt to the next Justicer, where they preached on the Pillery for want of a Pulpet, and were well whipped, and none did bewaile them. (59)

From silence to speech to preaching, the Dommerar's vocal revelation through pain is another triumph for Harman, who has distributed alms to the deserving poor as automatically and yet as naturally as he has ordered the torture of the body that would not speak.

In facing down the "poor naked wretches" and beggars he meets, Thomas Harman operates secure in the belief in his own righteousness. Only when he confronts the demonic other in the shape of Nicholas Genings do we begin to see how the exposure of the beggar's body also works as a kind of self-exposure. Harman's *text* shows us how Genings is Harman's own double, but the narrator never makes the connection. In the example of Harman and Genings, we begin to sense the truth of Lear's riddle to Gloucester: "Hark in thine ear: change places and, handy-dandy, which is the justice, which is the thief?" (*King Lear* 4.6.152–54).

Bedlam and Bridewell

THE two chief social institutions intended to bring relief to the poor and the mad in Tudor-Stuart England were Bridewell Hospital and Bethlehem (or Bedlam) Hospital. After Henry VIII's suppression of religious houses and seizure of their property, the City of London attempted as early as 1538 to regain control of those hospitals designated "for the aid and comfort of the poor, sick, blind, aged and impotent persons, being not able to help themselves nor having any place certain wherein they may be lodged, cherished and refreshed till they be cured and holpen of their diseases and sickness" (Allderidge 1979: 148). After protracted negotiations, Edward VI in 1553 granted a charter to the City of London establishing the Royal Hospitals of St. Thomas, Christ, and Bridewell; Henry VIII had refounded St. Bartholomew's in 1547, at which time the City also became the governor, but not the possessor, of Bedlam.[1] The four Royal Hospitals had their own elected governors, but the affairs of Bedlam were (as of 1557) simply managed by the governors of Bridewell. Bedlam and Bridewell were therefore intimately linked legally as well as in the popular imagination: "Bedlem and Bridewell," John

---

[1] See the useful summary in Allderidge (1979: 148). On the early history of Bedlam, see also Masters (32–47) and O'Donoghue (1929). For the history of Bridewell, see Innes, Pendry (1974: 1.40–53), Bowen (1798), Copeland, and O'Donoghue (1923). Copeland and O'Donoghue (both texts) are continually unreliable on details. See Allderidge's critique (1985) of the historiographical fallacies associated with Bedlam. Salgado (1977) brings Bedlam and Bridewell together in a chapter that offers a brief survey of popular conceptions of the two.

Howes reported in 1587, "ar nere kinsemen in condicions" (*TED*: 3.443).

The importance of both institutions is also indicated in part by the fact that the names of these specific hospitals immediately entered the language as generic terms: lunatics and insane asylums were known as bedlams, while institutions that reformed or punished vagabonds were known as bridewells. Bridewell and Bedlam were not just specific institutions, then, but cultural concepts, their names a kind of shorthand for the ways in which Tudor-Stuart society dealt with the poor. Both hospitals moreover quickly turned into prisons—an instance of how charitable intentions could be subverted and how the ideal of reform could become the reality of punishment and incarceration. As Foucault has shown, the movement from patient or indigent to prisoner is all too easy—indeed, the second is usually implicit in the first. Further, the clientele of both hospitals were, at one level of theory, the same: only the poor, who could receive no care from their families, were to be admitted to Bedlam, and lunacy was, in some documents, considered one of the allowable disabilities defining the "deserving poor," along with lameness and blindness (MacDonald: 6–7).[2]

In this chapter I will not attempt to write a history of each hospital, but rather to examine cultural representations of each—to see, for example, why Nicholas Genings would claim to have been in Bedlam but was himself imprisoned in Bridewell. I will also examine dramatic representations of these institutions, not only in casual allusions such as Jonson, Shakespeare, or Fletcher might make ("art thou bedlam?" Pistol asks Fluellen [*Henry V* 5.1.19]), but also in such linked plays as Dekker's *The Honest Whore, Part 1* and *Part 2*, whose final scenes are located in Bedlam and Bridewell, respectively. Such institutions are, first and foremost, conceived for the regulation of the body, before the "cures" for madness and poverty can take place. In the case of Bedlam, to which I now turn, the early modern discourse of madness intersects with, and is contaminated by, the discourse of poverty: the mad in Bedlam are doubly disabled because they are also poor.

---

[2] St. Katherine's provided for the better-off, as this passage in Jonson's *The Alchemist* indicates:

> *Lovewit.* The world's turned Bedlam.
> *Face.*   These are all broke loose,
>   Out of St Katherine's, where they use to keep,
>   The better sort of mad-folks.   (5.3.54–56)

Cf. also Stow (2.143–44).

Bedlam

Bedlam began its life in 1247 when the priory of St. Mary of Bethlehem was founded; the name of "hospice" or "hospital" was associated with it from about 1330, and its specialization in the care of the insane, particularly the "Lunaticque poore people" (*TED*: 3.442), may also be traced to the later fourteenth century (Allderidge 1979: 141–43). The hospital's history in this period is one of neglect and mismanagement, as Patricia Allderidge has shown, culminating in the misrule of the aptly named Keeper from 1619 to 1633, Dr. Helkiah Crooke (1979: 154-64). It was a grim place, whose inmates had "harde lodging and colde fare," according to a 1587 report (*TED*: 3.442)—"not fitt for anye man," as a 1598 report said. Donald Lupton summed up, in 1632, what many must have felt throughout this period.

> It seemes strange that any one shold recover here, the cryings, screechings, roarings, brawlings, shaking of chaines, swearings, frettings, chaffings, are so many, so hideous, so great, that they are more able to drive a man that hath his witts, rather out of them, then to helpe one that never had them, or hath lost them, to finde them again. . . . You shall scarce finde a place that hath so many men & woemen so strangely altered either from what they once were, or should have beene. (1632: 75–76)

Whipping and confinement seem to have become the hospital's chief functions—actually sanctioned as therapeutic tools—activities that Bedlam shared with Bridewell.[3] "Indeede I have heard," a character in Thomas Nashe's *Christ's Tears* (1594) reports, "there are mad men whipt in Bedlam, and lazie vagabonds in Bridewell" (2.181).

Bedlam's long history made it a household word in Tudor-Stuart England, a readily available symbol of both a certain kind of individual and

---

[3] Rosalind recommends "a dark house and a whip" for Orlando's "lunacy" (*As You Like It* 3.2.391), while Malvolio, though he is not whipped, is confined to "a dark room and bound" (*Twelfth Night* 3.4.137). MacDonald notes that although "flogging was certainly not the principal mode of therapy for madness during the seventeenth century," nevertheless (quoting Michael Dalton and Edmund Wingate) "men who whipped lunatics to bring them to their senses were exempted from legal punishment for assault, because they were no more guilty of a crime than parents who corrected their children" (MacDonald: 196). As Anselmo says of the inmates of Bedlam in Dekker's *The Honest Whore, Part 1*: "They must be usde like children, pleasd with toyes, / And anon whipt for their unrulinesse" (5.2.242–43). Allderidge indicates that whipping began "to be discounted as a regular treatment for lunatics" in the seventeenth century, at least by 1677 (1985: 27–28).

a specific institution.[4] As early as 1522, John Skelton could refer to Cardinal Wolsey as "Suche a madde bedleme / For to rewle this rea[l]me" (295), and Sir Thomas More remarked that "thou shalt in Bedlam see one laugh at the knocking of his own head against a post, and yet there is little pleasure therein" (1903: 7). More's comment, which suggests he has actually been in Bedlam, indicates one of its most peculiar features: it became an enormously popular place to visit, particularly in later periods when such distinguished visitors as John Evelyn, Richard Steele, Samuel Johnson, and William Cowper came to gawk at the lunatics, and recorded their impressions.[5] But visiting Bedlam was already a fashionable activity in the later sixteenth century; as merely one of many urban amusements, visiting Bedlam became for many a sign of shallowness. Thomas Lodge portrays (in 1596) a superficial town "gallant" who "haunts the cockpits, like a Gentleman followes the ordinaries; he is at Bedlam once a day I dare assure you" (40). Ben Jonson's urban dandies are frequently said to visit, as Haughty suggests in *Epicoene*: "And goe with us, to *Bed'lem*, to the *China* houses, and to the *Exchange*" (4.3.24–25).[6] In an ironically grand comparison, Richard Brathwaite links the Seven Hills of Rome to the "Seven sights in New Troy," or London: "Tombs, Guildhall giants, stage-plays, Bedlam poor, / Ostrich, Bear Garden, lions in the Tower" (Manley: 250). The "Bedlam poor" are thus just another form of popular entertainment, culturally equivalent to various urban curiosities, or to such theatricalized spectacles as bear-baiting or "stage-plays."

There was moreover a vogue in Stuart drama for scenes depicting a visitation to a madhouse, or the equivalent: John Webster's *The Duchess of Malfi* (1614) and Thomas Middleton and William Rowley's *The Changeling* (1623) are two of the more spectacular examples, but several plays in the Jacobean period also feature either a visit to a madhouse or a significant encounter with madness. Pug tells Ambler in Jonson's *The Devil Is an Ass* (1616) that "Your best song's *Thom o'Bet'lem*" (5.2.35),

---

[4] Napier, for example, routinely referred to his disturbed patients as "Bedlam mad" or "like a Bedlam" (MacDonald: 127, 130). The author of *Micrologia* refers to the specific institution but then broadens the term into a generic category: "but well consider, and we shall finde many Bedlems elsewhere, as in Court, City, Country, University, &c. Are there not Court Bedlems etc." (R.M.: D2ᵛ).

[5] Allderidge corrects Reed's often-quoted misinformation (Reed: 22–35) about entrance (or exit) fees and his fantastically high estimate of probable numbers of visitors (Allderidge 1985: 21–24).

[6] See comparable references in *The Alchemist*, 4.4.47–48; *Bartholomew Fair*, 1.2.54–55 and 1.5.23–25; *The Staple of News*, 4.1.12; and *The Magnetick Lady*, 5.5.37.

while in John Ford's *The Lover's Melancholy* (1628), one character, Cuculus, "Enter[s] . . . like a bedlam, singing" (3.3.54).[7] Some plays, moreover, moved their action quite specifically into Bedlam, such as Dekker's *The Honest Whore, Part 1* (1604) and *Northward Ho* (1607), and King James witnessed a performance, on 9 January 1618 at Theobalds, of an entire "Play . . . of Tom of Bedlem, the Tincker and such other mad stuffe" (McClure: 2.129).

Perhaps the most remarkable fact about Bedlam is that this hospital—the source of countless allusions in every kind of text, the wellspring of a well-known cultural stereotype, and the actual locus or inspiration of many scenes in Jacobean drama—rarely had more than 15 or 20 patients in it at a time, many of them very long term (Allderidge 1979: 145).[8] A 1598 report to the governors recorded 21 patients by name, and when the house was described as severely "overcharged" in a 1624 report, there were 31 patients in residence (Allderidge 1979: 152–53, 158); a 1611 report lists 30 patients (*SAL*: 24.206–7). Christ's Hospital, by contrast, contained 280 orphaned children in 1553 (Leonard: 34), and 2,730 persons passed through Bridewell between 25 March 1600 and 25 March 1601, with 172 still in the house on 28 March 1601 (Bowen 1798: 26).[9] Bedlam, in short, was an incredibly small institution to have loomed so large in the popular imagination.

Part of Bedlam's enormous cultural appeal may have derived from its locus as an intersection of both the poor and the mad, two of the most compelling and disturbing marginal social groups of the period. Moreover, it was not only a hospital but inevitably a prison as well; in a common synonymic usage of the period, Harman says the "Abram Man" has been kept in "Bethelem or in some other prison" (47). "Bedlam cures

---

[7] Even in a play as early as *Gammer Gurton's Needle* (c. 1553), the Vice is named "Diccon, the Bedlam," though he bears little resemblance to the type we are examining here. See Salkeld for discussions of several of these other plays, including *The Honest Whore, Part 1*; *Northward Ho!*, *The White Devil; The Duchess of Malfi*; and *The Changeling* (116–43). For Salkeld, "the common feature of all of these texts is their representation of the confinement of women. . . . the body on which the madness is sited is female. Bedlam becomes a vehicle for contemporary misogyny" (124). In my view, Salkeld tends to overstate his case, arguing a difference between dramatic and other cultural representations of Bedlam, which do not to my knowledge emphasize specifically *female* confinement; nor do the archival records suggest a preponderance of female inmates.

[8] Nor were there enough such facilities in any event, as Thomas Adams noted: "There are so few *Bedlam*-houses, and yet so many out of their wits" (1615: 64).

[9] Pearl figures for the later period 1640–60, an average yearly patient load of over 2,000 sick and aged persons at St. Thomas and St. Bartholomew, 450–900 orphans at Christ's, and about 1,000 vagrants and 200 apprentices at Bridewell (211).

not more madmen in a year / Than one of the counters [prisons] does,"
according to a character in Middleton and Dekker's *The Roaring Girl*
(3.3.79-80), marking Bedlam's comparability and inferiority at the same
time. Many of Bedlam's patients had, in fact, been first incarcerated in
Bridewell and then transferred to Bedlam (and vice versa).

Two distinct cultural stereotypes seem to have been generated from
the dismal confines of Bedlam. The first type is of course simply the
raving madman. "The stark, Bedlam madman," as Michael MacDonald
notes, was generally considered to be "dangerous, inclined to murder
and assault, arson and vandalism . . . his behavior and moods suggested
that he was helpless to govern the wild energy of his passions" (142).
"Many are kept here," Lupton noted in 1632, "not so much in hope of
recovery, as to keepe them from further and more desperate Inconve-
niences" (1632: 77). The existence of several very long-term patients
indicated in the 1598 and 1624 reports corroborates Lupton's observation that many patients "never think of getting out" (78). Bedlam contained the chaos of a small number of the mad, then, preventing its
eruption into the larger society.[10]

The second stereotype generated out of Bedlam, the one most relevant
to this study, is the Bedlam beggar, the Poor Tom or Abraham Man—
that is, the (usually) fraudulent madman beggar.[11] It was widely believed
that Tom o'Bedlam men were generally licensed to beg (and therefore
not subject to arrest), but there is no evidence, according to Beier, to
support this assertion (1985: 115). Nevertheless, the figure of the wandering mad beggar became a commonplace. The proliferation of such
figures in the discourse of poverty—in plays, archival documents, and
particularly in the rogue pamphlets—seems out of proportion to what
must have been their real numbers, perhaps because of a general cultural
fascination with madness.

It is easy to see why, in any event, Nicholas Genings would have claimed
to have been "a yeare and a halfe in bethelem" (Harman: 52), even if

---

[10] In *Perkin Warbeck* (c. 1625–34), Ford reverses the usual associations, linking the chaos
of the Scottish court with Bedlam: "The rare discord of bells, pipes, and tabors, / Hotch-
potch of Scotch and Irish twingle-twangles, / Like to so many choristers of Bedlam /
Trolling a catch" (3.2.4–7).

[11] The usual explanation for the term "Abraham" is that it "may come from a ward
in the hospital" (Beier 1985: 115); the earliest usage registered by the Oxford English
Dictionary is from Awdeley (1561). Allderidge makes no reference to the existence of
such a ward, though she notes an inmate in 1607 with the forename or nickname "Abraham" (1979: 154). Since the hospital had only two areas where patients slept at this time,
the term "ward" seems a little grandiose; Allderidge reproduces the original groundplan
of the hospital (1979: 146).

he did not know the Keeper's name, using his misfortune as a way of justifying his begging. The stereotypical Poor Tom was very well known for a remarkably long period. The earliest description is by Awdeley (1561): "An Abraham man is he that walketh bare armed, and bare legged, and faineth him selfe mad, and caryeth a packe of wool, or a sticke with baken on it, or such like toy, and nameth himselfe poore Tom" (3). Harman's description is very close:

These Abrahom men be those that faine themselves to have beene mad, and have bene kept either in Bethelem or in some other prison a good time, and not one amongst twenty that ever came in prison for any such cause: yet will they saye how pitiously and most extreamely they have bene beaten, and dealt with all. Some of these be merye and verye pleasant, they will daunce and sing; some others be as colde and reasonable to talke with all. These begge money; either when they come at Farmours howses they will demaunde Baken, either cheese, or wooll, or any thinge that is worthe money. And if they espye small company within, they will with fierce countenaunce demaund some what. Where for feare the maides will geve theim largely to be rid of theim. (47)

Harman goes on to tell of one "Stradlinge . . . the craftiest and moste dissemblingest Knave" of this sort he had ever encountered, who simulated having "a marveilous palsey, that both head and handes will shake when he talketh" (47–48). Archival evidence replicates these elaborate descriptions of deceit. In one case in 1578, one man confessed that he had for five months gone with a false license "feigning himself to have been in Bedlam this two years and a quarter for lunacy, and to beg for his fees" (Beier 1985: 116). There was thus a kind of standard "Bedlam looke," as Samuel Rowlands described it in 1613, with "shag haire, and staring eyes" (2.32). Richard West (1607) amplified the type: they

> Doe rage with furie as if they were so frantique,
> They knew not what they did but every day,
> Make sport with stick and flowers, like an antique.
> Stowt roge and harlot counterfeted gomme,
> One calls her selfe poore Besse the other Tom.

(F3)

(Poor Tom's female equivalent was Poor Bess, a common nickname of Queen Elizabeth.)

More than a century later, contemporary descriptions of the type varied little from those of Awdeley and Harman. John Aubrey reported on the phenomenon, with the legend of the begging license, in some detail:

> Till the breaking out of the Civil Wars, Tom o' Bedlam did travel about the country; they had been poor distracted men, but had been put into Bedlam, where, recovering some soberness, they were licentiated to go a-begging, *i.e.* they had on their left arm an armilla of tinn, about four inches long; they could not get it off; they wore about their necks a great horn of an ox in a string or bawdry, which when they came to an house for alms, they did wind, and they did put the drink given them into this horn, whereto they did put a stopple. Since the wars I do not remember to have seen any one of them.[12]

John Bunyan describes his conversion "from prodigious profaneness, to something like a moral life," as being "as great, as for a *Tom* of *Bethlem* to become a sober man" (15). As late as *The Academy of Armory* (1688), Randle Holme is still offering a variant of the long-standardized description. "The Bedlam" has "a long Staff, and a Cow or Or-horn by his side; but his Cloathing is more Fantastick and Ridiculous, for being a Mad Man, he is madly decked and dressed all over with Rubins, Feathers, cuttings of Cloth, and what not; to make him seem a Mad-Man, or one Distracted, when, he is no other then a Dissembling Knave" (3.161).

The phenomenon of the fraudulent Bedlamite endured late into the seventeenth century, then; the governors of Bedlam in fact found it necessary, in 1675, to state in public notice,

> Whereas several vagrant persons do wander about . . . pretending themselves to be lunatics under cure in the Hospital of Bethlem commonly called Bedlam, with brass plates about their arms and inscriptions thereon: These are to give notice that there is no such liberty given to any patients kept in the said Hospital for their cure, neither is any such plate as a distinction or mark put upon any lunatic during their being there, or when discharged thence. And that the same is a false pretense, to colour their wandering and begging, and to deceive the people. (Salgado: 198)

The pretense of Nicholas Genings was therefore not an isolated example, and Shakespeare's Poor Tom is merely the most famous instance of a tradition that spans more than a century.

The line dividing those who should be sent to Bedlam to begin with,

---

[12] *The Natural History of Wiltshire* 93; quoted in Wheatley: 1.176.

and those sent to Bridewell, was at times unclear and had little to do with the question of sanity. A report of 1601 referred to "William Barnes, a lunatic, who has been kept in Bridewell this 14 years" (*SAL*: 11.507). In some cases, Bedlam also seemed an appropriate place to incarcerate those who were perhaps simply seditious. In one case, on 6 June 1595, "a silkweaver, came to the Lord Mayor's house, using some hard speeches against the Lord Mayor in dispraise of his government. The Mayor said he was mad and so committeed [sic] him to Bedlam as a madman" (*SAL*: 5.249). But the mayor's action was resented by the silk-weaver's contemporaries, and when he was sent "towards Bedlam by some of his own servants . . . he was rescued by prentices and divers other to the number of about 200 or 300 persons."[13] The case of the silkweaver seems straightforward enough. Although insane people "were permitted freely to express normally unacceptable ideas," according to Michael MacDonald (143), there were certainly political limits to their speech and even, as in this case, an impulse toward defining a "normally unac-ceptable" idea as itself insanity.[14] We can see in this incident with the silkweaver an ideological appropriation of the concept of lunacy for po-litical ends. We can also see in the crowd's reaction a strong resistance to such a move.[15]

In a second case, in 1607, narrated by Sir William Waad, "a lewd fellow, one Bartholomew Helson," went about town, "giving himself forth to be Queen Mary's son, and oftentimes gathered people about him. Whereupon I caused him to be apprehended, and examined him." Helson said that "he was stolen from Hampton Court where he was born, with other words showing more seditious disposition than any kind of lunacy that I could perceive, though I hear sometimes he is possessed with that humour." Waad "committed him to Bridewell where he has remained ever since." But, "because the masters grow weary of him," Waad sent for him and through questioning, "cannot find he takes this course out of any distemperature malicious, but out of a knavish humour,

[13] Archer notes that the Lord Mayor, Sir John Spencer, was notoriously mean-spirited, and possibly corrupt (56).

[14] See MacDonald's discussion (156ff.) of the very narrow line drawn between religious enthusiasm and insanity at this time.

[15] By the same token, madness, Salkeld has argued, was "in the years leading up to the Civil War . . . increasingly used as a metaphor for political rebellion" (81). At the center of the metaphysics of sovereignty, he notes, "stood the body of the King, unifying social reality with a tropological force exerted by the metaphors of philosophy, theology, medicine and poetry. . . . The mythic ideal of the sovereign body is shown to be self-contradictory and self-defeating. Madness is the spectacular evidence of this crisis, signi-fying the failure of reason even at the heart of its ideology" (151–52).

being in want and a tall lusty fellow. Therefore I thought good to advertise you of his carriage, that you may either continue him there, or send him to Bedlem" (*SAL:* 19.177). Waad's uncertainty about how to deal with Helson is again instructive. The romance fantasy of royal birth he peddles might be relatively harmless had he not claimed Queen Mary, in particular, as his mother. Given his "seditious disposition" rather than "lunacy," he is rightly sent to Bridewell. But the second examination of Helson reveals that he may be merely crafty rather than deluded, his "malicious and knavish humour" and his poverty driving him to this fiction. Although his apparent sanity ought to indicate commitment to Bridewell, it is now left unclear whether Bridewell or Bedlam is the appropriate prison.[16] In some ways, Helson's "seditious disposition" is the very proof of his "lunacy." Ergo Bedlam. A similar, more transparently political imprisonment occurred as a result of an incident before King James at Theobalds in early May 1619. As one letter-writer explained, "a gentlemanlike fellow, one that had been a soldier," confronted James with "a message . . . from God!": "Thus saith the Lord, have I not brought thee out of a land of famine and danger into a land of plenty and abundance? Oughtest thou not therefore to have judged my people with righteous judgment? But thou hast perverted justice and not relieved the oppressed. Therefore, unless thou repent, God hath sent the kingdom from thee *and thy posterity after thee.*" After an interrogation revealed bizarre religious opinions, his "distraction or weakness" was confirmed, "his prophetical spirit [found] to be a spirit of phrenzy and madness," and so he was sent "to Bedlam, where he now is" (Birch: 2.156–57).

The charitable instincts of the founders of Bedlam and the post-Reformation governors and monarchs who supported it were thus inevitably compromised. The "hospital" for the poor could also serve as a "prison" for the poor, just as its twin institution, Bridewell, was transformed from a "house of correction" to a "prison" and site of torture; thus patients, or "prisoners," could easily be exchanged between these

---

[16] As Candido in Dekker's *The Honest Whore, Part 2* , says when the Constable takes him away:

> To Bridewell too?
> *Constable.* No remedy.
> *Candido.*   Yes, patience: being not mad,
> They had me once to Bedlam, and now I'm drawne
> To Bridewell, loving no Whores. (4.3.179–81)

The narrator of Dekker's *The Wonderful Year* (1603) likewise refers to a Dutchman "who (though hee dwelt in *Bedlem*) was not mad" (Dekker 1963: 1.121).

two institutions. Once they were inscribed in the discourse of poverty, then, the London mad could be classified as a social rather than a psychological problem, and official management could turn from the untreatable "mind diseased" (*Macbeth* 5.3.42) to the more easily managed body—disorderly, potentially seditious, and so the perfect candidate for incarceration.[17]

Locating a scene in a madhouse offered the Elizabethan and Jacobean playwright a convenient way of raising complex questions about the nature of sanity and insanity, of appearance and reality, of pathos and fraud. John Webster's horrific depiction of the mad in *The Duchess of Malfi* may resonate closely with modern sensibilities, but we ought also to recall that for many the spectacle of the lunatic poor was essentially comic. Dekker even engineers the comic resolution to *The Honest Whore, Part 1* (1604) so that the entire action of the long final scene takes place inside "*Bethlem* Monasterie . . . the scoole where those that loose their wits, / Practise againe to get them" (4.4.101–3).[18] The Keeper, Anselmo, expresses the contradiction of despair and humor that is typical of the period:

> . . . we have here some,
> So apish and phantastike, play with a fether,
> And tho twould greeve a soule, to see Gods image,
> So blemisht and defac'd, yet do they act
> Such anticke and such pretty lunacies,
> That spite of sorrow they will make you smile.
>
> (5.2.156–61)

Anselmo says that the true madmen "act" their lunacies, but Dekker's Bedlam, like virtually every other Elizabethan or Jacobean dramatic representation of a madhouse, in fact contains more sane people who "act" or counterfeit lunacy than actual madmen, for virtually every figure in the play is brought into Bedlam either as observer or as inmate. Dekker also moves the action of *Northward Ho* (1605) into Bedlam (in 4.3), but the scene is brief, perfunctory, and not integrated into the rest of the play; still, Bellamont is committed by a warrant against his will, though perfectly sane. In John Fletcher's *The Pilgrim* (1622), the madhouse

---

[17] For discussions of the body in Renaissance theories of madness, see MacDonald (passim) and Salkeld (55–61), for whom the mad body "devoid of normative meaning . . . signifies its emptiness through a semiotics of contradiction and disfigurement" (61).

[18] McPeek (82–86) argues that Dekker distinctly echoes Copland's *The Highway to the Spital-House* in the Bedlam scenes, though Copland's work is located at St. Bartholomew's rather than Bedlam.

scenes (3.7ff.) feature an "English Madman," a "Shee-foole," a "mad Scholler," and a "Welch mad-man," as well as "mad *Besse*," the "Parson," the "Prentize," and the "Justice," altogether comprising a microcosm of society. This madhouse, like most during the period, also contains the sane masquerading as the lunatic (primarily the heroine, Alinda), and inmates imprisoned against their will. This madhouse is unnamed—the play is set in Spain—but one of the Keepers notes, "We have few Citizens: they have bedlames of their own sir, / And are mad at their own charges" (4.3.18-19).

Bedlam was virtually always represented on the stage, then, as containing those who merely feigned madness as well as the lunatic; Donald Lupton noted the same phenomenon: "There's many that are so well or ill in their wits, that they can say they have bin out of them, & gaine much by dissembling in this kind: desperate Caitifes that dare make a mocke of judgement" (1632: 78). The city as well as the country therefore gives us "proof and precedent" (*King Lear* 2.3.13) of vagrants and counterfeit beggars who are "pretending themselves to be lunatics under cure in the Hospital of Bethlem commonly called Bedlam," as the 1675 notice warned, "a false pretence, to colour their wandering and begging, and to deceive the people." The history of the representations of Bedlam intersects the early modern discourse of poverty, leading to the complex figure of the madman-beggar.

Bridewell

In 1632, Donald Lupton remarked of Bridewell, "Heere's a Pallace strangly Metamorphosed into a prison" (39). Bridewell was the most important institutional expression of the Tudor-Stuart approach to the problem of the poor.[19] Although its history is briefer than Bedlam's, moreover, that history is filled with ironies that typify the period, including the unexpected social conjunction of the monarch and the beggar.

---

[19] For a valuable short history, see Beier (1985: 164–69); see also Slack (1988) and J. E. Thomas (163–77). Innes provides a useful history of the *concept* of the bridewell from 1555 to 1800, but her focus is less on Bridewell itself, in London, than the whole system of charitable relief and disciplinary punishment that spread throughout England in this period. In her view, bridewells "were penal instruments specifically designed to correct the faults of a servant class. In bridewell, those of the servant class who had shown insufficient respect for some aspect of the social or moral order might be subordinated to the authority of a (significantly named) bridewell 'master' and rudely reminded of the obligations attaching to their social position" (47). My argument is that the original London Bridewell had much broader, even contradictory functions.

Some of these ironies are conveniently set out in John Taylor's brief history (in *The Praise and Vertue of a Jayle and Jaylers*, 1623):

> *Bridewell* unto my memorie comes next;
> Where idlenesse and lechery is vext:
> This is a royall house, of state and port,
> Which th'eight King *Henry* built, and there kept Court.
> King *Edward* somewhat ere his timelesse fall,
> Gave it away to be an Hospitall,
> Which use the city puts it well unto,
> And many pious deeds they there doe doe:
> But yet for Vagabonds and Runnagates,
> For Whores, and idle knaves, and such like mates,
> 'Tis littell better than a Jaile to those,
> Where they chop chalke, for meat and drinke and blowes.
> In this house those that 'gainst their will doe dwell,
> Love *well* a *Bride* (perhaps) but not *Bridewell.*
>
> (1623: B4^{r-v})

Taylor's rendition is accurate, and Bridewell's rapid declension, from "royall house" to "Hospitall" to "Jaile," marks the cultural transformations of how the vagrant poor were to be dealt with.

Bridewell was "purposely builded [by Henry VIII] for the entertainement of the Emperour *Charles* the 5. who in the yeare 1522 came into this Citie," according to John Stow. "King *Henrie* himselfe," he continues, "oftentimes lodged there also," and a number of specific instances follow (1.70, 2.44). As part of the mid-century movement in London to deal with the poor already discussed, Bridewell was really the keystone, "the greatest innovation and the most characteristic institution of the new system," in one modern scholar's estimation (Leonard: 39). The most generous and humane of motives moved the citizens of London to petition the Privy Council in 1552 that the City be given the now-unused palace as "the situation and largeness thereof seemeth most meet and convenient for this purpose" (*TED*: 2.308). Bishop Ridley was quite direct in his appeal to Cecil in the same year: "Sir, there is a wide, large, empty house of the King's Majesty's, called Bridewell, that would wonderfully well serve to lodge Christ in, if he might find such good friends in the court to procure in his cause" (*TED*: 2.312).

Other hospitals existed to deal with orphans (Christ's), the insane (Bedlam), and the sick and aged (St. Thomas's and St. Bartholomew's), but there was no facility to care for beggars. The citizens argued a posi-

tion opposite to that which William Lambarde would argue in 1582: after
noting the failure of law alone to effect a social remedy, they observed
that "the greatest number of beggars" are

> fallen into misery by lewd and evil service, by wars, by sickness, or other
> adverse fortune, have so utterly lost their credit, that though they would
> shew themselves willing to labour, yet are they so suspected and feared
> of all men, that few or none dare, or will receive them to worke:
> wherefore we saw that there could be no mean to amend this miserable
> sort, but by making some general provision of work, wherewith the *willing*
> poor may be exercised; and whereby the froward, strong, and sturdy vag-
> abond may be compelled to live profitably to the commonwealth. (*TED*.
> 2.307)

In this refusal simply to blame all beggars for their own condition, the
citizens were well ahead of their time; and the only indication of the
employment of force is that sturdy beggars would naturally be "compelled" to participate in the new scheme.

The key to the entire project was the provision of work. Indeed, the
citizens referred to the proposed new institution as "an house of occupations"—"wherein shall be trained all the former sorts of people,
and those occupations shall be such as may be profitable to all the
king's majesty's subjects, and hurtful to none" (*TED*. 2.308). There was
no intention to make a profit (308), and the house, along with the
other royal hospitals, would have a fairly representative board of governors. "The present remedy to reform [beggars'] idle life shall be always the house of labour and occupations," they maintained
confidently (311). The citizens' arguments were in the end successful,
for Edward VI gave Bridewell to the City of London in April 1553, confirming it by charter in June, just a few days before he died; the mayor
and the Court of Aldermen actually took possession in 1555 (Stow:
2.45; Wheatley: 241).[20]

London's Bridewell soon became a model for relief efforts in other
cities, such as Ipswich, Cambridge, Lincoln, and York, and later the entire
country (Leonard: 40–46; Innes). The harsh statute of 1572 was to some
extent modified, or at least complemented by, the statute of 1576, which
for the first time ordered the provision of work on a national scale, including the establishment of houses of correction in every county, "to

---

[20] One German visitor in 1584 incorrectly reported that after Henry VIII "became
enemy of the emperor, he, to disgrace the latter, made it a place of confinement for
harlots and villains, who are kept there to the present day" (Bulow 1895: 233).

thentente everye suche poore and nedye person olde or younge able to doe any Worcke standing in necessitye of Releife shall not for want of Worcke goe abrode either begginge or committinge Pilfringes or other Misdemeanor livinge in Idlenes" (*TED*: 2.332). Anyone able to work and refusing to do so will be compelled to go, "there to be straightlye kepte, as well in Diet as in Worke, and also punisshed from time to time" (*TED*: 2.333).

Bridewell's record of success is very mixed indeed. On the one hand, it clearly did attempt to train the unemployed in useful occupations. A set of orders dated 1582 listed twenty-five distinct "artes" or occupations the inmates could be taught, from the "Spining of wollen yarne" to the "Making of Tennise balles" (*Orders*: B2ᵛ). Hospital records show, for example, that (on 23 January 1600) such trade masters as "a pinner, a wicker bottell maker, a button maker, a spinner of cotton wolle" lent their expertise to train the inmates (Bowen 1798: 24). An entry for 21 October 1602 shows another way in which the system was supposed to work. Richard Brookes, a "fustian weaver, engages to take during seven years next ensuing, forty vagrant boys and wenches of this city, as apprentices, to keep in diet, apparell, washing, and wringing: the said R. Brookes to receive with every of the said children at their coming, clean apparell; and ten pounds yearly" (Bowen 1798: 23).

Much of the "work" in Bridewell, however, revolved around two activities that became notorious and virtually indistinguishable from punishment. The prisoners were expected to beat hemp hour after hour, day after day—"labour hard enough," as Thomas Ellwood noted (Crump: 102), with whipping posts handy for use on those who flagged on the hemp-block. "If the Millers art you like not," as one ballad put it, "to the hempe blocke packe yee: / Thumpe, and thumpe, and thump apace, / for feare the whipper take yee" (Rollins: 41–42). In Philip Massinger's *The City Madam*, Luke threatens Shavem with

> a blew gown,
> And a whip to boot, as I will handle it
> Will serve the turn in Bridewell, and these soft hands,
> When they are inur'd to beating hemp, be scour'd
> In your penitent tears.
>
> (4.2.98–102)

Worse than beating hemp, though, was the "Millers art"—the mill, which had been set up in 1578 "to grind corn, which shall with eight men grind daily from 5 a.m. till 7 p.m. four quarters of corn" ("Extracts": 11.116). Beyond the sheer physical demands, which were enormous, the conditions associated with the mill—the noise, filth, fear—must have been unendurable, as we see in John Gerard's description of John Jacob, whom he visited in Bridewell in 1583: "He was wasted to a skeleton and in a state of exhaustion from grinding at the treadmill, a most pitiful sight. There was nothing left of him except skin and bones and I cannot remember having seen anything like it—lice swarmed on him like ants on a mole-hill" (5).

The author of *Micrologia* (1629) ironically captures Bridewell's fusion of a protocapitalist work ethic, punishment, and correction: "It is a well compacted Common-wealth of workers against their wils, where the awe of the whipstocke confines them to the laborious stroke of the hempe-blocke, and the turning of the wheele a daily Memento of turning over a new leafe" (R.M.: D5ᵛ). Despite some modest successes, Bridewell was not an effective cure for the disease of poverty, but a temporary local palliative. Bridewell was simply not large enough, nor securely funded—it was in fact "the most seriously underfinanced of the hospitals" (Archer: 190). The more successful it was, ironically, the more quickly it hastened its own failure, for the poor throughout the country came to London seeking relief, and the facilities could not sustain them (Leonard: 39-40; Beier 1985: 167–69). Even though "all London is but an hospitall"—so it seemed to John Howes in 1587—"a place of releife for the poore every one in ther kinde," still he insisted that "London cannot reliefe inglande" (*TED*: 3.431, 442).

The overloading of the London system of relief is quite understandable, even inevitable, but it does not fully account for the notorious reputation that Bridewell so quickly acquired. In another manuscript dated 1582, John Howes traces a corruption in Bridewell's governance to actions taken during the reign of Queen Mary: "The chaunge of Relligion" brought on "greate allteracon & chaunge" (Howes: 65, 63). The bishops, according to Howes, were responsible: "Theire mallice was moste chefely againste Bridewell" and "they did all they might doe to discountenance & to discreadit that house" because "it appearethe that Bridewell was a greate mote in theire eies & that theire owne consciences accused them of some fowle matters which they feared shoulde come to lighte by examinacon [i.e., sexual misconduct of priests discovered in the interrogation of prostitutes]" (71, 73, 72). Among the specific criticisms Howes later lodges against Bridewell in 1587 is that the governors have already lost sight of its original mission; the dialogue is worth quotation at some length here.

Dignitie. I woulde knowe of you the reason whie heretofore all those people before mencioned, as servingmen, soldiers and other honest
youthes, whose lacks have been the cause of theire loitering, have been
packte up and punnished alike in Bridewell with roges, beggers, strom-
pets and pilfering theves. This methincks goeth very harde that they
make no difference betwene bonum and malum, considering that the
very name of Bridewell is in the eares of the people so odious that it
killeth the creadit for ever, and a thousande to one if ever he or shee
comme to any preferment, having tasted of that soile; it is a sufficient
acquittance to barre them of all hope or meanes of preferment.

"Dutie" responds that the fault is not really in the governors, "because
they knowe not one man from another, neither can they judge of them
before they be examined," but "Dignitie" does not accept this reasoning.

Dignitie. Pretely answered; it is not the punishement which they receave
that I finde faulte withall, it is the place, which was ordained only for
Roges and common strumpetts [sic—of course, it was ordained for the
deserving poor]; it was not meant that any honest soldier or servingman
having any good qualletie shoulde be broughte to Bridewell, where
nothing is to be learned but lewdenes amoungest that generacion. And
althoughe it please god to laie the crosse of povertie upon them for
wante of service, will you presentlye condemne them for Roges? it were
very uncharetablie and not Christianlie done.

Dutie. I must confesse there is a fault, and it is partely as well for wante
of other place, as allso for lacke of maintenaunce. (*TED:* 3.439)

"Dignitie" also later observes that the governors have continued in term
too long (440) rather than constantly rotating through as originally
planned ("the eldest shall remain but two years" as a governor, *TED:*
2.309). There are several different accusations of financial mismanagement (*TED:* 3.440–41) as well.

Finally, Howes notes the governors' excessive interest in sexual misconduct, searching out sins that cannot be seen while overlooking the
poor who die in the streets before all men's eyes:

Suerly god can not but be angrie with us, that will suffer our Christian
Bretheren to die in the streates for wante of reliefe, and wee spende and
consume our wealthe and our witte in searching out of Harlotts, and leave
the worckes of faithe and mercie undone. And therefore it is not nor it
can not be that theire zeale is so greate in punishing of that, [of] which
Christe said to the woeman: let him that is not guilty throwe the firste

stone. But graunt it is good to punnishe sinne. So it is good to succour, healpe and to relieve the poore. And thereof they take theire names to be governors of the poore; it is a badde kinde of governemente to see them die in the streates. This is a greate abuse. (*TED*. 3.442)

In this latter complaint, Howes is referring to the period, particularly in the late 1570s and 1580s, when the governors of Bridewell consciously undertook a campaign against sexual immorality, particularly prostitution. Their willingness "to take action against wealthy or well-connected offenders," as Archer demonstrates, led at times to "highly embarrassing consequences to the City" (232); influence at court still counted for pardons, however.[21] By the 1590s, judging by the sharply reduced number of prosecutions of prostitutes and clients compared with the 1570s (Archer: 240–41), the sexual morality campaign had been considerably scaled back though not officially abandoned. In one of the sharper ironies of the period, Bridewell itself had briefly been turned into a brothel in 1602 when Stanley, as we saw in chapter 1, organized the "lewde women," who were allowed "to intertayne any that would resorte unto them."[22] In Thomas Middleton's *Your Five Gallants* (c. 1604–6), Bungler warns against commiting a boy pickpocket to Bridewell: "And as for Bridewell, that will but make him worse; 'a will learn more knavery there in one week than will furnish him and his heirs for a hundred year. . . . there's none goes in there a quean, but she comes out an arrant whore" (3.5.137–42).

The unnamed prison in Shakespeare's *Measure for Measure* (1604) to which Pompey is sent is a thinly veiled image of Bridewell; though the Duke expects that the bawd Pompey will there find "correction and instruction" (3.2.33)—the standard terms describing Bridewell's function—in fact Pompey finds all his old customers, "all great doers in our trade" (4.3.18), in a prison little different from "our house of profession" (4.3.1). The prison in George Whetstone's *Promos and Cassandra* (1578), one of the sources of *Measure and Measure*, is likewise recognizably

---

[21] See Archer (249–54) for a discussion of the role Protestantism may have played in this campaign. Griffiths uses Bridewell records to describe the "structure of prostitution" in Elizabethan London, but he understates the original founding purposes of Bridewell, and he overstates its connection to the punishment of prostitution; Bridewell came to have many different functions, as I argue here.

[22] Philip Stubbes (1583) told of a man named W. Brustar who, upon visiting Bridewell on business, "saw there a famous whore, but a very proper Woman, whom (as is said) he knew not; but whether he did or not, certen it is that he procured her delivery from thence, bailed her, &, having put away his owne wife before, kept her in his chamber, using her at his pleasure" (100).

Bridewell; though the name is never invoked, the inmates are the usual poor (*"one like a Giptian, the rest poore Rog[u]es,"* Bullough: 2.456) and loose women, and the beadle offers "a blew gown" and "whipping" to the inmates (464). (Whetstone dedicated his work to the chief scourge of London's vagrants, William Fleetwood.) The author of *Micrologia* (1629) begins his list of typical inhabitants of Bridewell with "the grand grosse Baud, Provocatious Pander, ungratious Letcher, [and] audacious Whore" before moving on to "rude Ruffians, Runnagates," and other petty criminals (R.M.: D5). As late as 1632 Lupton still ironically noted Bridewell's transformed function:

> In the outward Court were Carts not for the Husband-man, but for those that have used the unlawfull game of Venery; it seems to be contrary to nature, to make those draw which were made to beare, a strange invention to have such a new punishment, for such an old sinne. Me thinkes the house complains, *oh quam a dispari Domino.* (1632: 39)

Bridewell suffered in the eyes of many others not just because of its association with lechery, but because its name became a synonym for—and soon a generic term for—a harsh prison, vastly more notorious, in this respect, than Bedlam. In John Taylor's poem of 1623, Bridewell is quite routinely included as one of the eighteen "Jayles or Prisons" to be found in London, equivalent to the Tower, Newgate, the Fleet, the Counter, or the Clink. John Gerard recounted his servant's incarceration in Bridewell in the 1580s, in terms that would have been appropriate to any of the city's prisons. The servant was in solitary confinement:

> He said that he was given barely sufficient bread to keep body and soul together. His cell was narrow; it had thick walls; it had no bed in it and he had to sleep in a sitting posture perched on the window-ledge. For months he had not taken his clothes off. There was only a little straw in the place and it had been trodden flat, and now it was crawling with vermin and quite impossible to lie on. Worst of all, they left his excrement in an uncovered pail in that tiny cell, and the stink was suffocating. In these conditions he was waiting to be called out and examined under torture. (57)

Beyond its deplorable physical conditions, Bridewell had almost immediately upon its creation become known as a place of whipping and torture. In a typical synonymy, the Privy Council in 1596 ordered a group of prisoners to be carried to "Bridewell or some such prison of severe punishment" (*APC* 25:469). As Ben Jonson's Ursula says to Alice in *Bartholomew Fair* (1614), "You know where you were taw'd lately, both lash'd, and slash'd you were in *Bridewell*' (4.5.78–79). The "Beadle of Bridewell," in Samuel Rid's well-known rogue pamphlet of 1608, was known as "Martin Mark-all." In *Have With You To Saffron-Walden* (1596), Thomas Nashe describes how flogging in Bridewell was regulated (when the president of the Court of Governors let his hammer fall, the prisoners were taken to be whipped). His imaginary character, Don Carneades, is

> like a busie Countrey Justice . . . or rather, like a Quarter-master or Treasurer of Bride-well, whose office is to give so manie strokes with the hammer, as the publican unchast offender is to have stripes . . . [he] sets downe what proportion of justice is to be executed upon [the offender] and, when his backe hath bled sufficient, gives a signall of retrait. (3.21)

Another character described by Nashe in *Pierce Penilesse* (1592) is said to have "a backe so often knighted in Bridewell, that it was impossible for any shame or punishment to terrifie him from ill speaking" (1.190). In short, the beggars and vagabonds of London, according to *The Court of Conscience or Dick Whippers Sessions* (1607), could not evade the whip of Bridewell, "Nor yet defend your selves by all your shiftes, / From tasting of his franke and liberall gifts" (West: F3).[23] Shakespeare's Mistress Quickly and Doll Tearsheet are taken away to prison, undoubtedly Bridewell, by a beadle—a "filthy, famished correctioner," in Doll's words—who promises her in the usual grim phrase, "she shall have whipping cheer, I warrant her" (2 *Henry IV* 5.4.5, 20). "I dare scarce speak of Bridewell," one of Greene's female conny-catchers says (1592), "because my shoulders tremble at the name of it" (Judges: 224).

Bridewell's notoriety as a house of pain derives from two main sources. First, its function as a "house of correction" involved making "some general provision of work" for those able to do it, while those sturdy vagabonds who refused "may be compelled to live profitably to the commonwealth" (*TED*: 2.307). Prisoners were to be brought to Bridewell "for their reformation and not for perpetuall servitude," as one set of orders in 1582 specified (*Orders*: B2ᵛ). The terms of compulsion soon devolved into regular whippings, and the line between "correction" and

---

[23] In the ballad "Whipping Cheare" (dated 1612 by Rollins), "Gold and silver hath forsaken" the inmates, and "Twined whipcord takes the place, / And strikes t'our shoulders neerely" (Rollins: 41). Cf. the ironic trope of Bridewell as an inn, where the beadles "are ready waiters on your backs on any occasion, and their main service a full satiety of whipping-cheare" (R.M.: D4ᵛ).

"compulsion," work and punishment, was often blurred. The prisoners beat hemp and the beadles beat the prisoners: work was therefore rewarded with the same punishment as the failure to work. As Lupton put it,

> when men have here done their work, they are sure of their wages, a whip . . . some say there are many idle persons in it: strange! yet work so hard: It is thought there's scarce a true fellow in it, for they all lie hard: there's none can say hee workes for nothing, for they are all sure of payment. . . . they have taske-maisters to holde them to their worke: their whippe-maister is like a Countrey Pedagouge, they many times whippe better, then himselfe, and both take a pride in their office, they inflict that uppon others, which they deserve themselves. (1632: 40–41)

Ellwood described the technique of this "whipping cheer" in explicit detail:

> The manner of whipping there is, to strip the party to the skin from the waist upwards, and having fastened him to the whipping-post, so that he can neither resist nor shun the strokes, to lash the naked body with long but slender twigs of holly, which will bend almost like thongs, and lap round the body; and these having little knots upon them, tear the skin and flesh, and give extreme pain. (Crump: 103)

No doubt the mechanics of pain varied little over the decades.

Foreign visitors over a period of years confirm such accounts. Lupold von Wedd visited Bridewell in 1584, describing it as "a place of confinement for harlots and villains," where

> the men are forced to tread a mill, which is so constructed that as long as they tread it flour is ground by it. The males as well as the females are whipped twice a week; besides the latter must work very hard until they have done penance for their evil doings. (Most of the females are prostitutes, having been kept by men.) (Bulow 1895: 233)

Another German visitor in 1602 noted that men found "in illicit cohabitation" were whipped but then set free, while "the women are taken to a house especially appointed for the purpose, and are kept there sometimes for more than half a year, and twice a week they may expect to get a good whipping, but by paying 2 thalers and a half each time, they may escape these. Meanwhile, they earn their living by some hand-icraft" (Bulow 1892: 11).

Aside from the occasional foreign visitor or someone like the Puritan, Richard Rogers, who was "visiting the poore at Bridwell" on 16 April 1588 out of religious conscience (Knappen: 77), the texture of everyday life in Bridewell must have been exceedingly grim. The physical reality seems to have been as Thomas Ellwood, a prisoner in 1662, described it.[24] "Observing a door on the farther side, I went to it, and opened it, with intention to go in, but I quickly drew back, being almost affrighted at the dismalness of the place; for besides that the walls quite round were laid all over, from top to bottom, in black, there stood in the middle of it a great whipping-post, which was all the furniture it had." Distressed by the melodramatic theatricality of a "sight so unexpected, and . . . so unpleasing," Ellwood went through another door into "one of the fairest rooms that, so far as I remember, I was ever in"—Henry VIII's former dining room—"and no wonder, though it was now put to this mean use, it had for many ages past been the royal seat or palace of the kings of England" until Henry VIII abandoned Bridewell for Whitehall (Crump 94–95). The place of punishment and the site of royal feasting are con-tiguous, once again symbolically bringing together the lean beggar and the fat king.

Bridewell's notoriety was the result as well of its increasing use not simply as a place where vagrants and whores were thoroughly punished, but also as a major institution for all kinds of official punishments, rang-ing far beyond the quite specific limitations of its original charter. Thus, in 1600 one Mistress Fowler, an adultress who had plotted against her husband, was "to be carried to Bridewell and there to be often well whipped and afterward to have perpetual imprisonment" (Jeayes: 99). And we recall Bridewell's use as the holding tank for vagrant boys in the 1620s before they were shipped to Virginia.

The second main source of Bridewell's infamy derived from its use as a primary site for the state-sanctioned torture of criminal and political transgressors (though certainly second to the Tower in this regard) from

---

[24] The original Bridewell stood until it was partially burned in the Great Fire; New Bridewell was built in 1668. No contemporary paintings or drawings of the original Bride-well exist, except for the minute and relatively nondescript versions shown in various "long-view" drawings of London. Most historians believe that it looked like an earlier, smaller version of Hampton Court. Bridewell did have a "double courtyard," a layout "typical of Henry [VIII]'s palaces" (Gadd and Thompson: 257), and its "most unusual architectural feature" is said to have been "the Grand Staircase" (259). The foundation of Bridewell was excavated in 1978.

the late 1580s until the accession of James.[25] Torture was of course illegal under English common law, but it could be authorized by the monarch or the Privy Council until 1628, and it often was. By "torture" I do not mean the usual whippings or beatings. The chief conspirators in the William Hacket conspiracy of 1591, for example, were sent to Bridewell. The Privy Council ordered torture for Hacket himself by "the manackles and soch other tortour as you shal thinke good" (*APC:* 21.300); initially defiant, Hacket, according to Richard Cosin, after "beeing tortured, . . . sang another song" (62). Hacket's colleague, Edmund Copinger, died of mysterious causes in Bridewell the day after Hacket's execution, though the apologist Cosin claimed that Copinger had starved himself to death (72). Thomas Kyd, interrogated in Bridewell in 1593 with other suspects in the Dutch Church libel case, was to be put "to the torture in Bridewel, and by th'extremetie thereof . . . to discover their knowledge concerning the said libells" (*APC:* 24.222), as a result of which he implicated Christopher Marlowe as the owner of allegedly seditious documents found in Kyd's room. Again and again we read of the Privy Council ordering torture for prisoners of all kinds, especially those suspected of being Catholic or those having engaged in seditious activities. Bartholomew Steer, the ringleader of the abortive Oxfordshire Rising of 1596, was taken to Bridewell, and tortured and interrogated by Attorney-General Edward Coke himself, with the assistance of Solicitor-General Francis Bacon (Manning: 227; *APC:* 26.373–74). Prisoners are ordered moved in 1590 from Newgate, where the capacity for torture is evidently inadequate, to Bridewell, where they will "be put to the racke and torture of the manacles" and, it is hoped, "be compelled to utter all their followers" (*APC:* 19.69–70). In 1591, Thomas Clynton was ordered moved from the Fleet prison to Bridewell to be tortured by "the manacles and soche torture as is there used" (*APC:* 22.41–42), and in 1592 Owen Edmondes was moved from Marshalsea to Bridewell for "the torture accostomed in suche cases" (*APC:* 22.512). "The ordinarie torture there in Bridewell," as the Privy Council referred to it on 25 January 1596 (*APC:* 25.179), was evidently so well known that no further specification was needed. The role of Bridewell in the penal system was unambiguous: whenever transgressors "cannot be brought to confess the truth, then shall they be put to the manacles in Bridewell" (*APC:* 28.187–88).

Even this sorry legacy of official torture and unofficial cruelty does not

---

[25] On the general question of torture in the early modern period, with some specific references to Bridewell, see Langbein. Hanson offers an excellent analysis of official attempts to legitimate the use of torture, particularly in the cases of Catholic prisoners.

finally exhaust the functions of Bridewell, for the actual building had yet other uses. Incredibly, from a modern point of view, Bridewell seems also to have been a place of residence for some ordinary citizens, who signed leases as tenants and paid rent to the governors as if it had been any other apartment building—and indeed, as Ellwood's description (quoted earlier) indicates, as late as 1662 the palace could still dazzle (if you didn't wander through the wrong door) with its splendor. On 9 August 1561, John and Joan Rose, already living in Bridewell and making improvements to their quarters, signed a lease with the governors "during their natural life" for a rent of five pounds per year.[26] On 16 November 1568, however, "John Rose of bridwell" was ordered by the Court of Aldermen to "desiste and leve of that kinde of pastime that he there useth to make with puppetts and such other like things wherby greate numbers of people do thither resorte" (CLRO: *Repertories* 16/414). Rose had turned Bridewell into a theater, offering in the puppet shows the lowest form of dramatic experience. Rose thus takes his rightful place in the long line of entrepreneurial energies associated with Bridewell.

Offering housing in Bridewell could also be part of a package deal of benefits for employees; thus "Wm. Shackford, the clerk," was to move in on 27 April 1577 "to do the business of the house only," in return for free housing and an annual salary of twenty pounds ("Extracts": 11.112). A similar arrangement was made with Nicholas Alsopp, "chosen to be minister to this house," on 23 September 1603 ("Extracts": 12.69). Among Stanley's many abuses, during his brief rule over Bridewell, was that he and his colleagues "have taken into their own use the best rooms in the house such as were most fitting for setting prisoners and the poor at work"; more, they then proposed "to take and ever to take rent for divers rooms" rather than lodging prisoners ("Extracts": 12.38). Bridewell also routinely served as a storehouse for grains. During bad harvest years, as in the mid-1590s, the grain would be ground and "sold at slightly below the market rates in small quantities to the poor" of the City (Archer: 201).

Thus Bridewell was a royal palace, a house of correction and job training, a harsh prison, a place of torture, a favored site for non-noble political prisoners, a theater, a granary, a mill, a warehouse, and a desirable

---

[26] The lease allows Rose to "possess the rooms and place which he now possesseth that is to say one great chamber sometimes called the Chamber of Presence and of chambers over the same with a little room at the north-east corner of the same and all the rooms directly under the same great chamber and one peer [?piece] of the gallery which he also now possesseth both above and beneath and one plot of a garden lying between the churchyard of the said gallery and the nether part of the same" ("Extracts": 11.81).

rental space; for a brief time, it was also a whorehouse and "a common tapphouse of stronge beere." One character in *Locrine* (1595) even says of another, "I think you were brought up in the University of Bridewell, you have your rhetoric so ready at your tongue's end" (Kozlenko: 151). Created in an expression of Christian charity, Bridewell developed so many other functions that it became a kind of sordid microcosm of the whole society, a "stately and beautiful house" (Stow: 2.44) next to an open sewer (the Fleet ditch), a "labyrinth of misery" for one Catholic prisoner in 1598 (*SAL*: 8.394) but still possessing "one of the fairest rooms" in 1662, offering both hope and terror to the poor of the city. The "royal palace" become a "house of occupations" had by 1629, as a consequence of the Act of 1627 (3 Ch. I, c.5) degenerated into a spectacle of "shame," in which the prisoners,

> . . . (yoakt in Carts) . . . now must purge the street
> Of noisome Garbage, carry Dirt and Dung;
> The Beadles following with a mighty throng;
> Whilst as they passe the people scoffing say,
> Holla, ye pampred Jades of Asia.
>
> (R.M.: D6ᵛ)

The allusion to Marlowe's *Tamburlaine* not only emphasizes the theatricalism of this exemplary punishment—

> . . . the very shame will bring yee,
> (If ever) now to mend, else still ye must
> Drive, till ye sweat agen in Dirt and Dust,
> Barefac'd in publike view throughout the City;
> While all men laugh, and few or none will pitty—

but once again suggests the king/beggar inversion, since Tamburlaine's "Jades" were the conquered kings of Asia (R.M.: D6ᵛ). In a final irony of Bridewell, both prisoners *and* guards were to wear blue coats (Stanley had failed to follow this rule as well), suggesting their underlying identity as socially marginalized figures, excluded not by crime but by status.

Dekker's *The Honest Whore, Part 2* (1605) matches *Part 1*'s final scenes in Bedlam by offering the audience in *Part 2* "The Comicall Passages of an Italian Bridewell," as the title page notes. That there was anything comical at all about Bridewell would be a revelation to most today. The house's reputation is explicit in this exchange, in which Lodovico also describes typical inmate activities.

> *Lodovico.* Doe you know the Bricke-house of Castigation, by the River side
> that runnes by *Millan*: the Schoole where they pronounce no letter well
> but O?
> *Hippolito.* I know it not.
> *Lodovico.* Any man that has borne Office of Constable, or any woman that
> has falne from a Horse-load to a Cart-load, or like an old Hen that has
> had none but rotten egges in her nest, can direct you to her: there
> you shall see your Puncke amongst her back-friends, there you may
> have her at your will, for there she beates Chalke, or grindes in the
> Mill, with a whip deedle, deedle, deedle, deedle: oh little monkey.
> (5.1.13–24)

The inhabitants of Bridewell had long been colloquially known, in Thomas Lodge's phrase (584), as "bride well birdes" (1.51), and when Lodovico says, "Now to my Bridewell Birds, what Song will they sing?"
(5.1.34), it is clear that only a song of pain and suffering, the moan of
"O," was ever heard in Bridewell.

The entire final scene of the play takes place inside Bridewell, beginning with a long formal history of the place offered to the Duke by one
of the masters of Bridewell. The passage is taken directly from Stow's
account of the hospital's origin, beginning with the royal origin of the
house and the smart paradox, "Thus / Fortune can tosse the World, a
Princes Court / Is thus a prison now" (5.2.15–17). The population of
the house, the Master continues, swells when soldiers return from the
wars. The house also accommodates many others:

> The sturdy Begger, and the lazy Lowne,
> Gets here hard hands, or lac'd Correction.
> The Vagabond growes stay'd, and learnes to 'bey,
> The Drone is beaten well, and sent away.
> As other prisons are, (some for the Thiefe,
> Some, by which undone Credit gets reliefe
> From bridled Debtors; others for the poore)
> So this is for the Bawd, the Rogue, and Whore.
>
> (5.2.37–44)

The Master insists that everyone is there justly, and that the aim of punishment there was beneficent, "Not to take blowes alone, but to be made
/ And fashioned to some Charitable use" (5.2.52–53). "Thus," the Duke
pronounces in the complacent tones of the comfortable and powerful,
"wholsom'st Lawes spring from the worst abuse" (5.2.54).

Among the inhabitants of this Bridewell, in addition to the various people from the court there in disguise or as visitors, are one Bots, a pander; Mistress Horseleech, a bawd; and three whores (each in the traditional prisoner's "blue gown"), Dorathea Target, Penelope Whorehound (dressed first "like a Cittizens wife"), and Catyryna Bountinall. More than half of the play's final scene is given over to the successive introductions of these characters, with numerous moralizing comments on lechery and the decline of society. The Master expresses the contradictory values long associated with Bridewell:

> The Pander is more dangerous to a State,
> Then is the common Thiefe, and tho our lawes
> Lie heavier on the Thiefe, yet that the Pander
> May know the Hangmans ruffe should fit him too,
> Therefore he's set to beat Hempe.
>
> (5.2.246–50)

Dekker's Bridewell thus reflects only the obsession with lechery that Howes remarked on, with never a true vagabond in sight, nor any glimpse of "the manacles and soche torture as is there used." The only work done in this house of occupations is that of the oldest profession, the sort that Pompey had surveyed the year before in *Measure for Measure.*

Dekker also realizes the very mixed, often woeful effect Bridewell has on its prisoners. To Infelice's remark, "Me thinkes this place / Should make even *Lais* [a famous Corinthian courtesan] honest," the Master replies candidly, anticipating Lupton's comments twenty-seven years later.

> Some it turnes good,
> But (as some men whose hands are once in blood,
> Doe in a pride spill more) so, some going hence,
> Are (by being here) lost in more impudence.
>
> (5.2.254–57)

The characters in the play resolve their differences in Bridewell when their true identities are at last revealed and the plot is untangled. Only Bots is punished (like Lucio in *Measure for Measure*), "whipt . . . round about the Citty," as Genings was, and "then banisht from the Land" (5.2.452–53), but the others are unscathed by their experiences in Bridewell. As Candido confidently asks,

I was in Bedlam once, but was I mad?
They made me pledge Whores healths, but am I bad,
Because I'm with bad people?

(5.2.210–12)

In the real Bridewell, as Dekker well knew, the institutional influence all too frequently worked precisely counter to the ideal of reform. His remarks on prison in general, in *Villainies Discovered* (1616), illustrate what happened to Bridewell within a short time of its founding, with the "rare transformations" by which "it turns a rich man into a beggar, and leaves a poor man desperate" (Pendry 1968: 255).

The ironic spectacle of Bridewell reflected the inescapable conjunction of king and beggar: "We considered it a pity," one foreign tourist remarked, "that such a palace should be turned to such a mean purpose" (Bulow 1895: 233). It would be left to later generations to see more clearly the socioeconomic links between the "mean purpose" and the "palace," the whipping post and the king's Chamber of Presence. In the popular imagination, Bridewell, in Lupton's phrase, remained "the only Remembrancer of *Aegypts* slavery . . . they that come out of it neede not feare *Purgatory*, for it's thought to be a place of more ease" (1632: 41).

PART II

Shakespearean

Inscriptions

"The Perill of Infection":
Vagrancy, Sedition, and 2 *Henry VI*

As carriers of the social disease of poverty, the masterless men and women of the Tudor-Stuart period were continually subject to political quarantines of one type or another, from the simple expulsion from a single village, to confinement in houses of correction and forced transportation to the new colonies. The metaphor of disease was often taken quite literally: some authorities in London feared the theaters simply because they brought together large numbers of "the basist sort of people," as the Lord Mayor wrote in 1583, "many enfected with sores runing on them," who brought upon the city "the perill of infection" from the plague (*Collections* 63, 62). In a sermon of 1577, Thomas White made a simple, homonymic equation: "The cause of plagues is sin, if you look to it well, and the cause of sin are plays. Therefore the cause of plagues are plays."[1] "A Play," Henry Crosse wrote in 1603, "is like a Sincke in a Towne, whereunto all the filth doth runne: or a bile in the body, that draweth all the ill humours unto it" (Gurr: 217).

The fear of the plague was justified, the medical threat embodied in large crowds gathered together unquestioned. William Clowes also blamed "the licentious, and beastly disorder of a great number of rogues, and vagabondes" for the prevalence of syphilis in London (B1ᵛ). Yet a reading of complaints against the theater makes it clear that the threat of political "infection" was considered equally as serious as biological infection, because, the Lord Mayor wrote in 1592, "by the daily and disorderlie exercise of a number of players & playeng houses erected

---

[1] Quoted in the "General Introduction" to *The Complete Works of Shakespeare* (xliv).

within this Citie, the youth thearof is greatly corrupted & their manners infected with many evill & ungodly qualities" (*Collections* 68). As Clowes frankly acknowledged, mixing political and medical metaphors, the issue was also one of social class: "By meanes of which disordered persons, some other of better disposition are many times infected, and many more like to be, except there be some speedy remedy provided for the same" (B2). Sexual and social disorder thus mate in the trope of "infection," which is understood as the inverse energy of power: power operates *down* the social hierarchy, while social and political "infection" operate *up* the chain, threatening those of "better disposition."[2] Even for the "honest poor man," Nicholas Breton noted, "of the rich he is shunned like infection" (33).

The interrelation of poverty, the theater, and biological infection is of considerable importance in early modern England,[3] but in this chapter I mean to focus more narrowly on the figurative, political aspects of the trope of infection—the threat of popular rebellion. I will run the risk of some repetition, because I will consider separately two different but complementary discursive analyses of the political infection understood to be represented by masterless beggars and vagrants—the rural and the urban. This field of discourse includes a number of plays in the Elizabethan period which represent popular rebellion on the stage. Both sections of this chapter conclude with an an analysis of Shakespeare's *2 Henry VI*, arriving at the same end from different directions.

"The Nursery of Beggary": Enclosure and Rural Vagrancy

The movement to enclose common fields, already well under way at the beginning of the sixteenth century, was widely blamed as one of the primary causes of the increase in the number of vagabonds in this period. More substantial causal factors such as population growth and inflation, as we saw in chapter 1, were either invisible or not understood, but the enclosure of a common field was something that could be seen and its consequences felt. The central interpretive paradigm of the enclosure movement was lucidly set forth in 1516 by Sir Thomas More. In the famous account in Book 1 of *Utopia*, Hythloday describes the sheep "that used to be so meek and eat so little. Now they are becoming so greedy

---

[2] In a typical application of the disease trope, R.M. also describes Bridewell as "a free Hospitall for the Remedie of sundry diseases, whither many are brought, upon cure purg'd and past away" (D7).

[3] See the important work by Slack (1985) and Barroll.

and wild that they devour men themselves." Parasitical landowners have enclosed "every acre for pasture," leaving "no land free for the plow." A single "greedy, insatiable glutton . . . may enclose many thousand acres of land within a single hedge. The tenants are dismissed and . . . forced to move out." When their pittance of money is gone, he continues, "what remains for them but to steal, and so be hanged . . . or to wander and beg? And yet if they go tramping, they are jailed as sturdy beggars. They would be glad to work, but they can find no one who will hire them." What can such displaced men do, Hythloday asks, "but rob or beg? And a man of courage is more likely to rob than to beg." Thus a generation of thieves and beggars is created. The English lawyer is preparing a response to these accusations and promises, "I will demolish all your arguments and reduce them to rubble," when the Cardinal interrupts him (More 1975: 14–16).[4] This might be the only instance in literature, or life, when we would have wished to hear a lawyer speak more.

I would emphasize here these primary elements of More's, or Hythloday's, analysis: (1) Enclosures are initiated by "the nobility and gentry, yes, and even some abbots." (2) Their intention, spurred by rapacious greed, is to replace arable land with pasture for sheep. (3) Their tenants are always victimized by enclosure and cast into poverty. (4) The formerly honest and hard-working peasants are turned into thieves or sturdy beggars wandering the countryside. These four assertions in More's paradigm inevitably lead to some version of a pastoral communism as an eminently reasonable response to an intolerable economic and political situation. Economic historians have described any number of individual case histories that fit More's paradigm exactly, Sir Thomas Tresham's being one of the more notorious.[5] More's paradigm, moreover, is quoted approvingly and taken over in all its essentials by Marx in *Capital*, in a passage quoted in my Introduction, where this social upheaval is analyzed as an element of the transition to capitalist production, in which "the agricultural people, first forcibly expropriated from the soil," are whipped and tortured into "the discipline necessary for the wage system" (Marx: 808–9).

We should remind ourselves, however, that each generalization in More's paradigm is contradicted, or at least complicated, by considerable historical evidence:

[4] On the complex connections between enclosure and the increase in vagrancy, I have found the following particularly helpful: Leonard (73–74), Tawney (147–73, 213–30), Clay (1.67–101), Pound (7–11), Palliser (178–85), Thirsk, Penry Williams (180–85), and Manning (1988: 9–131).

[5] See the convenient account in Manning (1988: 237–41).

1. Enclosures were not always initiated by the nobility, gentry, or church, nor were enclosures defended only by the privileged classes. Indeed, in 1549 even the rebel Robert Kett proclaimed a wish to preserve some longstanding enclosures in the first article of his demands (Fletcher: 142).

2. The reason for enclosure was often technical agricultural innovation and improved efficiency of tillage rather than the wish to pasture sheep; and some acts of enclosure, as Manning has shown (1988: 93), were initiated by gentry against other gentry as part of more complex political, religious, or personal feuds.

3. Tenants were not always victimized; indeed, many formally agreed to enclosure.[6]

4. Not all displaced tenants turned into thieves or beggars. Moreover, enclosure was far from the only cause of vagrancy, even in rural areas, but was rather one of several complex social conditions that led to vagrancy.

What continues to stand out nearly five centuries later is not the historical accuracy of More's paradigm, though his account certainly was frequently if not always the case, but rather the interpretive power of that paradigm, its nostalgic vision—one might almost say fantasy—of an always already lost communal perfection. This power derives in part from the fact that the very term "enclosure" is so unstable in the period, used as an all-purpose signifier for virtually every negative socio-agricultural development, "at once too broad and too narrow" as R. H. Tawney once noted (216). As a metaphor in other discourses, enclosure was frequently something negative; as Flamineo cynically notes in John Webster's *The White Devil*, to take but one example, locking up one's wife is futile: "These polliticke inclosures for paltry mutton, makes more rebellion in the flesh then all the provocative electuaries [aphrodisiacs] Doctors have uttered since last Jubilee" (1.2.95–97).[7] Yet recent work in economic history has complicated every historical generalization about the enclosure movement in this period; indeed, "all attempts at generalization about the movement are hazardous," Thirsk notes (109). An apparent consensus among literary scholars that enclosure is *invariably* a negative needs to be contested, then, and the existence of a counterdiscourse, arguing the benefits of enclosure, needs to be reacknowledged. After

[6] See Thirsk (108–9) and Palliser (179) for examples; some "agreements" were clearly made under duress, however.

[7] For a discussion of the social and sexual metaphorics of enclosure, see Stallybrass, and the entire volume of essays edited by Burt and Archer.

briefly describing some of the contemporary arguments for and against enclosure, I will narrow my focus to one surprising point of agreement between these oppositional discourses and then follow that point into several dramatic representations of the 1590s. The point of agreement in the counterarguments involves the creation of "sturdy beggars," an epidemic of masterless men and women that seemed to many an uncontrollable, chaotic energy threatening the entire social order of both country and city.

The Thomas More paradigm held that enclosure creates vagrancy through depopulation. One opponent of enclosure a century and a half after More put the case exactly as More had seen it: "When these enclosures have made farmers cottagers, and cottagers beggars, no way of livelihood being left them, these poor with their families are forced into market towns and open fielded towns, hoping they may find some employment there." But the process merely snowballs, for the newly poor "lay such burthens upon open fields that they are not able to bear them," and so yet more wandering poor are created (*SCED*: 150). In addition to outright expulsion from newly enclosed commons, rising prices led to higher rents for the legitimate tenants, with the same results—the expulsion from the land of those who had always worked it. The hypocrisy and cruelty of the landowners is perfectly captured in John Taylor's 1621 vision, cited earlier in chapter 1, of the country lord who

> Ignobly did oppresse
> His Tenants, raising Rents to such excesse:
> That they their states not able to maintaine,
> They turn'd starke beggers in a yeare or twaine.
>
> (1621: C2)

Taylor's description of rising rents leading to impoverishment and beggary reflects hundreds of archival depositions. John Bayker's letter to Henry VIII, nearly a century earlier, told exactly the same story. "Is it not a petifull cais," he asked, "to come in to a litill vilage or towne wer that thaire haithe beine twentye or thirty howses and now are halfe off thaime nothinge but baire walls standing: is it not a petifull cais to se one man have it in his hands wiche did suffise ii or iii men wen the habitations were standinge" (Aydelotte: 145–47). The consummate dramatic exemplar of the type is no doubt Philip Massinger's Sir Giles Overreach (c. 1622), who shrugs off accusations that he is a "grand encloser / Of what was common, to my private use," his ears "pierced with wid-

ow's cries," while "undone orphans wash with tears" his threshold
(4.1.124–27). Overreach also unfolds plans of Machiavellian cleverness
"to hedge in the manor / Of [his] neighbor, Master Frugal" (2.1.27–
39). The enclosing landlord, as another writer put it, "loves to see the
bounds of his boundlesse desires; hee is like the Divell, for they both
compasse the earth about" (Lupton 1632: 107).

The painful economic realities of depopulating enclosure eventually
produced two stereotypical dramatic figures of oppression. First, as we
have seen, is "the grand Incloser of the Commons, for / His private
profit, or delight" (2.4.83–84), as Massinger terms the type in another
play, *The Guardian* (c. 1633). A second type of oppression is the greedy
farmer, much lower on the socioeconomic scale, as seen in *A Knack To
Know A Knave* (c. 1592), who has "raised the markets and oppress'd the
poor, / And made a thousand go from door to door."

In the counterdiscourse of enclosure in this period, however, arguments were made against excessive common waste ground, and *for*
enclosures because they were for "the general good of the commonwealth," as Sir Thomas Smyth said, "both in the breed of serviceable
men and subjects, and of answerable estates and abilities" (Knights: 99).
(Most of these arguments were made by the very landed interests that
stood to gain the most from enclosure, of course.) Sir Anthony Fitzher-
bert argued for enclosures in 1539 because the value of any piece of land
would be increased "by reason of the composting and donging of the
catell, that shall go and lie upon it both day and nighte," and because
enclosure would create "as many newe occupations that were not used
before" as were lost (*TED*: 3.23–24). In 1573 Thomas Tusser asked in
rhyme,

> More plentie of mutton and biefe,
>   corne, butter, and cheese of the best,
> More wealth any where (to be briefe)
>   more people, more handsome and prest,
> Where find ye (go search any coast)
>   than there, where enclosure is most?
>
> (*TED*: 3.64)

An anonymous pamphleteer in the 1650s argued more philosophically
on behalf of enclosure, in part because "husbandry is the fundamental
prop and nutriment of the Commonwealth," and, less convincingly, because there was "no example of common fields in all the divine word,
nor in any skilful author writing of husbandry, as Virgil, Tully, etc"

(*SCED*: 146). More mystically, he announced, "God is the God of order, and order is the soul of things, the life of a Commonwealth; but common fields are the seat of disorder, the seed plot of contention, the nursery of beggary" (*SCED*: 144).

In More's paradigm, then, enclosure causes beggars, but in the counterdiscourse it is the *failure* to enclose that causes beggars. In the aftermath of the Midlands Revolt of 1607, one member of the House of Lords argued, using the recurring metaphor, that "the nurseries of beggars are commons as appeareth by fens and forests," whereas "wealthy people [live in] the enclosed countries as Essex, Somerset, Devon, etc" (*SCED*: 107). The anonymous pamphleteer quoted earlier argued that "common fields are the seed plots of contention" because "there is much unrighteous dealing," and "every man being for himself, he that thrives on his farm thriveth commonly by hurting his neighbor, and by his loss" (*SCED*: 145). "Common of pasture," argued one Elizabethan surveyor, was a "maintaining of the idlers and beggary of the cottagers," and King James proposed in 1610 that the House of Commons move against the numerous cottages on commons and in forests which were "nurseries and receptacles of thieves, rogues and beggars" (Hill: 41). Enclosure, as always, was in the eye of the copyholder.

Tudor and Stuart governments regulated enclosure from a complex of often contradictory motives, then: the obligations of Christian charity, the need to increase agricultural productivity, and the need to ensure social and political stability in the body politic, among others. Parliamentary actions were often, on the surface, simply contradictory: acts against enclosures were passed and investigatory commissions formed to expose abuses, even while acts *for* enclosure were being passed for the benefit of individual landowners, frequently members of Parliament themselves—simply another form of "robbery," in Marx's view (796). The interests of capital were thus being served on several fronts, with official discourse at odds with specific practices; the public correction of egregious abuses permits the continuation of more systemic corruption.

Whether one argued for or against enclosures as state policy, however, the common specter of social discord was the nightmarish vision of a new-created race of masterless men, of beggars and vagabonds wandering the roads, homesteading on the dwindling common wastes, poaching and fence breaking at will. Ironically, vagabonds had even been hired to participate in local enclosure riots by the disputants (Manning 1988: 163). As More noted, "a man of courage is more likely to rob than to beg." One anti-enclosure writer in 1550 put it, "And now they have nothinge, but goeth about in England from dore to dore, and axe their almose for

Goddes sake. And because they will not begge, some of them doeth steale, and then they be hanged, and thus the Realme doeth decay" (*TED*: 3.56). It was exactly this state of affairs that concerned government authorities, for the swarms (in the usual dehumanizing metaphor) of beggars in the countryside were, like their city cousins, also thought to be ready material for riot and insurrection. Enclosure, or the lack of enclosure, led to beggars and masterless men, and *they* certainly led to sedition.[8] And sedition could never be tolerated. In a telling analogy, the parliamentary speaker of 1607 quoted earlier wondered whether the alleged causes of the Midlands Revolt—depopulating enclosures—ought to be redressed immediately, lest encouragement be given to such rebellion, and he reminded his listeners that "in Edward the sixth his time the remedy was not pursued until two years after the rebellion of Kett" (*SCED*: 107).

Although no large-scale political rebellion occurred in this period, at least after 1549, nevertheless there were frequent eruptions of civil disorder, particularly in the 1590s, both in the country, with the abortive Oxfordshire Rising of 1596 as perhaps the most notorious act of sedition, and in London, as we shall see. Public and private rhetoric in this period was often highly inflammatory; memories of Robert Kett or Jack Cade were frequently recalled, particularly in connection with enclosure riots and related acts of sedition. In Thomas Lodge's *Wits Miserie and the Worlds Madnesse* (1596), the personification "Sedition, the Trouble worlde," is active in religion and politics, both in the city and "in the countrie, [where] hee stormes, and railes, against inclosures, telling the husbandmen that the pleasures of their Lords, eates away the fat from their fingers; and these rackt rents . . . are the utter ruine of the yeomanrie of England: the conclusion of his talke alwaies is insurrection, and commotion. . . . This is hee that saith that warre is a good tree, and bringeth forth good fruit, namelie store of good crownes: and it is a paradox of his, That it is better [to] live a Rebell then die a begger" (4.67).

Such voices were heard frequently during the disastrous harvest failures of the mid-1590s, particularly in Oxfordshire. In the ringleader of the Oxfordshire Rising, Bartholomew Steer, Tudor authorities found exactly the threat to political and social order they had always imagined. A group of poor petitioners there was reported to have said that "if they Could not have remedie, they would seek remedie themselves, and Cast

---

[8] On the development of the sedition laws, see Bellamy (1979) and Manning (1980, 1988). As Manning notes, "the enclosure riot remained the preeminent form of social protest during the period from 1530 to 1640" (1988: 27).

down hedges and ditches, and knocke down gentlemen." Steer told his interrogators "the poore did once Rise in Spaine and Cutt down the gentlemen, and sithens that time they have lived merily there." In England, he believed, "there would be somewhat adoe shortlie in this Countrie, more then had beene seene a greate while, for that manie would Rise. . . . It was but a monthes work to overrun England." Steer's ultimate vision of a national rising, though it would turn out to be only a hallucination, involved leveling the "hedges and ditches" of local enclosures, then marching on London itself, as Wat Tyler, Jack Straw, and Jack Cade once had done, and joining up with the mobs who had recently rioted in the city: "When the prentices heare that wee bee upp, they will Come and Joine with us . . . he was rather induced to thinck the same," his interrogator reported, "by reason of the late intended insurrection in London, and that certain Prentices were then hanged" (Walter: 98, 108, 107–8).

Steer's dream of a rural-urban proletarian solidarity was a hopeless one, in the view of the anonymous author of *A Students Lamentation* (1596), a supposed insider's account of the apprentices' riots, though from a counterrevolutionary perspective. Even princes have failed in acts of sedition, the author notes, "and shall vulgar people, nay inconsiderate boys have any hope to prosper in tumultuous riots? No assuredly, for as the great escape not, the baser cannot choose but perish. Of Jacke Straw, Will Waw, Wat Tiler, Tom Miller, Hob Carter and a number more such seditious inferiour ringleaders to seditions and conspiracies most notable, what hath been the end? Misery, destruction, and shame" (*Students*: B2ᵛ).[9]

The association of masterless men and certain forms of sedition was quite close, then, particularly when enclosure was an issue. The rebel Falconbridge in Thomas Heywood's *1 King Edward IV* (c. 1599), to take an example from drama, is at some pains to distinguish himself from the usual kind of sedition, invoking a social class contempt which demonstrates the allegedly "natural" association of the poor with rebellion, but distinguishes theirs from his own:

> We do not rise like *Tyler, Cade,* and *Straw,*
> *Bluebeard* and other of that rascal rout,
> Basely like tinkers or such muddy slaves
> For mending measures or the price of corne,

[9] The passage continues: "All these at the beginning would be Reformers, a wrongs forsooth they went about to right: but when they had got head, what wrong did they not count right?" (B2ᵛ).

> Or for some common in the wield of Kent
> Thats by some greedy cormorant enclos'd,
> But in the true and antient lawfull right
> Of the redoubted house of *Lancaster.*
>
> (Thomas Heywood: 1.9)

The litany of economic injustices, particularly enclosure, which might justify rebellion, and has done so in the past, is not relevant; rather, like most actual risings in the period, this one is led not by the peasantry but by a discontented nobleman. Both dramatists and civil authorities nevertheless accepted the equation between masterless men and sedition, as Shakespeare's Henry IV articulates it:

> And never yet did insurrection want
> Such water-colors to impaint his cause,
> Nor moody beggars, starving for a time
> Of pell-mell havoc and confusion.
>
> (*1 Henry IV* 5.1.79–82)

The inherent lawlessness of the vagrants of the countryside is dramatized in several plays of the 1590s, such as *Woodstock* (c. 1591–94) and especially *The Life and Death of Jack Straw* (c. 1593), discussed later. Jack Cade's revolt in Shakespeare's *2 Henry VI,* however, is perhaps the most directly connected to the issues of vagabondage and enclosure. Edward Hall's *Union of the Two Noble and Illustre Famelies of Lancastre and Yorke* (1548) makes Cade's ancestry plain: on Cade's return to London, "divers idle and vacabonde persons resorted to him from Sussex and Surrey, and from other partes to a great number. Thus this glorious Capitain, compassed about, and environed with a multitude of evil rude and rusticall persones, came again to the plain of Blackeheath" (Bullough: 3.114). Moreover, in one of the rogue pamphlets of the period, *Martin Mark-all* (c. 1608), Cade is in fact said to be the "originall and beginning" of the Regiment of Rogues of the kingdom—more or less the ur-vagabond. Cade's rebellion and march on London are joined, in this version, by the "Rakehels and Vagabonds . . . [and] masterlesse men" of Kent (Rowlands: 2.44–45). In another rogue pamphlet, Dekker's *O per se O* (1612), contemporary rogues and beggars are said to be like "Jack Cade and his rebellious ragamuffins" (Pendry 1968: 287). So, too, Shakespeare's Cade, in *2 Henry VI,* is followed by an army of vagabonds, "a ragged multitude / Of hinds and peasants, rude and merciless" (4.4.32–33). Cade himself is said, in the comic asides of Dick Butcher and Smith the

Weaver, to have all the hallmarks of a rural vagabond: he was "born, under a hedge," his father's house was "but the cage," and he is himself a "valiant" beggar, who has been "whipped three market days together," and been "burnt i' the hand for stealing of sheep" (4.2.50–61). In elaborating the fantasy that he is the son of Edmund Mortimer, finally, Cade himself offers that he is the older, hitherto unknown child, who, "being put to nurse, / Was by a beggar-woman stol'n away" (4.2.137–38).

Cade's genealogy is clear enough, and his political platform, though lunatic in some of its details, is also familiar in its claims. His assertions that "seven halfpenny loaves [shall be] sold for a penny" and that he will "make it felony to drink small beer" are meant to be comical, but he also demands that "All the realm shall be in common" (4.2.63–66), which he repeats later, even more generally: "And henceforward all things shall be in common" (4.7.17). Here Cade sounds like his fellow rural rabble-rouser, the infamous Parson Ball in *The Life and Death of Jacke Straw* who, we will see later in this chapter, argued for all things in common: "It were better to have this communitie, / Than to have this difference in degrees" (lines 84–85).

As might be expected, the same Tudor authorities who passed laws restricting enclosures in an attempt to preserve common fields and wastes and reduce the numbers of displaced poor were at the same time frightened of the idea that *all* things should be in common. Few were willing even to entertain such radical solutions as one reformer proposed: "Unless private property is entirely done away with, there can be no fair or just distribution of goods, nor can mankind be happily governed" (More 1975: 31). Thomas More, to return to where we began, proposes an economic solution that follows quite logically from the enclosure paradigm he established. In *2 Henry VI*, Cade's solution— "all things shall be in common"—also follows from the grievances of the commons.

In one telling incident in *2 Henry VI*, the petitioners in Act 1 mistake Suffolk for the Lord Protector, and among the complaints Suffolk reads is one explicitly against him: "Against the Duke of Suffolk, for enclosing the commons of Melford." The petitioner defends himself from the angry duke by noting, "I am but a poor petitioner of our whole township" (1.3.23–26). At this point, at least in the early Quarto version of the play, *The First Part of the Contention*, Suffolk "teares the papers" and says:

> So now show your petitions to Duke *Humphrey.*
> Villaines get you gone and come not neare the Court,
> Dare these pesants write against me thus[?]
>
>   (B2ᵛ)

Suffolk's act of enclosure is Shakespeare's invention, not present in any of the sources. In Hall's narration, Suffolk is vaguely said to have "vexed, oppressed and molested the poore people," merely "for lucre of money," but enclosure is nowhere specifically mentioned (Bullough: 3.109). It is fitting that Suffolk's agrarian exploitation is linked to the conditions that helped create the rebellious multitude that now calls for his head.

But not all enclosures are inherently evil, as we have seen. Shakespeare counterbalances Cade's desire to have all things in common with the antithetical agrarian position of Cade's nemesis, Alexander Iden of Kent, in whose enclosed garden Cade is slain. An experienced poacher, the "originall of vagabonds," Cade climbs over the "brick wall" into the garden, like any famished beggar looking for food. Iden is described as "the lord of the soil," who holds his "fee simple" as an "inheritance my father left me" (2 *Henry VI* 4.10.7–25). Iden is designed as the virtuous contrast to the usual rural oppressors, the "greedy cormorants" who rapaciously enclose or raise rents. Rather, Iden is a Horatian figure, an ideal of the landowner protecting his property: "I seek not to wax great by others' waning, / Or gather wealth, I care not with what envy. / Sufficeth that I have maintains my state / And sends the poor well pleased from my gate" (4.10.20–23). His charity is such that he forbears "to combat a poor famished man," but when challenged slays the trespasser, only then discovering it is Cade, at which point all his charitable instincts vanish as he proceeds to mutilate and behead the corpse. Cade's headless body is dragged "unto a dunghill," where it will presumably help one day to fertilize the gardens and enclosed fields of Kent. But in *The First Part of the Contention*, Iden accuses Cade of trespassing in somewhat different terms: "Thou hast broke my hedges, / And enterd into my ground without the leave of me the owner" (G4).[10] Recasting the historically contested term "hedges" as a "brick wall," and the "ground" as a private "garden," the Folio version ensures that Iden will be seen not as a potential encloser, a "greedy cormorant," but an emblematic version of the happy rural man. The Folio also adds several lines to Iden's initial speech about rural contentment, including his charity to the poor, as well as Cade's extremely explicit reference to the "fee simple" and Iden's right to impound him as a trespassing "stray." Iden's Eden is

---

[10] My colleague James R. Siemon first pointed out this detail to me; see his fine essay (1994) on this scene.

thus more firmly established as legitimate in the Folio text, as one kind of enclosure is idealized and another condemned.[11]

In some accounts of Cade's rebellion, such as Polydore Vergil's, there is no reference to Iden at all: Cade was simply "taken soone after, and lost his life for his labour" (Ellis: 86). In *The Mirror for Magistrates*, Iden is portrayed as the active seeker of Cade, motivated not by self-protection but by "hope of money [which] made him stur his stumpes" (*Mirror.* 176). Here, Cade's carcass does not rot in the fields of Kent, but is returned to Southwark, where his "parboilde quarters" (176), like those of any traitor, are mounted on poles for public view. The intensifying emphasis on Iden as Cade's nemesis, at least in Shakespeare's version, culminates in the return of "Captain" Cade's *caput* (Cade had ironically prophesied that "men shall hold of me *in capite,*" 4.7.118–19), to confront the monarch he would have replaced: "The head of Cade?" Henry exclaims, "O, let me view his visage, being dead, / That living wrought me such exceeding trouble" (5.1.68–70). Here the lean beggar (Shakespeare has also invented the fact of Cade's famine) mirrors the weakened monarch, who is also, in political terms, all head and no body. Reasserting the hierarchical values that Cade had threatened, Henry asks Iden "what is thy degree?" (5.1.73), and has Iden "kneel down," then "Rise up a knight" (5.1.78). The knighting of Iden plays out the acceptable version of the fall and "rise" that Cade—his very name suggests falling—had threatened.

Cade is vanquished, at least on the London stage circa 1592, but his memory continued to live within the culture, as did his associations with masterless men and rural revolt. The recurring argument in the Tudor-Stuart discourse on enclosure was that masses of beggars and masterless men in the countryside stood ready to join their cousins, the loose apprentices and vagrants in the cities, in armed rebellion. Polydore Vergil described Cade and his men alluring "unto them on every side, in hope of spoile, an huge number, as well citizens as countrey people" (Ellis: 84). The descendants of Cade were allegedly immediately at hand in figures such as Bartholomew Steer of Oxfordshire. Whatever the facts about sedition from the top, the enduring myth in Tudor-Stuart political discourse was of sedition from below. Francis Bacon described the masses

---

[11] As Greenblatt observes, in this scene "status relations . . . are being transformed before our eyes into property relations, and the concern . . . for maintaining social and even cosmic boundaries is reconceived as a concern for maintaining freehold boundaries. Symbolic estate gives way to real estate" (1983: 25). Cartelli's essay on the play provides an illuminating analysis of class conflict in the play and a subtle consideration of the play's mixed ideological positioning.

of masterless men as "a seed of peril and tumult in a state" (11.252), and in his essay on sedition offered a Brechtian warning: "The rebellions of the belly are the worst" (6.409).[12] It is this fear that gave shape to much of the Tudor-Stuart discourse of enclosure, and helped produce in Shakespeare's Jack Cade one rebellion of the belly, the poaching vagabond, "ready to famish! These five days have I hid me in these woods and durst not peep out, for all the country is laid for me. But now am I so hungry that, if I might have a lease of my life for a thousand years, I could stay no longer" (4.10.2–6). The conflicts in 2 *Henry VI* enact a characteristically Shakespearean ambivalence, reflecting both sides of the contemporary enclosure debates—inventing enclosure abuses and giving the rebels legitimate grievances, but at the same time undermining the rebels' ideological position through excess and ridicule. Still, though Cade's end is an ignominious one, he spoke on the London stage as one of the "hungry," "ready to famish," more likely to rob than to beg.[13]

The "Prophane Spectacles" of Urban Disorder

The public theaters of London were understood by Tudor-Stuart authorities to be loci of disorder and infection, the natural home of the urban followers of Cade.[14] The public theaters, the Lord Mayor wrote in 1595, provide a place for "the refuse sort of evill disposed & ungodly people about this Citie . . . to assemble together"; the theaters are "the

---

[12] Bacon notes two fundamental causes—"the matter of seditions is of two kinds; much poverty and much resentment" (6.408)—and recommended, as prevention, that government suppress, "or at the least [keep] a strait hand upon the devouring trades of usury, ingrossing, great pasturages, and the like," while at the same time working (he does not say how) toward "the improvement and husbanding of the soil" (410).

[13] Shakespeare himself, in 1614, was embroiled in an enclosure dispute surrounding his Welcombe property, which eventually led to hedge breaking by citizens of Stratford and Bishopton and a prolonged legal action settled by no less a figure than Chief Justice Coke, who, in 1616, ruled that William Combe "should never enclose nor lay down his common arable land" (Schoenbaum: 285). But Shakespeare's way would be different from Cade's: shortly before the dispute began, Shakespeare had prudently entered into an agreement guaranteeing compensation to him or his heirs for any loss suffered "by reason of anie inclosure or decaye of tillage there" (Chambers: 2.142). Hawkes comments insightfully on the "ambiguities and contradictions" of this dispute and Shakespeare's ambiguous role (or nonrole) in it (7–13). Shakespeare was equally careful in his will to leave these properties to his daughter Susanna.

[14] Among the many recent works of cultural materialism and New Historicism that take up these issues, see particularly Mullaney, who demonstrates in detail how, in the Liberties of London, "the spectacle of the outcast and the marginal traditionally held sway" (26). Howard's 1994 book takes up the larger question of the theater and its place in social struggle of the period.

ordinary places for all maisterles men & vagabond persons that haunt the high waies to meet together & to recreate themselfes" (*Collections* 77). Throughout the period 1580–1600, the Lord Mayors pleaded with the Privy Council to ban the theaters altogether, only to be told that the queen, "beinge pleased at sometimes to take delighte and recreacion in the sight and hearinge of them," would permit their existence because "it is Considered that the use and exercise of suche plaies not beinge evill in it self may with a good order and moderation be suffered in a well governed estate" (*Collections* 82, 81).

No monolithic authority, then, spoke with a single voice on this issue. For some, the performance of a play is "not . . . evill in it self," while for other authorities, particularly in London, the very existence of the theaters was seen as leading to "most ungodly confederacies" (*Collections* 64). The risk of political infection was thought to be strong in part because the memory of older insurrections, such as the riots on May Day, 1517, would not die: the Lord Mayor in 1583 wrote against gatherings at the Theatre because of "the danger of disorders at such assemblies the memorie of ill May daie begon upon a lesse occasion of like sort" (*Collections* 62–63), and the Recorder, William Fleetwood, wrote in 1586 of one city "insurrection" of apprentices that he had found "all things as like unto Ill May Day, as could be devised in all manner of circumstances, *mutatis mutandis*; they wanted nothing but execution" (Long: 51).[15] Nearly seventy years after Ill May Day, 1517, the reverberations of that seditious riot still seemed present—and a few years after these reminders, a collaborative play, *Sir Thomas More*, would represent on the stage the same Ill May Day riot.[16] The prospect of this dramatic plot caused Sir Edmund Tilney, Master of the Revels, to censor it: "Leave out . . . the insurrection wholy with the Cause ther off," he wrote on the top

[15] As will be seen in the documents quoted in this chapter, "apprentices" was usually a term of contempt equal to, and essentially identical with, "masterless men." Beier notes that the dependency of the master/apprentice relation "was subject to a multitude of upheavals that actually caused vagrancy" (1985: 23).

[16] Harold Jenkins argues "c. 1590–93 for the original composition and c. 1594–5 for the revision" (*Book*: xliii); most scholars agree with these dates. Metz accepts the conclusion that "the original composition . . . took place circa 1592–93" and argues that "because of the unrest of [May] 1593, the play was temporarily set aside," and then permanently abandoned, "probably without having been produced, because of the serious anti-alien disturbances of 1595 with the resultant executions" (495). Melchiori takes "1592–94 as the limiting dates of composition, with Tilney's (single or double) intervention at 1593–95" (306); the additions, he believes, can be dated "not later than 1593–94, fairly close to the composition of the original text" (307). McMillin argues the original play was written "between the summer of 1592 and the summer of 1593" and specifically reflected "the crisis over aliens" (72); he then argues that the revisions were written a decade later (92), except in the case of Hand D (135ff.).

of the first page, "& [b]egin with Sir Tho: Moore att the mayors sessions with a reportt afterwards off his good service don being Shrive off London uppon a mutiny Agaynst the Lumbards only by A shortt reportt & nott otherwise att your own perilles" (Gabrieli and Melchiori: 17).

The threat of popular disorder, particularly in London, was felt to be extremely high in the late Elizabethan period. Roger B. Manning describes an "epidemic of disorder" in London between 1581 and 1602.[17] He cites "no fewer than 35 outbreaks of disorder" in this period, of which approximately one-third can be attributed to "economic distress" and several others directed against gentlemen and lawyers; but the largest category (14 insurrections and riots), Manning notes, "protested the administration of justice" (202), and included acts of violence against city authorities. The period 1590–95 was particularly unstable, culminating in "the most dangerous and prolonged urban uprising in England between the accession of the Tudor dynasty and the beginning of the Long Parliament" (208), namely, the riots of 1595.[18] The theaters were frequently blamed as a gathering site for these insurrections, and although no full-scale rebellion ever took place in London, still the Lord Mayors' complaints were not entirely groundless. Even an enterprise as daft as the rising undertaken by William Hacket and his colleagues on 16 July 1591 was understood to depend on the "many handes of the common multitude" in whom "tumult and sedition" would be moved (Cosin: 57); the authorities had heard boasts of "a hundred thousande handes for the advancement of their cause," though this move failed because the "common multitude ... did better keepe themselves out of this action then was expected: Yet the danger thereof was great" (85).

One notorious incident, a riot in Southwark on 11 June 1592, illustrates all the social instabilities of the early 1590s, particularly the threat allegedly posed by masterless men, and the contradictory ways in which city authorities responded to it. The Lord Mayor reported to Lord Burghley that he had found "great multitudes of people assembled togither & the principall actors [even the metaphors implicate the theaters] to bee certein apprentices of the ffeltmakers gathered togither out of Barmsey street & the Blackfriers with a great number of lose and maisterlesse men

---

[17] Manning (1988: 187). For a thorough reappraisal of the "crisis" in London, see Archer (1–17).

[18] For details of governmental actions to control the crisis of the years 1594–97, when there were three successive harvest failures, see Power, who notes that there was only a single "outbreak of mass violence" during these years, in 1595 (381). Rappaport, on the other hand, stresses the general stability and lack of violence throughout the period.

apt for such pourposes.'"[19] The fray began when the "Knights Mareschalls men" attempted to serve a warrant upon a feltmonger's servant who was committed to the Marshalsea prison without cause. A move was made to block these authorities, for "restraining of whome the sayed apprentices & maisterles men assembled themselves by occasion & pretence of their meeting at a play which bisides the breach of the sabboth day giveth opportunitie of committing these & such like disorders" (*Collections* 71). The Lord Mayor went on to admit that the marshal's men had however with "a most rough and violent manner provok[ed] them by such hard dealing to contend with them which otherwise would obey in all duetifull sort" (71). The pretense of "meeting at a play" had been merely the excuse, not the cause of the riot—which had in fact been provoked by the same authorities who quelled it; nevertheless, it was reason enough to argue for the closing of the theaters as breeding grounds for sedition. The mere performance of a play on a Sunday, a "breach of the sabboth day," was itself an instance of public disorder and lawlessness.

The lesson to be learned here, according to the Lord Mayor Sir William Webbe, was that "such tumults beeing once raised by disordered multitudes ar rather to bee quenched & suppressed by policie for the present time, then farther to bee kindled by violent means" (*Collections* 72). Webbe's expiation of the apprentices was countered by the Privy Council's request that the Surrey justices undertake a more rigorous examination than the Lord Mayor's, which was "very partiallie taken and to[o] favora[b]ly in theire behalfe" (*APC* 23.19).

[19] Richard Wilson details the economic conditions surrounding the "militant clothing industry of London in the 1590s" (1986: 171) which may have led to the sardonic identification of "Jack Cade the clothier [who] means to dress the commonwealth, and turn it, and set a new nap upon it" (*2 Henry VI* 4.2.4–6). Wilson points out that "as on Evil May Day, the economic crisis inflamed anti-alien sentiment as the problems of unemployment and immigration became enmeshed" (173). But Wilson further claims that Shakespeare *himself* "invested £ 30 in a consignment of 'knyt stockynges,'" thereby appearing "in the hated role of middleman" in 1598 (171). However, Wilson has apparently simply misread the "yow" of Adrian Quiney's letter as referring to Shakespeare when it clearly throughout refers to the addressee, his son Richard Quiney. Shakespeare is referred to in the letter as a possible source of money, but the investment ideas are all Quiney's. There is certainly no evidence here that Shakespeare was "tipped . . . off" (171) by Quiney, or that he knew the destination of the money he was to provide. Nor is there any evidence that Shakespeare "invested" money in this scheme: Wilson is conflating two different letters. The second refers to the idea of buying the stockings, but in the first, Richard Quiney is asking Shakespeare for a loan to help relieve "all the debettes I owe in London" (Chambers: 2.102). Schoenbaum concludes, moreover, that "Shakespeare never received" the letter (238). Wilson uses Shakespeare's alleged involvement in the cloth-buying scheme to claim that he had "a personal stake in these capitalist developments" (171) and so had a direct financial ax to grind in ridiculing Jack Cade, but the evidence does not support such an association.

Three years later, in the even more turbulent year 1595, the Lord
Mayor—now Sir Stephen Slany—was blaming not only the very existence
of the theaters, but their content, for the 1595 incident, because they
contain

> nothing but profane fables, Lascivious matters, cozonning devizes, &
> other unseemly & scurrilous behaviours, which ar so sett forthe; as that
> they move wholy to imitation & not to the avoiding of those vices which
> they represent which wee verely think to bee the cheef cause aswell of
> many other disorders & lewd demeanors which appeer of late in young
> people of all degrees, as of the late stirr & mutinous attempt to those
> fiew apprentices and other servants who wee doubt not driew their infec-
> tion from these & like places. (*Collections* 77)

The analysis of Lord Mayor Webbe, who placed the *cause* of the 1592
rebellion as originating in large part with the legal authorities themselves,
is reversed in the analysis of Slany, who now places the theaters themselves as "the cheef cause" of the 1595 apprentices' riot.[20] An interrogation of prisoners in the Marshalsea, reported on 23 October 1592,
reveals why the 1592 Southwark riot seemed so threatening, and why it
was seen to have so much potential for social chaos: "When the apprentices were unruly, and would have broken up the Marshalsea, Rich. Webster, another prisoner there, said they could not agree because they had
no head, and that if they had one, all the commons would rise, for they
all disliked the State and Government" (*CSPD* 1591–94: 252).

Slany's reading of the apprentices' riot represents a clear example of
demonization by a central authority. The very physical existence of the
theaters as a gathering place, and the "prophane spectacles" (*Collections*
63) shown there, become equally offensive. The evidence suggests a continuing fusion of masterless men, sedition, and the theater. Several plays
of the period 1590–95 even represent riots like Ill May Day in which
masterless men were alleged cause or accomplice, but the conflicting
interpretations of the authorities outside the theaters are matched by
those dramatized inside them.

Three famous risings comprise the central events in several plays in

---

[20] Cook usefully reminds us of the "fairly obvious bias" (245) of the London authorities' accounts of urban disorder; their bias is of course part of my argument. D. J. Johnson
explains how a dispute over the jurisdiction of the Marshalsea was part of the problem
of interpretation (228). Patterson provides an excellent analysis of the historiographical
issues at stake in competing interpretations (i.e., Manning 1988 versus Richard Wilson
1986) of the 1592 riot; her work is essential reading on this topic.

the tumultuous period 1590–95: the rebellion of Wat Tyler and Jack Straw against Richard II (in *Woodstock*, c. 1591–94, and in *The Life and Death of Jack Straw*, c. 1593)[21]; the Ill May Day rising of 1517 (in *The Book of Sir Thomas More*, c. 1592–93); and Jack Cade's rebellion against Henry VI (*2 Henry VI*, c. 1592).[22] The chief figures in these risings—Tyler, Straw, Parson Ball, Cade—are continually linked together in all kinds of documents in the period. In *The Arte of English Poesie* (1589), for example, George Puttenham described the rhetorical figure of *amphibology* ("or the Ambiguous") as the figure that misleads people in rebellion:

> as that of Jacke Straw, & Jacke Cade in Richard the seconds time, and in our time by a seditious fellow in Norffolke calling himself Captaine Ket and others in other places of the Realme lead altogether by certaine propheticall rymes, which might be constred two or three wayes as well as that one whereunto the rebelles applied it. (Puttenham: 260–61)

Puttenham's historical compression—placing Cade with Straw in the reign of Richard II rather than of Henry VI—is a typical discursive formation, in which all previous acts of sedition are contemporaneous, and simultaneous with whatever current disorder exists. Dekker offers a comparable fusion in 1609, when he describes a rebellion certain to be put down: "But a number of *Jack-strawes* being amongst them, and opening whole Cades of councell in a cause so dangerous, they were all turned to dry powder, took fire of resolution, and so went off with this thundring noise, *That they would dy like men, though they were but poore knaves*, and counted the stinkards and scum of the world" (Dekker 1963: 4.110). Thus Cade and Straw become contemporaries, even co-conspirators, in a timeless discourse of treason and conspiracy.

In *Woodstock*, the rebellion against Richard II is the central question, though neither Tyler nor Straw is specifically mentioned. Again, rebellion is here split into two forms, a division along class lines: on the one hand, the threat from the commons, which must be suppressed at all costs; and on the other hand, the threat from the nobility—the displaced uncles of

---

[21] Tyler and Straw were originally one person; for an analysis of how the folk-name Straw took on a life of its own, see Pettit.

[22] The Arden edition of *2 Henry VI* argues for a date of 1590 (xlvi), and the Riverside and Oxford editions argue for 1590–91. Born has presented a good case for "between March and August 1592" (334), but the New Cambridge editor is in my view most convincing that "the whole sequence [parts 1, 2, and 3] was *written* some time before March 1592" (68)—i.e., before the feltmongers' riot. Richard Wilson (1986: 176) argues that *2 Henry VI* was written after the riot, as a direct response by a playwright supposedly hostile to popular protest.

Richard II. As the play begins, we are told that "the Commons murmur gainst the *dissolute* king / Treason is whispered at each common table" (1.1.157–58). Richard's actions, and those of his henchmen Bushy, Bagot, Green, and Tresilian, are seen as the direct cause of serious disorder among the poor: "Those late oppressions rise / To set the Commons in a mutiny / That London even itself was sacked by them" (1.3.123–25). "The men of Kent and Essex do rebel" (1.3.233): these traditional rural hotbeds of sedition provide an opening for the discontented uncles to take out the parasitical counselors: "Take open arms. Join with the vexed Commons / And hale his minions from his wanton side. / Their heads cut off, the people's satisfied" (1.3.247–49). As David Bevington has pointed out, "Lancaster and his allies never aim at replacing Richard himself. This seemingly important disclaimer of regicide offers little consolation to the orthodox, however, for every major rebellion of the sixteenth century protested its loyalty to the crown" (253). The virtuous Woodstock rejects the plan, while Richard's Queen Anne works to undo the causes of rebellion among the poor engendered by her husband. The reek of *noblesse oblige* is overpowering:

> Distressed poverty o'erspreads the kingdom:
> In Essex, Surrey, Kent and Middlesex
> Are seventeen thousand poor and indigent
> Which I have numbered; and to help their wants
> My jewels and my plate are turned to coin
> And shared amongst them.
>
> (2.3.18–23)

The Duchess of Gloucester reassures the queen that "England's not mutinous: / Tis peopled all with subjects, not with outlaws" (2.3.38–39), yet the nobles go out of their way to control them. In the queen's charity "of needful clothing / To be distributed amongst the poor" (2.3.59–60), though, we can see the habitual Tudor move to treat the symptom and not the cause of poverty, to merely contain disorder. Even as they are being isolated and threatened by Richard, moreover, the uncles are scrambling to protect the king and defuse the legitimate anger of the poor. York urges that each of them return home before the people rise, and "seek to restrain them from rebellion— / For what else can be looked for? Promise redress: / That eloquence is best in this distress" (3.2.94–96). These desperate efforts succeed, as Woodstock reports that Queen Anne's "charity hath stayed the Commons' rage / That would ere this have shaken Richard's chair, / Or set all England on a burning fire" (4.2.58–60). The threat of a commons' revolt is horrific to the author of *Woodstock*; even those nobles who would themselves plot a rising against Richard's retinue, and who will themselves be quelled or murdered by Richard, work to suppress the commons' rebellion lest it contaminate their own political aims. In a final ghastly irony, when surrounded by Richard and his men, Woodstock fears it is the beginning of a peasants' rebellion: "Ha, soldiers! Afore my God, the Commons all are up then: / They will rebel against the king, I fear me, / And flock to me to back their bold attempts" (4.2.159–62). Still fearing rebellion from below, he is led away to his murder by those above him—by Richard himself.

The anonymous author of *Woodstock* clearly shows that Woodstock's middle way, and his virtues of plainness and honesty, would avert disorder and preserve the highest values of the kingdom. Indeed, his murder is not *his* tragedy so much as it is the kingdom's. We are also clearly shown that disorder from below is heinous and to be averted by any means possible, except the removal of its root cause from above. And yet Richard has been made so awful, the murder of his uncle so terrible, the despoliation of the kingdom so profound, that a case for aristocratic rebellion is not only present, but plausible. The rejection of peasant rebellion is partly an issue of social class, but more complexly an exorcism of one mode of violence which permits another, higher form, to flourish.

The anonymous author of *The Life and Death of Jack Straw* begins from a very different ideological position than does the author of *Woodstock*. Here Richard II is a beneficent figure of order, truly "Gods visgerent here on earth" (line 439), and blameless for the rebellion; the "murmuring to rise" does not result from his actions, as it does in some versions. What is truly different in *Jack Straw*, however, is the terrifying, even hysterical representation of the rebels, and their ability to call up the Kentish commons. The incendiary speech of Parson Ball is everything that city and national authorities feared, and exactly what the Lord Mayors would want kept off the London stages:

> England is growne to such a passe of late,
> That rich men triumph to see the poore beg at their gate.
> But I am able by good scripture before you to prove,
> That God doth not this dealing allow nor love.
> But when *Adam* delved, and *Eve* span,
> Who was then a Gentleman.
> Brethren, brethren, it were better to have this communitie,
> Then to have this difference in degrees:

....
And make division equally,
Of each mans goods indifferently,
And rightly may you follow Armes,
To rid you from these civill harmes.

(lines 78–109)

Jack Straw of course agrees ("Wee will have all the Rich men displaste, / And all the braverie of them defaste," lines 113–14), as does Wat Tyler ("Wele be Lords my Maisters every one," line 127), in a kind of all-star chorus of sedition. Here is the very Tudor nightmare of "the Multitude a Beast of many heads" (line 188), spouting communistic doctrine of leveling all "difference in degrees," rising without real provocation or aristocratic leadership.[23] It is mere chaos. The rebels are moreover continually linked with vagabonds and masterless men: "Who would live like a beggar, and may be in this estate[?]" (line 247). The contempt the nobles hold for the rebels is profound, and it seems excessive even by the usual standards of class division; Morton calls them "men of no great account, / For they bee none but Tylers, Thatchers, Millers, and such like" (391–92).

The danger represented by the rebels widens considerably when they leave their stronghold in Kent and attack London itself. What was only a brief reference in *Woodstock*—"even London itself was sacked by them"—becomes in *Jack Straw* a profound civil violation. Straw and his colleagues are seen to be not only rebellious but representatives of utter lawlessness. "They have spoilde all Southwarke, let out all the prisoners, broke up the Marshalsea and the Kings bench, and made great havocke in the Burrowe here" (590–93). The Marshalsea was of course where the feltmonger's servant was committed, provoking the Southwark riot of 1592; the link to *Jack Straw*, perhaps written shortly after that riot, is suggestive. But if the Knight's Marshall's men did not serve their warrants with "good discretion and moderate usage" (*Collections* 71), Richard's agents in *Jack Straw* are, if once rude, fundamentally blameless. The London mob of 1592 confronted the prison, but the marshal's men "beeing within the Mareschalsea issued foorth with their daggers drawen & with

---

[23] Forty years earlier, the voice of Crowley's "pore man of the contrey" resembles that of Parson Ball in *Jack Straw*, and the fears of his rich man, one of the "gredie cormerauntes," constitute the standard Tudor social nightmare, in which the peasants "knowe no obedience, they regard no lawes, thei would have no gentlemen, thei wold have al men like themselves, they would have al thinges commune! Thei would not have us maisters of that which is our owne!" (Crowley: 142).

Bastianadoes in their hands beating the people" (*Collections* 72) and drove them away, whereas Straw's mob succeeds in storming the prison. *Jack Straw* thus shows what *almost* happened in 1592—a mob engaging in an ultimate violence against the very idea of society, by "burning up Bookes and matters of records" (line 651), as Tom Miller makes a bonfire of "Bonds and Indentures and Obligations" (781), randomly destroying anything that represents civil order: "Althat I saw either in the Guild-Hall or in any other place" (783). The author of *Woodstock* kept the commons' rising against Richard safely offstage, isolated in Kent, but the author of *Jack Straw* brings riot into the heart of the City itself, into its legal center, Guildhall, and shows that rebellion is not merely political but metaphysical. The Lord Mayors who served in Guildhall already knew this.

The rebels are eventually overcome, mostly by Richard's skillful use of pardons and threats. Ball and Tyler are executed, but in the most famous episode of the entire rising, Straw is killed by Walworth, the Lord Mayor. This scene—the ideological counterpart to Iden's slaying of Cade—was memorialized in another, more official, dramatic forum. The civic pageant for Lord Mayor John Allot—who was, like Walworth, a member of the Fishmonger's Company—was mounted in 1590 by Thomas Nelson. This celebration of civic virtues in London glorified the commonwealth: "Peace," "Wisdom," and "Science and Industry," among others, speak their turn, when suddenly a quite different set of characters appears. First Richard II asks Walworth's help against "this rebels pride," then Straw himself appears:

> Jacke Strawe the rebell, I present, Wat Tyler was my aide,
> Hob Carter and Tom Miller too we all were not afraid,
> For to deprive our Soveraigne king, Richard the second namde,
> Yet for our bad ambitious mindes by Walworth we were tamde,
> He being Mayor of London then soone danted all our pride,
> He slew me first, the rest soone fled, and then like traitors dide.
>
> (Bullough: 3.137)

The terms associated with Straw in this civic pageant are merely the platitudes of civic religiosity: "pride," "ambitious minds." The author of the play *Jack Straw*, on the other hand, understood his man to be something far less conventional and much more irrational than the wooden figure in Nelson's device.[24]

[24] On Nelson's pageant, see Bergeron (1971: 132–34 and 1968). In Samuel Rowlands's "Hell's Broke Loose" (1605), Jack Straw appears again, as a Ghost speaking the Prologue to the story of John Leyden, the Anabaptist heretic. Straw never "consorted with that

In *Sir Thomas More*, the events of Ill May Day 1517, which Tilney wanted deleted in their entirety, are precipitated by the commons' resentment of aliens; the bill of complaint drawn up by Lincoln registers the "extreme poverty" of the citizens, caused by "aliens and strangers [who] eat the bread from the fatherless children, and take the living from all the artificers, and the intercourse from all merchants, whereby poverty is so much increased" (1.1.109–14). Soon the "rebellious rout" (1.3.84) rises up in an angry but at times carnivalesque mood: as the rioters consider firing the houses of the Lombards, Doll says "we may as well make bonefires on May day as at midsummer; we'll alter the day in the calendar, and set it down in flaming letters" (2.1.36–38).[25] The real grievances of the commons are as usual soon overwhelmed by spreading chaos and a distinct antiauthoritarian impulse—they have "released / Sundry indebted prisoners" from both the Counters (2.2.3–4), and then "broke open Newgate, / From whence they have delivered many prisoners, / Both felons and notorious murderers, / That desperately cleave to their lawless train" (2.2.11–14). Sir Thomas More nevertheless sees the good side of "these simple men" (2.2.34), and in the famous scene that follows—likely written by Shakespeare—he persuades them to lay down their weapons. His argument to the crowd is completely orthodox: if they were to have their way and "sit as kings in your desires" (2.3.83), expelling the aliens from the city (their "insolence" is incidentally nowhere to be seen in More's sentimental vision of "the wretched strangers, / Their babies at their backs,"—2.3.80–81), they would merely have established a "pattern" by which "other ruffians" would "shark on you, and men like ravenous fishes / Would feed on one another" (2.3.88–93). Bearing the present injustice is thus the better course. Rising against the King, moreover, is rising against God. (More's own resistance to the king's authority in religious matters is lightly glossed over at the end.) Paired with this positive appeal is the threat of the king's malice: what would they do, More asks, if the king were to banish them? They would become despised aliens themselves. Finally, More promises the king's pardon if they will lay down their arms. In a nicely symmetrical turn, the chief rebels are then returned to be confined in the very prisons they had assaulted. In a fantasy of contrition, Lincoln declares that "obedi-

---

slave," he notes, "but that in name, and nature wee agree" (Rowlands: 1.9). As in the Hacket case (Cosin: 87–96), religious and political subversion are conflated: "Hee, to have all things common did intend: / And my Rebellion, was to such an end. / Even in a word, wee both were like apointed, / To take the Sword away from Gods Anointed" (Rowlands: 1.9–10).

[25] See Pettit and Bristol (1985) on the associations of folk ritual and social disorder.

ence is the best in each degree" (2.4.59) on the scaffold just before his execution. "Whensoe'er we talk of ill May day," Doll declares in celebration, "Praise More" (2.4.157–58).

Whenever the Lord Mayors of the 1590s talked of Ill May Day, however, praising More was perhaps furthest from their minds; rather, there was a dread of the kind of popular urban rebellion that could be quelled only by violence rather than rhetoric. The play about More "stresses the way in which trouble can be forestalled through royal generosity," as Bevington points out (255), but the off-stage enlightened Henry VIII contrasts strikingly with his daughter Elizabeth in the early 1590s, who seems to have taken a very hard line indeed on public disorder, frequently reprimanding mayors and sheriffs for inadequate zeal in rounding up vagrants or punishing rioters, even commanding the provost-marshall in 1595 "to carry out summary executions" (Manning 1988: 210). More's theatrical certainty of the mercy and goodwill of the sovereign found a very confused echo in a government whose own violence was understood to have made things worse[26], while Elizabeth herself donated 200 pounds to be distributed to the poor in January 1596, and 300 pounds again on 15 March 1597 as part of the governmental response to the food crisis (Power: 375–76). A ballad depicting Elizabeth's sympathy for the people's suffering because of the scarcity of goods was nevertheless suppressed by the Lord Mayor in June 1596 lest it further provoke the discontent (Power: 380). *Sir Thomas More*'s depiction of quelled Ill May Day violence was further reflected in the events surrounding May Day 1593, when tension between apprentices and foreigners in London again rose, and one immigrant, the aptly named Peter Coale, was charged with "threatening to set the city on fire" (Manning 1988: 204).

We have already seen how Shakespeare's representation of Jack Cade in 2 *Henry VI* derives in part from a rural discourse of enclosure, vagrancy, and sedition, and it should by now be clear as well that it also derives from the urban context of the 1590s, when rebellions were being staged in the theater as well as in the streets. In the urban discourse, civic authorities feared a fusion of rural and urban forces of the kind Bartholomew Steer dreamed of. In 2 *Henry VI*, Jack Cade's rising against Henry VI originates, as usual, from above: reaching out to the traditional hotbed of discord, York has "seduced a headstrong Kentishman, / John Cade of

---

[26] Manning goes so far as to argue that "royal interference in the affairs of the city of London not only complicated the problem of preserving public order, but also provoked popular protests" (1988: 202).

Ashford, / To make commotion, as full well he can, / Under the title of John Mortimer" (3.1.356–59). The commons are as always depicted as a chaotic energy ready to erupt, "like an angry hive of bees / That want their leader, scatter up and down / And care not who they sting in his revenge" (3.2.125–27). The commons even threaten to storm Henry's palace to seize Suffolk (3.2.246). Into this extremely volatile atmosphere comes Cade, "with infinite numbers" (4.2.30s.d.) of followers. The association of Cade with vagabonds and masterless men was traditional, as we saw earlier in this chapter. Parson Ball's inflammatory communism in *Jack Straw* is reflected here, however, in Cade's comically inept utopianism: "The three-hooped pot shall have ten hoops . . . in Cheapside shall my palfrey go to grass. . . . there shall be no money. All shall eat and drink on my score" (4.2.64–73). The real suffering and grievances of the poor, the injustices perpetrated by the nobles, the ineptitude of Richard: all these energies lose their force when embodied in Cade's buffoonery, although the grievances *are* spoken on the stage.

2 *Henry VI* offers in Cade's rebellion an uneasy dialectic between a grotesque low comedy that tends to deflate the social threat, mocking the legitimacy of its complaints, and a genuine dread of the class warfare Cade calls down on the kingdom. Cade declares,

> We will not leave one lord, one gentleman;
> Spare none but such as go in clouted shoon,
> For they are thrifty honest men and such
> As would, but that they dare not, take our parts.

Told that they "are all in order," marching toward them, Cade makes a memorable reply: "But then are we in order when we are most out of order" (4.2.179–85). Later, however, in scenes that must have resonated strongly with the contemporary street scenes in London, Cade and his men promise to have the "[Lord] Mayor's sword borne before us" (4.3.13), move to "break open the jails and let out the prisoners" (4.3.14–15) and, like the rebels in *Jack Straw*, threaten to "burn all the records of the realm" (4.7.13–14).

Earlier in the play, Shakespeare plays out two parallel enactments of the vagrant/disorder relation that Cade more flamboyantly represents. In the first, the conflict between Thomas Horner and his assistant Peter Thump, Shakespeare presents a model of hierarchical inversion, with the "prentice" overthrowing his "master"—indeed, accusing him of "high treason" (1.3.182). When the king establishes a trial by combat to resolve their conflict, this aristocratic ritual seems to favor Horner, since the apprentice "cannot fight" (1.3.216). But Horner shows up drunk, and Peter, who is urged to "fight for credit of the prentices" (2.3.71), strikes Horner down. Between the announcement and the action of the duel, moreover, Shakespeare inserts the scene (2.1) in which the sturdy beggar Saunder Simpcox is exposed.

   The story of the exposure of the supposedly blind beggar's "miracle" derived from John Foxe's *Actes and Monuments* (1583) or, less likely, Richard Grafton's *Chronicle* (1569), but both took their account from Sir Thomas More's *Dialogue of the Veneration and Worship of Images* (1529). In all these accounts, the sturdy beggar is only "blind"; Shakespeare invents Simpcox's second affliction, lameness, and shows him borne in "*between two in a chair*" (*2 Henry VI* 2.1.65s.d.). The object of the anecdote in Foxe is twofold: to illustrate the "craftye working of false miracles in the clergye" and to demonstrate "the prudent discretion of this high and mighty prince," Gloucester (Bullough: 3.127). In Foxe's account, the encounter is strictly between Gloucester and the beggar; there is no indication that the king is even present. In Shakespeare the focus shifts to the gullible king, however, who expresses belief in the miracle even before Simpcox enters. Henry begins to question Simpcox, accepting all his answers with religious platitudes, but Gloucester soon takes over, cleverly exposing the logical contradictions in Simpcox's narrative. In effect, Gloucester plays Harman to Simpcox's Genings, exposing the fraudulent beggar to a gullible (and here, kingly) audience. In Foxe, moreover, Gloucester exposes the false beggar through linguistic means alone (how can he know the names of colors if he has been blind, etc.) but in the play, Gloucester reaches for a device that reflects contemporary practice far more accurately: "My masters of Saint Albans, have you not beadles in your town, and things called whips?" (2.1.139–40), and an ominous "*Beadle with Whips*" (line 149s.d.) soon enters. Simpcox reasserts his lameness, but "*After the Beadle hath hit him once, he leaps over the stool and runs away; and they follow and cry* 'A miracle!' " (line 156s.d.). The punishment for Simpcox and his wife comes directly from the statutes: "Let them be whipped through every market town till they come to Berwick, from whence they came" (lines 161–63). The wife's claim—"Alas, sir, we did it for pure need" (line 160)—falls on the usual deaf ears and stony hearts. The pleasure taken in the exposure is exactly like Harman's in the story of the Dommerar we saw in chapter 2: "You shall se a miracle wrought anon. For I once . . . made a dumme man to speake." Through the "miracle" of torture, "he that was both deafe and dume coulde in short time both heare and speake" (Harman: 58–59). In both Harman and Shakespeare, "none did bewaile" (Harman: 59) the false beggars.

Why does Shakespeare overdetermine Simpcox's fraudulence, then, not only doubling it, but making it manifestly ludicrous? Surely one of his aims was to expand the encounter's range, not merely making it a vehicle to demonstrate Gloucester's perception, but, in bringing the king into the frame of Foxe's account, to stage a confrontation between lean beggar and fat king. The meeting of Henry and Simpcox does not of course have the power that the meeting between Lear and Edgar will have, but both scenes reveal the monarch's inability to "read" an inversion of his own image. Henry's figurative blindness and impotence are mirrored in Simpcox's claims of literal blindness and lameness, in a kind of comic version of the "king's evil," but which cannot be cured by the king because he himself is the cause.[27]

Just as powerful as the symbolic nature of the king-beggar encounter are the tangible issues of political control at stake. Shakespeare invents the beadle and his whip because they are the incarnations of the power of the state to control its vagrants and masterless men—and Simpcox is just a comical version of the "Rakehels and Vagabonds . . . [and] master-lesse men" (Rowlands: 2.44–45) whom Jack Cade mobilizes for insurrection. The structural placement of the Simpcox scene, between the servant/master inversion of Thump and Horner, is also suggestive of the general slackening of hierarchical power in the play.[28] Shakespeare does not explicitly link Simpcox and Thump/Horner to Cade, but culturally and historically the rural beggar and the urban apprentice constituted the demonized mob, "moody beggars, starving for a time / Of pell-mell havoc and confusion." A further instance of hierarchical subversion,

---

[27] Howard perceptively observes that "the association of Simpcox with St Albans' shrine forges a link between his actions and deceptive Catholic practices" (1994: 132), and concludes that Simpcox "represents the charlatanry and deception springing up, Hydra-headed, in the absence of a powerful authority at the head of the state. As in the anti-theatrical tracts, the victims of cultural chaos are often written as its primary instigators" (1994: 133).

[28] For Bernthal, however, the Thump-Horner episode's "ideological function is apparently to prove the divine sanction of Henry VI's kingship—and kingship in general—in that a weakling such as Peter could survive trial by combat only through divine intervention" (44), but this function is somewhat undermined by "Tudor England's prevailing social nightmare—betrayal to the authorities by friends, servants, family" (44). Rackin remarks that "Shakespeare's entire reconstruction of the [Thump-Horner] incident seems designed to raise the issue of providential justice but withhold an answer" (50–51). Howard sees the Thump-Horner combat as "calculated to produce the same effect of power's exposure of truth" (1994: 136) as seen in the exposures of Simpcox and Eleanor Cobham in 1.4 and 2.4. My reading of the scene obviously stresses different ideological concerns than Bernthal and Rackin do; I am also skeptical of Bernthal's claim about the "prevailing" social concern of Tudor England.

placed within the frame of the Thump-Horner conflict, is offered in the appearance of the witch Margery Jordan and the two priests in 1.4; although they have been under surveillance and are quickly captured, her prophecies will come true. The very fact of their existence suggests the weakening of hierarchical power and the anxieties attending it. The Margery Jordan scene enacts in terms of gender and religion what we see more fully realized as a class issue with Thump/Horner, Simpcox, and Cade.

The representation of rebellion in the play thus veers between the horrific and the comic: even those who teach reading and writing, or speak Latin, to return to Cade himself, are condemned. Again, the grotesque comic contradictions of Cade (he himself speaks in Latin at 4.7.118) vitiate the actual social injustice, on which Cade is almost eloquent:

> Thou hast appointed justices of peace to call poor men before them about matters they were not able to answer. Moreover, thou hast put them in prison, and because they could not read thou hast hanged them, when indeed only for that cause they have been most worthy to live. (4.7.38–44)

One can debate how seriously any of Cade's complaints might have been taken by the audience, but that is in effect the point: Cade's complaints were real ones, frequently heard outside the theaters, but this representation of Cade tends to subvert their political and ideological power.[29] Yet Cade's followers, the rabble of the city, are in the end everything that the Lord Mayors feared: fickle, chaotic, without direction, bloodthirsty ("the rascal people, thirsting after prey, / Join with the traitor, and they jointly swear / To spoil the city and your royal court," 4.4.51–53). Even Cade is astonished at their mutability: "Was ever feather so lightly blown to and fro as this multitude?" (4.8.54–5).

It is well known that Shakespeare conflated his sources in his depiction of Cade, combining events from the rebellion of Tyler and Straw with those of Cade, so that the worst features of Tyler and Straw were transferred to Cade. The effect was to fuse these distinct acts of rebellion.[30]

---

[29] Patterson brilliantly describes the play's employment of "ventriloquism . . . the trope of reported speech" (41) as a means of permitting the expression of a genuine voice of popular protest.

[30] See Bullough (3.89–100) for a concise summary; Pugliatti has usefully analyzed the patterns behind Shakespeare's variations from his sources.

Cade, in short, is further demonized so as to invalidate, or at least qualify, his claims of social injustice. This deliberate ideological mystification has led to many conflicting claims about Shakespeare's own politics.[31] But Shakespeare, as we have seen, was not alone in his ambivalence toward such figures.

The walls of the London theaters constituted a boundary which to some extent excluded the social disorder of the time: the riots were near the theaters, but not in them; the theaters were at times the occasion, but not the cause, of riots. They existed in marginal zones of the city in which disorder flourished, and all the Fleetwoods in London could not finally contain this energy. Yet the walls of the theaters at the same time also defined a space within which representations of civic disorder were mounted on the stage. In these plays, disorder from below is invariably condemned, though its causes are admitted; disorder from above is frequent, as in real life, but its removal is not permitted. Thomas Nashe, writing in 1592, had it almost exactly right: noting that some petitioners of the Privy Council object against plays that "they corrupt the youth of the Cittie, and withdrawe prentises from their worke," Nashe points out that the players wish just the opposite. "They heartily wishe they might bee troubled with none of their youth nor their prentises; for some of them (I meane the ruder handicrafts servants) never come abroade, but they are in danger of undoing." Nashe goes on to argue that the plays of this period never crossed the line of sedition: "and as for corrupting them when" the youth and apprentices come to the theater, "thats false; for no Play they have, encourageth any man to tumults or rebellion, but layes before such the halter and the gallowes" (1.213–14). Nashe may

---

[31] Richard Wilson attacks the applause which, in earlier criticism, so often accompanied Shakespeare's humbling of Cade, and attempts to implicate Shakespeare himself in a web of economic self-interest leading to "this character assassination" (1986: 170); but see note 19 above. Weimann has described Cade's political saturnalia as "a case of the mocker mocked, the inversion of the inverter" (240). Rackin has recently argued the "containment" position: "Thus, despite the vividness of Cade's characterization and the real social ills his rebellion addresses, Cade is finally reduced to a mechanism for ideological containment" (216). Hattaway, on the other hand, sees Shakespeare as "not a pillar of the establishment . . . but himself a radical" (15). Bristol argues that "conventional historicist criticism" (i.e. Tillyard, Reese) has seen the play as containing "an unambiguously inscribed political ideology which enables the audience . . . to understand Jack Cade as a pathetic, ludicrous and potentially vicious aberration" (1985: 89). Bristol's position, however, is close to the one I argue here: "Despite these strategies of ideological containment, however, the speeches of Cade and his followers constitute a powerful political and discursive indiscretion" (89). In the end, he argues, the expression of popular resentment "escapes being totally repressed" (90). I see the issue here as less a subversion/containment dichotomy being worked out in the writer's ideological practice than the unexamined coexistence of these forces.

be right about the eventual fates of Cade, Straw, and Tyler, but their lives, rather than their deaths, continued to preoccupy the authorities. The continuing failure of rural and urban risings could never slay the ghosts of Straw and Cade; indeed, it was paradoxically essential for city authorities that their memories be kept alive as examples of failure even as representations of their rebellions were censored or suppressed.

Both London and national authorities, whatever their other disputes, did agree on the menace posed by masterless men, and this widespread concern culminated in the great vagrancy and poor relief acts of 1597–98. Still, the evidence, both within and without the theaters, suggests that the masterless men of London and the countryside were never more than a *potential*, waiting to be energized by a higher force. Yet those "who move the common sort to sedition," Cecil remarked to the Privy Council in 1599—ignoring the history of the previous decade—are not the nobility. "I have no fear of men of worth; when has England felt any harm by soldiers or gentlemen or men of worth? The State has ever found them truest. Some Jack Cade or Jack Straw and such rascals are those that have endangered the kingdom" (*CSPD* 1598–1601: 352). The comment was made, ironically, not in regard to a lower-class uprising of masterless men, but in a discussion following the Earl of Essex's Irish disaster. Barely a year later, Essex would instigate the most notorious, and perhaps the most serious, rising of this period. It began with—what else?—the commissioning by some of the rebels of a performance of a play about Richard II, but it ended with the fantasized army of vagabonds and masterless men, along with the proper citizenry, failing to appear.[32]

[32] After Simon Forman went to the Globe Theatre on 30 April 1611 to see "Richard the 2" (evidently not Shakespeare's, but yet another version), his first thoughts were ones we've come to expect: "Remember therin howe Jack Straw by his overmoch boldnes, not being pollitick nor suspecting Anye thinge: was Soddenly at Smithfeld Bars stabbed by Walworth the major of London, & soe he and his wholle Army was overthrowen" (Chambers: 2.339).

"Would Not the Beggar Then Forget Himself?":
Christopher Sly and Autolycus

When Rivers suggests to the future Richard III that he and his followers would follow Richard, "if you should be our king," Shakespeare's
Richard recoils in his usual false sincerity, "If I should be? I had rather
be a peddler!" (*Richard III* 1.3.148–49). The contemporary depth of disgust in Richard's invocation of his symbolic opposite may also be seen
reflected in the Maid's initial encounters with the Peddler in *The Pedler's
Prophecy* (1595):

> I never knew honest man of this occupation,
> But either he was a diser, a drunkard, or a maker of shift,
> A picker, a cutpurse, a raiser of simulation,
> Or such a one as runne away with another mans wife.
> ....
> [A type of men] whose whole trade is idlenesse:
> Dicers, drunkards, makers of strife,
> Very sincks and sentences of all wickednesse.

> (A4ᵛ, B)

The low reputation of peddlers in the period derived not only from em-
pirical evidence but from legal theory as well, for the statutes defining
vagrants invariably included, like the 1597 law (39 Eliz. I, c.4), "all Juglers Tinkers Peddlers and Petty Chapmen wandring abroade" (*TED:*
2.355).[1] Here we see that though a peddler holds an "occupation," he

---

[1] The language of the 1572 statute (14 Eliz. I., c.5) is virtually identical: "all Juglers
Pedlars Tinkers and Petye Chapmen" (*TED:* 2.329).

is *defined* by statute as a vagabond; so too jugglers[2], tinkers, and others. Though they are not on the public dole, do not (usually) beg in the streets, and generally support themselves, such occupations are nevertheless legally and socially condemned. The real objection is that they are "wandring abroade"—literally vagrant (a peddler, one writer said in 1631, is "a wandring starre," *Cater.* 8). They are not bound through guilds to a master-apprentice hierarchical relation, to a fixed place or to a fixed wage.

Such free-lance economic activity was considered harmful in other ways as well. In *Love's Labor's Lost*, for example, Berowne complains of Boyet,

> This fellow pecks up wit as pigeons pease,
> And utters it again when God doth please.
> He is wit's peddler, and retails his wares
> At wakes and wassails, meetings, markets, fairs;
> And we that sell by gross, the Lord doth know,
> Have not the grace to grace it with such show.
>
> (5.2.316–21)

Recasting the dandified Boyet as a peddler is an insult in class terms, but a more concrete objection is that he "utters" or sells whenever the time seems appropriate, earning "retail" at the expense of those who "sell by gross," or wholesale.[3] This violation of economic convention is repeated in the peddler's infiltration of various seasonal festivals and in his seeming ubiquity; as one character in *The Pedler's Prophecy* says, "there be too many such runnagates at these days, / All the whole world with such idle persons doth flow" (C3^{r-v}). The peddler was thus a loose cannon on the economic ship: unregulated, mobile, transgressive. Tinkers were little better. Indeed, "a sort [i.e., gang] of tinkers" (3.2.277) forms part of the mob in *2 Henry VI*, and Robert Greene tells a conny-catching tale of "a tinker, that went about the country" and practiced the "black art" of the picklock (Salgado 1972: 227). "A Tinker," as one writer put it, "is

---

[2] For "juggling," or legerdemain, see Samuel Rid's how-to manual, *The Art of Juggling or Legerdemaine* (1612); Rid plagiarizes freely from Reginald Scot's *The Discovery of Witchcraft* (1584). For a dramatic example of a beggar con-man practicing juggling, see Fletcher and Massingen's *Beggars' Bush* (3.1.62–96), where Prig tricks the "Boores."

[3] The Arden edition of *Love's Labor's Lost* quotes from Gabriel Harvey (1592) and William Covell (1595) in illustrating "by gross" as a term for wholesale, in opposition to "retail" (155). Dekker (1609) has the same conjunction of terms—one sells "by the gross" and another "buys his sport by the penny and like a haggler is glad to utter it again by retailing" (Pendry 1968: 98).

a mooveable: for hee hath no abiding place; by his motion hee gathers
heate, thence his cholericke nature" (*Overburian*: 34).[4]

Peddlers and tinkers were simply vagabonds, different from Counterfeit Cranks or Dommerars only in the details of their transgressions. In
The Highway to the Spital-House, "Copland" and the Porter rank peddlers
like any other stereotype of beggar.

> *Copland*
> Come none of these pedlars this way also,
> With pack on back, with their bousy speech,
> Jagged and ragged, with broken hose and breech?
> *Porter*
> . . . .
> . . . out of the spital they have a party stench.
> And with them comes gatherers of cony-skins,
> That chop with laces, points, needles and pins.
>
> (Judges: 23–24)

Some master thieves, Gilbert Walker reports in *A Manifest Detection of
Dice-Play* (1552), "follow markets and fairs in the country with peddlers'
footpacks, and generally to all places of assembly" (Kinney: 83).
Awdeley describes both types: "A Swigman goeth with a Pedlers pack"
(5), and "a Tinkard leaveth his bag a sweating at the Alehouse, which
they terme their Bowsing In[n], and in the meane season goeth abrode
a begging" (5). Most tinkers, Dekker says in *The Wonderful Year* (1603),
are "base, rascally . . . with a ban-dog and a drab at their tailes, and a
pike-staffe on their necks, [and] will take a purse sooner then stop a
kettle," though his story concerns a "devout" one (1963: 1.142). A man
disguised as a tinker in Robert Armin's *The History of the two Maids of More-
clacke* (1609) enters "*in a tawny coate like a tinker, and his boy with budget
and staffe, Toures tincks upon his pan drinking*" (C3ᵛ). The wandering tinker
in Francis Beaumont and John Fletcher's *The Coxcomb* (c. 1609) is more
threatening, however, as he enters "*with a Cord*" (2.2.1.s.d.) and his doxy,
Dorathy; frustrated by all the locked doors, they circle Viola menacingly,

---

[4] In a more benign characteristic, tinkers were also said to be innately musical, in some
accounts even the ur-musicians: "From his Art was Musicke first invented, and therefore
is hee alwaies furnisht with a song; to which his hammer keeping tune, proves that he
was the first founder of the Kettle-drumme" (*Overburian*: 35); "his Musicke is alwayes a
paire of woodden Organs under a Peinthouse, or a Crosse which he loves not to see;
beside his daily practice of the voice set and sung to the Tabering on a Kettle" (R.M.:
C6ᵛ). Shakespeare makes nothing of this tradition in Sly, and little beyond Autolycus's
singing itself.

with many sexual comments, and finally bind her, before abandoning her (2.1.28–93).

Harman, as usual, amplifies these two rogue types considerably. If "dronken" tinkers, also called "Prigs," see any old kettles or pewter about, they "quicklye snappeth the same up, and in to the booget [i.e., budget, or pig-skin bag] it goeth round" (59), just as Autolycus, who sings "If tinkers may have leave to live, / And bear the sow-skin budget" (*The Winter's Tale* 4.3.19–20), describes himself as a "snapper-up of unconsidered trifles" (4.3.25–26). Such tinkers, Harman notes, mingle "with a litle worke for a coulour," or pretense, and so "they live with deceite." The "swadder or Pedler," Harman likewise concedes, is "not all evile, but of an indifferent behaviour"; they themselves fear the stronger beggars such as Upright Men because "they have often both wares and money of them" (60). Evidently uneasy with their ambivalent status, Harman nevertheless accepts their mere status as criminal: "But for as much as they seeke gaine unlawfully against the lawes and statutes of this noble realme, they are well worthy to be registred among the number of vacabonds" (60).

With his usual combination of plagiarism and invention, Dekker (in *O per se O*, 1612) describes, in the familiar metaphor, the "swarms of locusts" who flock to the Deerhurst Fair, with a resonant political analogy: "If you look upon them you would think you lived in Henry VI's time, and that Jack Cade and his rebellious ragamuffins were there mustering" (Pendry 1968: 287). Dekker's vision of the fair is like something out of Dante, with more than one echo of *The Winter's Tale* and foreshadowing of Jonson's *Bartholomew Fair*. At Deerhurst, "None here stands crying 'What do you lack?' for you can ask for nothing that is good but here it is lacking. The buyers and sellers are both alike, tawny sunburnt rascals, and they flock in such troops that it shows as if Hell broke loose. The shopkeepers are thieves and the chapmen rogues, beggars and whores" (Pendry 1968: 288). In the usual projection of hierarchy, Dekker also describes how one "is chosen the Lord of the Fair, who is commonly the lustiest rogue in the whole bunch," leading his mob "from alehouse to alehouse" (288) in a drunken inversion of a royal procession. Such fairs always end in riot and violence, he concludes: "Here lies a rogue bleeding, there is a *mort* cursing, here a *doxy* stabbing with her knife. And thus this fair which begins merrily ends madly, for knaves set it up and queans pull it down" (Pendry 1968: 288). Dekker ironically ends his own book by identifying himself with such vagrants: "Enough of this, and he that desires more pieces of such pedlary ware may out of this little pack fit himself with any colours. *Vale!*" (Pendry 1968: 308).

The peddler and the tinker, then, were as clearly defined vagrant stereotypes as the Counterfeit Crank. In fact, at times, according to one writer, the peddler who fears impressment will resort to all the usual deceits of a Genings: he will "stirre his stumpes: but if that will not serve, he turnes counterfeit cripple, and as one cut off by the stumps, he cants his maimes most methodically: and this practice hee most constantly retaines till the coast be cleare" (*Cater.* 139). Like other vagrants, they blear the honest man's eye: the peddler was a "raiser of simulation," the tinker "live[s] with deceit." These vagabonds employ the standard canting language, "babbling French," as Copland says, but speak as well their own more specialized rhetoric; the Tinker's "tongue is very voluble, which with Canting proves him a *Linguist*" (*Overburian.* 35). They are also associated, like other types of masterless men, with disorderly mobs in country and city, even linked to Jack Cade as potentially rebellious subjects (Cade's wife is also said to be "a peddler's daughter," *2 Henry VI* 4.2.44). Peddlers and tinkers are distinguished from most other vagrants, however, by the fact that they have an "occupation," though "they seek gain unlawfully against the laws and statues of this noble realm," as Harman noted; they are thus marked more by their tendency to rob than to beg. Overbury's Tinker ironically "observes truely the Statutes, and therefore hee had rather steale then begge . . . and [he is] so strong an enemie to idlenesse, that in mending one hole, he had rather make three then want worke" (*Overburian.* 35). In some ways, peddlers and tinkers figure as prototypes of early capitalist entrepreneurs, yet contemporary discourse in general ranks them as petty criminals and inveterate frauds, experienced practitioners of various "black arts," like their cousins the Dommerar and the Abraham Man. Residual feudal values thus criminalize their entrepreneurial economic self-sufficiency, serving as one additional marker of the period's obsession with socioeconomic transgression. Perhaps the most telling description of all is R.M.'s ironic vision of a tinker "in the summer season . . . most frequent to be seene at the Royall Exchange of a Bush or hedge" (C6ᵛ). The central symbol of the emergent new economy, the institution presiding over, but not really controlling, exchange transactions of capital, is thus fused with what is taken to be its economic and philosophic opposite, the tinker, in a metaphor of condescension.[5] Yet the tinker's mobility reflected capital's liquidity—

---

[5] Dekker says "the theatre is your poets' Royal Exchange," where the Muses are merchants, "players are their factors," and gallants and courtiers are "the soundest paymasters and . . . the surest chapmen" (Pendry 1968: 98). As Knights observes, "It was international finance that first made capital mobile. It was international finance that prepared the way for the doctrine of complete economic freedom. . . . All that Gresham

indeed, it proceeded from the same forces—in ways that were not yet understood. The bourse and the beggar are, once again, two dishes, but to one table.

Given their pedigrees of thievery and deception, then, we might expect that the representations of tinker and peddler in Shakespeare's plays would be as darkly edged as that of Poor Tom, but such is not the case. Instead, Shakespeare seems to move in the opposite direction, offering us the genial warmth of Snout the Tinker in *A Midsummer Night's Dream* rather than, say, a vicious Jonsonian cheat whose trickery mocks the stupidity of his victims. The purpose of this chapter is to consider in some detail the two chief Shakespearean exemplars of this vagrant type, Christopher Sly in *The Taming of the Shrew* and Autolycus in *The Winter's Tale.*

The Taming of a Tinker

Christopher Sly identifies himself to the lord by reciting a comical curriculum vitae that firmly locates him geographically and socially: "Am not I Christopher Sly, old Sly's son of Burton-heath, by birth a peddler, by education a cardmaker, by transmutation a bearherd, and now by present profession a tinker?" (Ind. 2.17–20). And he further cites as a reference "Marian Hacket, the fat alewife of Wincot," to whom he owes the substantial sum of fourteen pence for the ale he has drunk. Stage directions and speech headings of the Folio text of *The Taming of the Shrew*, however, identify him more simply as "Begger" and "drunkard," generic rubrics which include all of Sly's announced "profession[s]." Sly's career path follows a rather low arc, its endpoints of peddler and tinker legally and socially identical. As a "bearherd," however, Sly has begun the first small step toward the world of professional entertainer, a rural version of the quasi-theatrical urban spectacles on display at the Beargarden; perhaps this phase of his career accounts for his garbled allusions to *The Spanish Tragedy* (Ind. 1.9). But Sly's "education" as a "cardmaker"—that is, one who made cards for combing wool—is the most ironic of his occupations, since the enclosure of common lands to pasture sheep, as the More paradigm explained, led to depopulation and an increase in vagrants—hence, to wandering beggars like Sly himself.[6]

[who built the Royal Exchange] and the financiers who followed him represented, therefore, would be completely alien to the peasants and small masters who still formed more than three quarters of the population of England. The ideas of the local community were not those of the Royal Exchange, and a clash was inevitable" (44–45).

[6] Boose situates the play in the context of "a vast cultural circulation of the anxieties of displacement that arose from the enclosure era" (203), linking the concepts of "hus-

Sly denies that he is descended from "rogues. Look in the chronicles: we came in with Richard Conqueror" (Ind. 1.3–4), but when the lord tells him he has awakened from a dream, he is happy enough to renounce his "present profession," and in blank verse rather than prose: "Upon my life, I am a lord indeed, / And not a tinker nor Christopher Sly" (Ind. 2.72–73).[7]

I have written elsewhere (1985: 41–50) on the energies of metamorphosis in *The Shrew*, with particular emphasis on the various forms of transformation enacted in the Induction; Sly's attempted metamorphosis into a lord is mirrored in the transformation of the boy page who dresses like Sly's lady, in the multiple allusions to Ovid's *Metamorphoses* (including the transformations of Cytherea, Io, and Daphne), and in the transforming effects experienced by an audience watching a play (Ind. 1.93–97; 2.127–32). The relation between these modes of transformation in the frame plot and what happens to Kate and Petruchio in the inner plot is a complex issue, the subject of my earlier study and many other critics as well.[8] But here I want to focus more narrowly on Sly's social and economic status and the class issues involved in his metamorphosis into a lord.

The rogue pamphlets of Harman, Dekker, and Robert Greene echo official documents, such as Edward Hext's letter to Burghley in 1596, in describing the histrionic abilities of certain vagabonds, some of whom counterfeit mutilation and degradation, as we have seen, but also others who "play the role" of the proper citizenry, and even infiltrate the legal system. Their role playing is supposedly so perfect that no one can distinguish them by external signs. But Sly is clearly not such a beggar, for he seems to have no histrionic gifts at all, and his lower nature continually reveals itself in his new role. The lord anticipates that Sly,

> . . . if he were conveyed to bed,
> Wrapped in sweet clothes, rings put upon his fingers,
> A most delicious banquet by his bed,
> And brave attendants near him when he wakes,
> Would not the beggar then forget himself?
>
> (Ind. 1.36–40)

---

bandry" and the ownership of common lands to the situation of women, particularly Kate. See also Stallybrass on this question. Boose goes on to show how "the disgruntlements of class are being transferred into the space of gender" (213) in *Shrew*. Her reading of Sly overlaps with mine at several points.

[7] None of the details of his "profession" is present in *The Taming of A Shrew*.

[8] Two recent, and quite different, discussions by Sirluck and Hager (26–33) are useful.

The expectation is that when Sly awakens, they will "persuade him that he hath been lunatic, / And when he says he is [i.e. now], say that he dreams, / For he is nothing but a mighty lord" (Ind. 1.62–64).

Sly's inability to "forget himself" into a new social role—or at least convince the audience that he can play the part—may remind us of Bottom (another weaver) and his similar incapacity in *A Midsummer Night's Dream*, but it should also be noted that Sly's situation is not exactly identical with those of Dekker's and Fleetwood's rogues, whose counterfeiting reaches only into the ranks of the middling sort. Shakespeare makes Sly attempt something far more difficult, to become "a mighty lord." The social and economic gaps between the tinker and the lord are about as large as could be imagined. Though the tinker is legally condemned for his "profession," the lord has none at all, an "idleness" permissible only in the aristocracy. The lord's avocation is hunting, not for food but for sport. His concern for his overheated dogs, one of whom he would not lose "for twenty pound" (Ind. 1.20), an enormous sum, does not extend to the human being he discovers sleeping: "O monstrous beast, how like a swine he lies! / Grim death, how foul and loathsome is thine image!" (1.33–34). The lord cares for his "dog" but now prepares to trick the "swine" by inverting his social position.

The world of the lord is one of spectacular conspicuous consumption, sensual indulgence, and practiced indolence, as close to the grotesque parody of Sir Epicure Mammon in Jonson's *Alchemist* as it is distant from Sly's "small ale" (Ind. 2.1) here. The lord commands the huntsmen—evidently now not his equals but his social inferiors—to see to the details of the jest:

> Carry him gently to my fairest chamber,
> And hang it round with all my wanton pictures.
> Balm his foul head in warm distilled waters,
> And burn sweet wood to make the lodging sweet.
> Procure me music ready when he wakes,
> To make a dulcet and a heavenly sound.
> And if he chance to speak, be ready straight,
> And with a low submissive reverence
> Say, "What is it your honor will command?"
> Let one attend him with a silver basin
> Full of rosewater and bestrewed with flowers;
> Another bear the ewer, the third a diaper,
> And say, "Will't please your lordship cool your hands?"
> Someone be ready with a costly suit,

> And ask him what apparel he will wear;
> Another tell him of his hounds and horse,
> And that his lady mourns at his disease.
>
> (Ind. 1.45–61)

All this because "he is nothing but a mighty lord." Yet it is not Sly's past life that can be thought of as a "dream" here, but rather the one the lord describes, which is a fantasy of hierarchical power and privilege.

The dream of class privilege, soothed by the murmurs of "low submissive reverence," is punctuated by the arrival of the players, who "offer service to your lordship" (Ind. 1.77). They had better receive the lord's patronage, too, otherwise these players will violate the same vagrancy laws—in the same paragraph, in fact—that defined tinkers and peddlers as vagabonds.[9] The lord calls for a play, the players exit to prepare, and the lord instructs that "Barthol'mew my page" be "dressed in all suits like a lady," to pretend to be "Lord" Sly's wife. Again the language emphasizes the comic inversion of the hierarchical, and now specifically marital, power. The page's proper conduct, we are told, should be "such as he hath observed in noble ladies / Unto their lords":

> Such duty to the drunkard let him do
> With soft low tongue and lowly courtesy,
> And say, "What is't your honor will command,
> Wherein your lady and your humble wife
> May show her duty and make known her love?"
> And then with kind embracements, tempting kisses,
> And with declining head into his bosom,
> Bid him shed tears, as being overjoyed
> To see her noble lord restored to health,
> Who for this seven years hath esteemed him
> No better than a poor and loathsome beggar.
>
> (Ind. 1.104–22)

Now the "submissive" fantasy of class privilege merges with the patriarchal dream of the "humble wife," easy to "command," dedicated to "duty." These positions are normalized, in the lord's plan, while Sly's

---

[9] Skura offers a fine reading of the Induction, through the trope of the "Player King as Beggar in Great Men's Houses" (99–106). She points out that while the Lord is "necessary to realize Sly's fantasies, . . . Sly is also necessary for the Lord to work out his own" (103).

ordinary position is no better than, and legally, no different from, that of a "poor and loathsome beggar."

When Sly awakens into his fictive lordship, however, it becomes clear that no matter what "apparel" or "costly suit" he wears, he cannot be mimetically transformed into the elevated social position of the lord. Promises of fantastic sensual indulgences, including erotic Ovidian transformation scenes, are summoned up to encourage the befuddled tinker, but clothes, it is clear, do not make the gentleman, though Sly continues to try. It has often been noted how Sly's attempt to command his "Lady's" obedience anticipates Petruchio's with Kate, but the key passage again brings together both marital and class hierarchies:

> *Sly.* Are you my wife, and will not call me husband?
> My men should call me "lord"; I am your goodman.
> *Page.* My husband and my lord, my lord and husband,
> I am your wife in all obedience.
>
> (Ind. 2.102–5)

Sly's wonderfully blunt command—"Servants, leave me and her alone. / Madam, undress you and come now to bed" (Ind. 2.113–14)—is no different from the lord's commands earlier, except that they are not obeyed. Instead, the players are announced, and Sly dispenses mock-aristocratic grace ("Marry, I will let them play it") but also reveals his confusion over the exact nature of this entertainment: "Is not a comonty a Christmas gambold or a tumbling trick? . . . household stuff?" (Ind. 2.133–36). The beggar is thus, as always, a kind of spectacle himself, an object lesson and source of amusement for the lord no less than the official entertainers, the players.

In the anonymous play *The Taming of A Shrew*, as is well known, Sly is seen and heard again at the end of the play, the frame plot closing securely; once more dressed in his "owne apparell," Sly promises to try out the shrew-taming lessons on his own wife. He speaks of his experience as Bottom does in *Midsummer Night's Dream*: "I have had / The bravest dreame to night, that ever thou / H[e]ardest in all thy life" (Bullough: 1.108). But in *The Shrew*, by contrast, there is no awakening or demystification of Sly, who has vanished textually from the play. In a way, then, Shakespeare at last fulfills the beggar's own fantasy, "I would be loath to fall into my dreams again" (Ind. 2.123), and he remains in the apparel of a gentleman.

Autolycus: A "Gentleman Born"

After Simon Forman saw a performance of *The Winter's Tale* at the
Globe on 15 May 1611, he reported the Leontes-Polixenes plot with
some care, explicitly noting the abandonment and recovery of Perdita.
Yet Forman notoriously did not mention any of the spectacular stage
effects from the second half of the play—no Chorus of Time (though
he does note that Perdita is sixteen years old), no bear, no eating of
Antigonus, no great statue scene; he does not even note Hermione's
apparent death, much less her rebirth. But one feature of the second
half of the play struck his attention greatly, and he devoted considerable space to it:

> Remember also the Rog that cam in all tottered like coll pixci and howe
> he feined him sicke & to have bin Robbed of all that he had and howe
> he cosened the por man of all his money, and after cam to the shep sher
> with a pedlers packe & ther cosened them Again of all their money And
> howe he changed apparrell with the kinge of Bomia his sonn, and then
> howe he turned Courtier &c.

The message of all this was clear to Forman: "Beware of trustinge feined
beggars or fawninge fellouss" (Chambers: 2.341). Autolycus is an entirely
different kind of "feined beggar" than Poor Tom, of course—not a lunatic but the cheerful peddler, part of the tradition of the merry beggar.
He enters singing of the red blood reigning in the winter's pale and the
sweet birds, O how they sing.

Although Autolycus's character seems derived primarily from literary
sources—something of the picaresque, a little of the Vice (Felperin: 217–
18), and a great deal of a tradition that romanticized the freedom and
openness of the tramp's life, as we saw in the first chapter—still, the
language Shakespeare has created for him receives its life from a number
of other wellsprings. The songs link Autolycus with a popular tradition
of festive natural celebration; many analogous songs have been reported
with the same peddler's cry, "What do you lack?"[10] On the other hand,
the language of Autolycus also reveals a strong indebtedness to the
conny-catching pamphlets of Robert Greene, not only in the specific trick

---

[10] See, for example, *The Pedler's Prophecy*: "What lacke you, what buy you, any good
pinnes etc" (D3), as well as the Dekker reference from *O per se O* quoted in the first
section of this chapter. Gerrard's song in *Beggars' Bush*—"Bring out your Cony-skins, faire
maids to me" (3.1.97–113)—is part of the same tradition. As one writer noted of the
peddler, "What doe yee lacke is his ordinary intergatory" (*Cater.* 138).

which Forman recalled (which seems to come from *The Second Part of Conny-catching* [1591]), but in the vocabulary and diction of his language.[11] Autolycus is given many of the specialized terms of the thieves' trade: "doxy," "pugging" (or "prigging"), "die and drab," "prig," "cut-purse," "I picked and cut most of their festival purses," and so forth. More, his voice is both unique in its colloquial eccentricities and almost Jonsonian in its sharp familiarity with the conventions of thieving: "You might have pinched a placket, it was senseless. 'Twas nothing to geld a codpiece of a purse. I could have filed keys off that hung in chains. No hearing, no feeling, but my sir's song, and admiring the nothing of it . . . had not the old man come in with hubbub against his daughter and the King's son and scared my choughs from the chaff, I had not left a purse alive in the whole army" (*The Winter's Tale* 4.4.612–21).

Autolycus's language is Shakespeare's closest approximation to beggar's cant. He is indeed a merry-hearted, jovial vagabond, but he also knows that "Gallows and knock are too powerful on the highway; beating and hanging are terrors to me" (4.3.28–29). He can flourish now because "I see this is the time that the unjust man doth thrive" (4.4.677–78). In placing his character so precisely in this particular social context, Shakespeare inevitably invokes questions of class privilege and social identity—issues that concern the other characters in Bohemia as much as they do Autolycus.

While much criticism has in the past been concerned with the relative attractiveness of Autolycus as a character,[12] his structural function in the play has also been frequently described in formalist terms.[13] Yet Autolycus

---

[11] Autolycus's links to the traditions of vagabondage were briefly described in McPeek (237–46). A far more compelling account of Autolycus's historical and social contexts is provided in Mowat's essay, which authoritatively discusses the "texts and infracontexts" of *The Winter's Tale* 4.3 in particular, and of the character in general. Mowat emphasizes the specific use of the term "rogue" to refer to Autolycus (64–66), whereas I believe he is more clearly marked in the tradition of the peddler.

[12] Opinion about Autolycus's character has varied considerably. For Knight, Autolycus "is spring incarnate; carefree, unmoral, happy, and sets the note for a spring-like turn in our drama" (100). Berlin claims that, as Autolycus is the representative of "the lowest, the underworld . . . the audience feels no sadness about his plight, because he *is* a rogue, because his spirit is essentially merry, and because the audience is not sympathetic toward him at the play's end. Shakespeare casts no moral opinion against him" (228). Vickers, however, finds that Autolycus's "attitude and especially his images reveal a boasting superiority which is less attractive" (414).

[13] Tillyard argues that Autolycus is "organic to the whole country scene, and that it would collapse into an over-sweetness of sentiment without him. . . . His delinquencies, like the pastoral realism, keep the earthly paradise sufficiently earthly without disturbing the paradisiac state" (Muir: 86). Frey sees his structural function in similar terms: Autolycus is "a figure who mediates humorously between the claims of Polixenes and those of Perdita and Florizel. He excites a laughter whose result is always to lessen the tension

appears not in an eternal and unreal springtime but in the particular historical context of Jacobean England. David Kaula has demonstrated how "the terminology Autolycus applies to his wares [e.g., "trumpery," 4.4.600] belongs to the verbal arsenal of anti-Catholic polemical writing in Reformation England" (289), and he argues that as "the cunning merchant of popish wares" (292), Autolycus is intended to be "a counterpart to Perdita" (293), setting up a binary distinction between "the artificial and the natural, the predatory and the charitable, the licentious and the chaste" (294).[14]

One thread of Kaula's argument is directly relevant to my topic here: his observation that "Autolycus' 'popish' associations seem to be limited to his peddler's role" (301). But this association is completely predictable, given the essential transgressiveness of the peddler to begin with. Kaula quotes from several Protestant writers who link Catholic icons with peddlers' wares. One of them is Samuel Harsnet ("the trinkets, toyes, & pedlars ware in the Popes holy budget" [Kaula: 289]), from whose work Shakespeare quotes some years earlier in *King Lear*. Another writer claims, in 1602, that "Romish wares" are

> sent abroad among the common people, both Protestants and Papists in London and in the countrey, & that, by certain women Brokers and Pedlers . . . who with baskets on their armes, shal come and offer you other wares under a colour, and so sell you these, where they see and know any likelihood to utter them. . . . under the habit of such, many young Jesuites, and olde Masse-priests range abroad, and drawe disciples after them. (Kaula: 291)

Here, there is transgression on many levels: not only religious and economic, but gender-related as well, for if anyone should not be errant, it is a woman, even "certain women." Yet as Alice Clark has noted, "in

---

between opposing forces: age and youth, pretension and reality, greed and charity, wrath and forgiveness, lion and lamb" (148). Cox, however, describes in some detail the parallels between Autolycus and Leontes, concluding that "the story of Autolycus, self-robber and self-deceiver, is a springlike variation of the winter story of Leontes" (298).

[14] Kaula's argument becomes unconvincing, for me, when it pushes over into explicit allegory: so Perdita's "betrothal to Florizel is meant to represent, on one level of symbolism, the union between Christ and his Bride" (296), and Perdita is equated with "the Virgin Mary" (297). I also see the binary distinctions Kaula lists as deconstructed within the play. Hamilton attempts, with mixed success, to place Autolycus in the historical context of the Union debates of 1604–10: he "is not a Scot exactly, but he is a refiguration and an acknowledgment of a social and political phenomenon in which the Scottish people were implicated and one that was threatening the English system of legitimation" (244).

some districts the trade [of peddler] was almost [a] monopoly" of women (206).

In the great fantasy of paranoia, the "people" have been infiltrated by papists, peddlers, and women, each of whom works through a disguise, and operates through deceit, "under a colour." Even when something innocuous is being peddled—ballads, for example, rather than heresy— the same rhetorical negatives are invoked, as in one work of 1592, which complains of the "Ballad-seller, [who] hath a whole Armie of runnagates at his reversion, that swarme everie where in *England*, and with their ribauld songs infect the Youth of this flourishing Commonweale."[15] Chettle (also 1592) echoes this vision in Anthonie Nownow's comment in *Kind-Hartes Dreame*:

> I am given to understand, that there be a company of idle youths, loathing honest labour and dispising lawfull trades, betake them to a vagrant and vicious life, in every corner of Cities & market Townes of the Realme singing and selling of ballads and pamphletes full of ribaudrie, and all scurrilous vanity, to the prophanation of Gods name, and with-drawing people from christian exercises, especially at faires markets and such publike meetings. (15)

Thus, even these peddlers, often employed by the stationers themselves to distribute their printed commodities, "swarme," in the usual metaphor, and "infect" parts of the body politic.

Peddlers were known to frequent "wakes and wassails, meetings, markets, fairs," as Berowne noted in *Love's Labor's Lost*, while a "petty Countrey Faire" itself was said to be little more than "the publication of some few Pedlers packs distinguisht into Boothes" (Saltonstall: 49); thus Autolycus's appearance at a sheep-shearing festival is conventional. Wassails, fairs, and sheep-shearing festivals were public sites outside the normal boundaries of surveillance and control, and thus they were socially marginal in every sense of the term. Jonson's *Bartholomew Fair* (1614) is a catalogue of every "enormity" imaginable at such a fair.[16] Shakespeare's Autolycus combines in one character two of Jonson's—Nightingale the ballad-seller, who works in league with Edgeworth, the cutpurse. The commercial activity such peddlers engage in, though statutorily illegal, is considerable and quite welcomed by the customers. Peddlers such as Autolycus are condemned in part, then, because they enable a redefini-

---

[15] E. de Maisonneuve, *Gerileon of England* (1592), A4; quoted in the Arden edition of *The Winter's Tale* (100).

[16] See Stallybrass and White on the cultural significance of Bartholomew Fair.

tion of the very concept of the marketplace—no longer closed but open, not static but fluid, not fixed in its elements but "placeless," in Michael Bristol's term (1991: 163). They represent, in short, the transgressive fluidity of capital.

Perhaps the central paradigm of the feudal conception of work, enshrined (or embalmed) in the London craft-guilds and in the codifications of the Statute of Artificers, is the master-apprentice relation. But the peddler, both cause and symptom, heralds a different kind of economy, in which a different paradigm operates: "Come to the peddler; / Money's a meddler, / That doth utter all men's ware-a" (*The Winter's Tale* 4.4.321–23). Money talks: money can "utter," both speak and put on the market, *all* "ware." The peddler is the embodiment of this medium of exchange, this "meddler." To "meddle" also carries the sense "to mix (wares) fraudulently" (OED v.1b) and "to have sexual intercourse (with)" (OED v.5)—perhaps from the standard contemporary pun on "medlar," the pulpy apple synonymous with the female genitals.[17] Sexual meddling is therefore a refraction of economic meddling. All these associations may also be seen at play in the Pedler's speech in John Heywood's *The Foure PP* (c. 1531): "Why, dost thou nat knowe that every pedler / In every trifull must be a medler?/ Specially in womens triflinges" (lines 217–19). Money is the "meddler," Autolycus says, and the peddler's profession participates in an economy of alleged corruption linked to several other types of transgression.

Autolycus's personal history, moreover, mimics the declension from an older to a newer form of service: "I have served Prince Florizel," he tells the audience, "and in my time wore three-pile, but now I am out of service" (4.3.13–14). Now, for Autolycus, "My traffic is sheets" and "my revenue is the silly cheat" (4.3.23, 27–28). Poor Tom, too, was once "a servingman, proud in heart and mind" (*King Lear* 3.4.84), but is now "nothing." Since being "whipped out of the court," Autolycus reports (in the third person) of his career that he has been "an ape bearer, then a process server, a bailiff. Then he compassed a motion of the Prodigal Son and married a tinker's wife . . . having flown over many knavish professions, he settled only in rogue" (4.3.87–97).

As an accomplished, role-playing rogue, Autolycus has certainly mastered more than the role of peddler. In his initial encounter with the

---

[17] Cf. *Coriolanus* (4.5.49–52): *Third Servingman:* "Do you meddle with my master?" *Coriolanus:* "Ay, 'tis an honester service than to meddle with thy mistress"; and *Romeo* (1.2.39–40): "It is written that the shoemaker should meddle with his yard." For "medlar," see *Romeo* (2.1.35–37), *Measure for Measure* (4.3.172), *As You Like It* (3.2.116–18), and *Timon* (4.3.309–15).

Clown, Autolycus does an excellent version of Nicholas Genings, as he falls to the ground in apparent agony:

> *Autolycus.* O, that ever I was born! [*He grovels on the ground*]
> *Clown.* I' the name of me!
> *Autolycus.* O, help me, help me! Pluck but off these rags, and then death, death!
> *Clown.* Alack, poor soul! Thou hast need of more rags to lay on thee, rather than have these off.
> *Autolycus.* O sir, the loathsomeness of them offends me more than the stripes I have received, which are mighty ones and millions. (4.3.49–57)

Another Shakespearean character also has "the falling-sickness": "He fell down in the marketplace, and foamed at mouth, and was speechless" (*Julius Caesar* 1.2.252–53). But Julius Caesar's infirmity is meant to be real, while Autolycus is anything but speechless. Indeed, he claims that he has been robbed and beaten, "my money and apparel ta'en from me, and these detestable things [his garments] put upon me" (4.3.60–62). Claiming that his "shoulder blade is out," Autolycus picks the Clown's pocket as he is helped to his feet.

This scene's language of "rags," "apparel," "garments," and "horseman's coat" reflects Shakespeare's emphasis on the rogue's shifting, unstable identity and his histrionic gifts.[18] Simon Forman's account of the play, quoted earlier, marked three distinct kinds of "apparel" for Autolycus: first, he "cam in all tottered like coll pixci"[19]; afterwards he came to the sheep-shearing "with a pedlers packe"; and finally, "he changed apparrell with the kinge of Bomia his sonn, and then howe he turned Courtier &c." In this last phase, the beggar and the king(-to-be) once again confront one another, and the mirroring of inversion is played out in an outright exchange of clothing. And like Christopher Sly trying to become a "great lord," Autolycus is to be "turned Courtier." When Camillo and Florizel approach Autolycus to exchange clothing, Camillo remarks that they will exchange only "the outside of thy poverty" (4.4.635). As we have repeatedly seen, though, the outside of poverty is always the least authentic of cultural signs; even the "millions" of

---

[18] See my comments elsewhere on the metamorphoses of Autolycus and those in the play as a whole (1985: 210–25). Mowat points out the inversion of the Good Samaritan story here (61–62).

[19] The Arden editor glosses "coll pixci" as "Colle- or Colt-pixie = hobgoblin, particularly in the form of a ragged (tattered) colt which leads horses astray into bogs, etc." (xxii).

"stripes" Autolycus claims to have received were frequently faked, and he never shows them anyhow.

As the gentles speak the language of the theater—"play," "part"— Camillo advises Perdita to "disliken / The truth of your own seeming" (4.4.655–56), a practice she is already unwittingly engaged in, and which is being extravagantly enacted by Autolycus. His self-transformation into a courtier begins when he takes off a false beard ("Let me pocket up my peddler's excrement," 4.4.716–17), and announces himself to the Clown and Shepherd in high astounding terms, almost Falstaffian in their mock-pomposity:

> Whether it like me or no, I am a courtier. Seest thou not the air of the court in these enfoldings? Hath not my gait in it the measure of the court? Receives not thy nose court odor from me? Reflect I not on thy baseness court contempt? Think'st thou, for that I insinuate to toze from thee thy business, I am therefore no courtier? I am courtier cap-a-pie, and one that will either push on or pluck back thy business there. Whereupon I command thee to open thy affair. (4.4.733–41)

While the Clown thinks "this cannot be but a great courtier," his father the Shepherd reflects more observantly that "his garments are rich, but he wears them not handsomely" (4.4.751–54).

"Garments" and "apparel" continue to be the subject when we next see the rustics at the court of Sicilia. They now wear new clothing and claim the same transformation of social class that Sly and Autolycus did: "See you these clothes? Say you see them not and think me still no gentleman born. You were best say these robes are not gentleman born. Give me the lie, do, and try whether I am not now a gentleman born" (5.2.132–35). These jokes may have been meant to reflect the phenomenon of the great number of newly made "gentlemen" in King James's court, but there is an equally strong connection to Shakespeare's interest throughout the play in whether a "gentleman" is "born" or made, natural or constructed. The Clown reports a comically confusing nexus of kinship relations: "I was a gentleman born before my father; for the King's son took me by the hand and called me brother; and then the two kings called my father brother; and then the Prince my brother and the Princess my sister called my father father" (5.2.140–44). Like the famous debate in 4.4 over the priority and value of art and nature, the Clown's speech further blurs the categories of distinction. Yet clothes, again, do not make the gentleman. In a final irony, Autolycus and the clowns reverse position again, and he enters "courtly" service again to his new "good masters" (5.2.175), the Clown and the Shepherd.

Autolycus is hardly a Grand Rogue or Upright Man in Harman's terms: "On the highway," he admitted, "gallows and knock are too powerful . . . beating and hanging are terrors to me." He projects his memory of such "terrors" onto the rustics in a comic but disturbing set-piece when he threatens them.

> If that shepherd be not in handfast, let him fly. The curses he shall have, the tortures he shall feel, will break the back of man, the heart of monster. . . . Some say he shall be stoned; but that death is too soft for him, say I. . . . He has a son, who shall be flayed alive; then, 'nointed over with honey, set on the head of a wasp's nest; then stand till he be three-quarters and a dram dead; then recovered again with aqua vitae or some other hot infusion; then, raw as he is, and in the hottest day prognostication proclaims, shall he be set against a brick wall, the sun looking with a southward eye upon him, where he is to behold him with flies blown to death. (4.4.772–95)

Such tortures far exceed what any beggar might legally receive, though the testimony of some former prisoners in Bridewell, we saw, was chilling enough.[20] The only way to escape such torture, as Autolycus notes, is to approach the prince. Shakespeare's conclusion to this line of action in the play resonates suggestively with the passage in *Lear* that exposes "the great image of authority" (4.6.158ff.). Here, the Clown says of Autolycus, "He seems to be of great authority. Close with him, give him gold; and though authority be a stubborn bear, yet he is oft led by the nose with gold. Show the inside of your purse to the outside of his hand" (4.4.803–7).

The nature and validity of authority, in both legal and social categories, are thus brought into question by the very presence of the beggar: poor implies rich, low implies high, "nothing" implies "all." The lean beggar serves not just as an antithesis to the fat king, but as an opposing principle to all authority that derives from the sociopolitical hierarchy that maintains and justifies the monarchy, the court, and the social gradations ramifying from it. "What authority surfeits on would relieve us," says the First Citizen in the opening scene of *Coriolanus* (1.1.15–16). Here the reality of hunger among the poor is not genially transformed, as it is in

---

[20] The literary source of this torture is probably Boccaccio's *Decameron* 2.9 (Arden *The Winter's Tale* 132), but oral traditions of contemporary Spanish cruelties might also have been in the background.

the cases of Sly and Autolycus, but fully staged in a Shakespearean version of Bacon's dictum that "the rebellions of the belly are the worst."[21]

> If they would yield us but the superfluity while it were wholesome, we might guess they relieved us humanely. But they think we are too dear. The leanness that afflicts us, the object of our misery, is as an inventory to particularize their abundance. Our sufferance is a gain to them. Let us revenge this with our pikes ere we become rakes; for the gods know I speak this in hunger for bread, not in thirst for revenge. (*Coriolanus* 1.1.16–23)

"The leanness that afflicts" the poor, in the Citizen's dialectic, is at the same time the sign of the patricians' "abundance." The patricians are fat, overflowing, surfeited, indifferent to the poor: they "suffer us to famish, and their storehouses crammed with grain; make edicts for usury to support usurers; repeal daily any wholesome act established against the rich; and provide more piercing statutes daily, to chain up and restrain the poor. If the wars eat us not up, they will" (1.1.78–84). The "statutes" are "piercing," not just in the general sense, but as we have seen, in the literal ways in which beggars' bodies were marked and punished. Yet this rebellion, in Menenius's famous allegory, turns out not to be one of the belly, which is said to signify the beneficent Senators of Rome, but the "great toe," because like it, they are the "lowest, basest, poorest" of the rebellion (1.1.155–56).

Shakespeare's general allusion in this scene to the Midlands Revolt of 1607 has often been noted, perhaps most brilliantly by Janet Adelman, who illuminates the play's underlying dynamic of rebellion, hunger, and violence.[22] As Manning shows (1988: 229–46), the rising in 1607 began as enclosure riots and soon spread to wider forms of disorder and violence before it was suppressed. Although the contemporaneity of the allusion in *Coriolanus* is clear enough, it is also significant that one of Coriolanus's lines attacking the mob ("You cry against the noble Senate, who, / Under the gods, keep you in awe, which else / Would feed on one another," 1.1.185–87) echoes a line from the similar insurrection scene, probably by Shakespeare, in *The Book of Sir Thomas More*, where "men like ravenous fishes / Would feed on one another" (2.3.92–93). Whether this allusion is understood as a specific one, or as a coincidental

---

[21] Leinwand reminds us that the mob in *Coriolanus* is made up of "citizens" of the "middling sort": "Only their hunger may temporarily align them with either the poor or with those just a step ahead of poverty" (1993: 296).

[22] For an early study, see Pettet; see also Patterson (135–46).

reference to the familiar political trope of "big fish eats little fish," it continues the recurring discursive formation of the beggar or masterless man or woman as essentially constituted by his or her body—indeed, as one of the lowest levels on the food chain.

Coriolanus dismisses the hunger of the poor along with their "proverbs": "That hunger broke stone walls, that dogs must eat, / That meat was made for mouths, that the gods sent not / Corn for the rich men only" (1.1.205–8). Hunger and poverty are, if not technically synonymous, nevertheless inevitably linked, and Shakespeare constantly associates the wandering poor with the kind of starvation that leads to political danger. The citizens of Rome in *Coriolanus* "are all resolved rather to die than to famish" (1.1.4–5), and Richard III can think of no greater insult than to call Richmond's troops

> A sort of vagabonds, rascals, and runaways,
> A scum of Bretons and base lackey peasants,
> Whom their o'ercloyed country vomits forth
> To desperate adventures and assured destruction.
> . . . .
> These famished beggars, weary of their lives,
> Who, but for dreaming on this fond exploit,
> For want of means, poor rats, had hanged themselves.
>
> > (*Richard III* 5.3.316–19, 329–31)

Again, these beggars are in opposition to plenitude, though the "o'ercloyed country," having much too much its fill of such figures, must vomit them forth; famished themselves, they are paradoxically also a nauseating food to others. And "rebellion . . . hurly-burly innovation . . . [and] insurrection" are fueled, as Henry IV warns, by "moody beggars, starving for a time / Of pell-mell havoc and confusion" (*1 Henry IV* 5.1.74–82). Thus the hungry hunger for chaos, which will leave them yet hungrier and more desperate. The same kind of "loud rebellion" threatens in *Henry VIII*, where

> The clothiers all, not able to maintain
> The many to them 'longing, have put off
> The spinsters, carders, fullers, weavers, who,
> Unfit for other life, compelled by hunger
> And lack of other means, in desperate manner

> Daring th'event to th'teeth, are all in uproar,
> And danger serves among them.

(1.2.29–37)

This last reference to the social unrest arising from widespread unemployment in the wool industry returns us to Sly and Autolycus, who
had adapted to rather than rebelled against their subjection. Sly, we recall, had once worked as a "cardmaker," and Autolycus finds his greatest
success as a cutpurse at a sheep-shearing festival—the end product, so to
speak, of the socio-agricultural revolution of the enclosure movement
which, it was argued, created vast numbers of vagabonds such as Autolycus himself. While Jack Cade was "ready to famish," "so hungry that,
if I might have a lease of my life for a thousand years, I could stay no
longer," and claims to be "vanquished by famine, not by valor" (2 *Henry*
VI 4.10.2, 4–6, 74), Autolycus is a source of plenitude, commercially
speaking. "He utters [tunes] as [if] he had eaten ballads" (4.4.184–85),
we are told, and his peddler's pack is a "silken treasury" (4.4.350), a
cornucopia of consumer products, as eagerly desired "as if my trinkets
had been hallowed and brought a benediction to the buyer" (4.4.604–
5). Sly, as we saw, was offered a vision of sensual and gustatory plenitude
("A most delicious banquet by his bed," *The Taming of the Shrew* Ind. 1.38)
which is inverted in the inner plot in Petruchio's strategy of starving Kate
to tame her. The associations she makes by now seem inevitable:

> What, did he marry me to famish me?
> Beggars that come unto my father's door
> Upon entreaty have a present alms;
> If not, elsewhere they meet with charity.
> But I, who never knew how to entreat,
> Nor never needed that I should entreat,
> Am starved for meat, giddy for lack of sleep,
> With oaths kept waking, and with brawling fed.

(4.3.3–10)

Such deprivation can only be comparable to the life of a beggar, it seems,
but Kate's confidence in their receiving "present alms" is not always
borne out in Renaissance England: she obviously never met anyone like
Timon of Athens, who advises "Hate all, curse all, show charity to none,
/ But let the famished flesh slide from the bone / Ere thou relieve the
beggar. Give to dogs / What thou deniest to men" (*Timon* 4.3.532–35).

Cade's attempted ascent to a kind of peasant kingship and Poor Tom's elevation (as we will see) to the position of "learned justice" are therefore comically mirrored in Sly's and Autolycus's reversals in status from vagabond tinker and peddler to lord and gentleman. These doubled inversions suggest that the beggar's status in these plays is not only to speak the voice of the dispossessed, which they do insistently, and not only to offer a sociopolitical impersonation of the voice and values of those above them, but also to be that force which naturally seeks to *rise*, and so constitutes a deeply politicized energy.[23] The presence of the beggar always engages the question of social class. Even Christopher Sly, the most passive figure in this group, begins to imagine the impossible: "I am a lord indeed, / And not a tinker nor Christopher Sly" (Ind. 2.72–73). But the beggar, in the end, is never permitted fully to "forget himself," and all the mock-elevations are eventually overturned.

[23] Though they are very different characters, Cade, Poor Tom, Sly, and Autolycus share many common attributes in their language: it is almost exclusively prose, highly colloquial, filled with puns and dramatic irony, semantically and syntactically unstable, invariably refracting the imagery and thematic concerns of the "high" language of the plays. But beyond the obvious political themes *in* their language, the most political aspect of it is that it exists at all. For more on their language, see my essay (1992).

CHAPTER SIX

"The Base Shall Top th'Legitimate": King Lear and the Bedlam Beggar

WHEN Tudor playwrights represented beggars on their stages, the beggars tended to be of two types: either the genuine, usually unnamed poor, or the histrionic counterfeiter. The boundary between these two categories was in general quite strong—until, that is, Edgar turned into Poor Tom in *King Lear*. One early dramatic representation of a sturdy beggar—of the type known as the Counterfeit Crank, like Nicholas Genings—may be seen in Francis Merbury's *The Marriage between Wit and Wisdom* (c. 1571–78). Here the inherent fraudulence of the sturdy beggar is merged with the traditional histrionic counterfeiting of the Vice. The Vice's name in this play is Idleness, who tells us,

> marry my masters she [his mother Ignorance] sent me the
> counterfait crainke for to play
> & to leade witt Severities sone out
> of the waye.
>
> (lines 212–215)

As the Counterfeit Crank, the Vice enters with the familiar beggar's appeals:

> give me one peny or a halfepeny
> for a poore man that hath had
> greate losse by sea
> & is in great misery
> god save my good master & my good dame

> & all the householder
> I pray you bestowe your almes of a poore man
> nye starved with colde
> now I am a bould begger
> I tell you the stowtest of all my kin.
>
> (lines 1138–47)

He exits and reappears with a useful stage prop as a sign of his status—a stolen "porridge pot a bout his nect." Later, he is captured by Inquisition, the stolen pot is identified, and he suffers the standard fate of beggars: "lett him be whipte up & downe the towne next markit day" (1253–55). But Idleness escapes, of course, and triumphs, like Mosca in *Volpone*, "I am of that condition / that I cane turne into all / coullers like the commillion" (1354–56). Those who "list [choose] not to work," he concludes, "let them follow me" (1385–86).

The beggar as con-man is a relatively common figure in the drama, but the fantasy of the sturdy beggar's histrionic omnipotence is in some texts of the period also fused with an intense romanticizing of the beggar's life, as we saw in chapter 1—the man *chooses* to counterfeit a beggar not because it is his nature to deceive (like the Vice), or because a relatively high level of wealth can be secured, but because the life of the beggar is claimed to be actually superior to that of the rest of us. This delusion of course flies in the face of the reality of social conditions, and it seems a perfect illustration of how those comfortably placed within the social hierarchy rationalize the continued exclusion of the marginal. Beggars are thus usually either demonized by the prevailing discourse or their suffering suppressed through idealization. In Robert Wilson's *The Three Ladies of London* (c. 1581), for example, three beggars—Tom Beggar, Wily Will, and Simplicity—enter singing cheerfully, and Tom tells the audience,

> Now truly, my masters, of all occupations under
>   the sun, begging is the best;
> For when a man is weary, then he may lay him
>   down to rest.
> . . . .
> Why, an emperor for all his wealth can have but
>   his pleasure,
> And surely I would not lose my charter to liberty
>   for all the king's treasure.
>
> (347–48)

Wily Will naturally agrees.

> Shall I tell thee, Tom Beggar, by the faith of a
>   gentleman, this ancient freedom I would not forego,
> If I might have whole mines of money at my
>   will to bestow.
> Then, a man's mind should be troubled to keep
>   that he had;
> And you know it were not for me: it would make
>   my valiant mind mad.
>
> (348)

As they approach the gate of the house of Lady Lucre, the three beggars fashion the standard beggars' pleas—"Good gentle Master Porter, your reward do bestow / On a poor lame man etc" (349). Not only do they receive no alms, but eventually Fraud converts them into outright highwaymen.

When beggars who are *not* counterfeitors or romanticized—that is, the "real" thing—appear on the Elizabethan stage, as in *A Knack To Know A Knave* (c. 1592), however, all the Tudor anxieties about the poor seem energized in close proximity. In this play we are given a character, Bishop Dunstan, who actually obeys the biblical edicts of charity.

> The poor man never yet went from my door,
> But to my power I did relieve his want:
> I was no farmer that enrich'd myself,
> By raising markets and oppressing poor.
>
> (541)

We are also shown one of these greedy farmers, whose credo is "Therefore learn to provide for yourself; let God provide for the poor" (546). When a neighbor, a "poor man," enters, he is dismissed with contempt by the farmer (who nevertheless tries to steal the title to the poor man's cottage). When "Honesty and a Beggar" meet the dishonest priest later in the play, their encounter is telling:

Beggar. I beseech you, good master, for God's sake, give one penny to the poor, lame, and blind; good master, give something.

Priest. Fie upon thee, lazy fellow, art thou not ashamed to beg? Read the blessed saying of St Paul, which is, Thou shalt get thy living with the sweat of thy brows, and he that will not labour is not worthy to eat.

Honesty. [Aside] Ay, but he remembers not where Christ saith, He that giveth a cup of cold water in my name shall be blessed.

(578–79)

In John Fletcher's *The Pilgrim* (c. 1621), in a similar scene, the virtuous Alinda asks her maid Juletta, "What Poor attend my charity today, wench?"

> *Juletta.* Of all sorte, Madam; your open handed bounty
> Makes 'em flock every houre: some worth your
> pitty,
> But others that have made a trade of begging.
> *Alinda.* Wench, if they ask it truly, I must give it:
> It takes away the holy use of charity
> To examine wants.
>
> (1.1.95–101)

When four true beggars are brought onstage, the Porter roundly condemns them:

> O the infinite Seas of porridge thou hast swallowd!
> And yet thou lookst as if they had bin but Glisters;
> Thou feedst abundance; thou hadst need of sustenance;
> Almes do you call it to relieve these Rascals?
>
> (1.2.18–21)

Even Alinda's father, Alphonso ("an old angry Gentleman" in the Dramatis Personae), scoffs at the louse-ridden beggars and puts away his money; he grudgingly relieves them only when told "the wrongs ye do these men, may light on you" (line 80). Alinda enters next, berates the Porter—"Do you make sport sir, with their miseries?"—and orders them served immediately (line 94). A different charitable impulse is played out in the anonymous *Raigne of King Edward the Third* (c. 1590–93) when "*sixe poore Frenchmen*" enter just as Edward begins the siege of Calais. These "wretched patterns of dispaire and woe," like "gliding ghosts, / Crept from your graves to walke upon the earth" (lines 1680–82), are the "deseased, sicke and lame" (line 1686) of the besieged city who have been expelled so as not to be a drain on the dwindling supply of food. Edward points out that as they are enemies, he can simply put them "to the sword" (line 1693), but in a royal gesture of magnanimity offers them charity instead, ordering Derby to "Command that victuals be appointed them, / And give to every one five Crownes a peece: / The Lion scornes to touch the yeelding pray" (lines 1699–1701).

Whatever the depth of social awareness or empathy for the poor in these plays, their authors move toward no form of social or economic analysis. Rather, the movement is usually toward the exposure of the good or evil individual beneath the disguise. Thus Idleness is unmasked and Tom Beggar and his friends are sent packing. In *A Knack To Know A Knave*, the real beggar leaves with nothing, while the scoundrels Coney-catcher, the Farmer, and the Priest are individually punished by Honesty. In play after play, then, the voice of the beggar—the destitute, the dis-possessed, the marginalized—is occasionally heard but not, so to say, fully received. But things are much different in *King Lear*.

In one of the central epiphanies of his long, painful journey, King Lear falls to his prayers on the heath while the storm rages about him:

> Poor naked wretches, whereso'er you are,
> That bide the pelting of this pitiless storm,
> How shall your houseless heads and unfed sides,
> Your looped and windowed raggedness, defend you
> From seasons such as these?
>
> (3.4.28–32)[1]

In the past, Lear has taken "too little care of this," he says, but in his promise to "expose thyself to feel what wretches feel," he begins a tor-turous process of self-regeneration. In the next moment, the monarch is brought face to face with one of his kingdom's lean beggars, the wan-dering lunatic Poor Tom. Shakespeare's powerful encounter between monarchical power and social marginality physically enacts more than a century's worth of symbolic confrontations, but this representation comes with a major difference: the humbling of Lear, the king's descent to the level of the beggar, is not only a critical moment in the play, but a skep-tical one—part of an important Shakespearean interrogation of the dis-

---

[1] Bevington bases his text on the Folio, but includes much from the Quarto in what is now termed a "hybrid" or "conflated" text. The problem of the "two-text" *Lear* is not my subject here, although the character of Edgar underwent some alterations in the Folio version of the play—see Warren's path-breaking article, as well as Blayney and Taylor and Warren's *The Division of the Kingdoms*. The alterations in Edgar's part—such as the deletion of his soliloquy at the end of 3.6—do not in general affect my argument in this chapter, and I indicate in the notes where I have diverged from Bevington's text, or where there is a significant distinction between Folio and Quarto readings. For an analysis of the interpretive implications of the two-text theory, particularly in the case of Edgar, see my 1988 essay.

courses of poverty and power. Lear's remarkable prayer is part of a powerful dramatic process that will expose the arbitrariness of class, power, wealth, and so identity. The beggar and the king's confrontation, facing one another in similar positions of deprivation, deconstructs the traditional binaries of authority and subjection, wealth and poverty, identity and nothingness. What this confrontation means for Lear, and for the play generally, can best be registered by first examining Edgar's role in the play in some detail.

Edgar's passage through *King Lear* is relatively clear in its outlines—from naive son to outcast beggar to restored son, heir, and finally, perhaps, king. It is the curve of a romance plot, though it never feels like one. The nature of Edgar's "inner" changes, on the other hand, is an entirely different question; whether he possesses what may be called a consistent inner self has been widely debated. Much of the difficulty in discussing Edgar stems from the series of roles he plays in the middle of the play which seem embodiments (if that is possible) of negation and self-alienation, most cryptically expressed in a string of orphic negatives, from "Edgar I nothing am" (2.3.21) through "in nothing am I changed / But in my garments" (4.6.9–10) to "Know my name is lost" (5.3.124). The play's eerie calculus transforms these negatives into the positive assertion of identity Edgar makes to Edmund at the end of the play: "My name is Edgar, and thy father's son" (5.3.172)—and yet even this positive assertion is characteristically ambiguous. We will never be able to explain everything about Edgar—the mystery of things is too great in his case—but his role in the play becomes clearer when we look more closely at his disguise as Poor Tom, the Bedlam beggar, and when we realize that the play's persistent interrogation of the human body's place in the natural and social orders culminates in Poor Tom's suffering body. We will also see how a link between Poor Tom and Edmund helps clarify Edgar's situation in the play.

My emphasis on Edgar here is not a detour from the main line of the play, for Edgar is the chief point of contact between the Lear and the Gloucester plots. Edgar even received equal billing in the first published version of the play, the 1608 Quarto, whose title page reads: "M. William Shak-speare: His True Chronicle Historie of the life and death of King Lear and his three Daughters. With the unfortunate life of Edgar, sonne and heire to the Earle of Gloster, and his sullen and assumed humor of Tom of Bedlam." If Shakespeare did not compose this title—and he probably did not—at least his publisher recognized the importance, and the notorious appeal, of Edgar. Moreover, the paired antithetical attributes given to Edgar on the title page—the "sonne and heire" on the one hand, and the "sullen and assumed humor of Tom of Bedlam" on the other—mark the boundaries of cultural possibility for Edgar.

The first reference to Edgar in the play is Gloucester's response to Kent's praise of Edmund: "But I have a son, sir, by order of law, some year elder than this, who yet is no dearer in my account" (1.1.19–21). This as yet unnamed son—for whom the phrase "by order of law" takes the place of a name—has a legal but perhaps not an emotional advantage in his father's affections over his bastard brother Edmund. The next reference to Edgar—his very naming in the play—is in Edmund's opening soliloquy, where he is called "Legitimate Edgar" (1.2.16), as if the epithet were part of his name. Certainly for the "sonne and heire," created "by order of law," the central fact of his nature seems to be that he is "legitimate." Fine word, legitimate. Edgar's nature seems essentially indistinguishable from the order of law, but in depicting Edgar's dispossession and abasement, the play will suggest that "legitimacy" might be a legal, not a biological category; written, not natural. If one is "got 'tween the lawful sheets" (4.6.116), the adjective "lawful"—a social construct—counts for more than the verb; and the "lawful sheets" might be a play on 'legal documents' as well. The ideas of legitimacy and inheritance seem by turn incorporated in the natural body and arbitrarily empowered by the social order. The issue of legitimacy is most clearly articulated in the relationship between Edgar, the "sonne and heire to the Earle of Gloster," and Edmund, whose illegitimacy marks him (like Goneril's steward, Oswald) as the "son and heir of a mongrel bitch" (2.2.21–22).

Edgar's role as son and heir—the two are not exactly synonymous, we see, since Edmund is also a son but not an heir—figures as the very key Edmund will use to unlock his father's fears; Edmund will himself enact the fantasy of father-replacement which Gloucester would have expected from Edgar. What Edmund wants to do is become someone else, almost anyone else, because he cannot stand himself. His goal is to become Edgar, and he does, and then he becomes his father as well, dispossessing him as he himself was dispossessed. Edmund therefore does not really want to overthrow the legal order when he asks "Wherefore should I / Stand in the plague of custom and permit / The curiosity of nations to deprive me[?]" (1.2.2–4). Instead, he wishes to render the social order arbitrary, dissociated from the order of nature, and to stand where the order of law has instead placed his brother. Throughout the play, he will speak and write in the stolen or forged voices of his brother and father, endeavoring to replace them by becoming them.

The key moment in Edmund's displacement of Edgar as heir occurs in the famous passage in 1.2, after his now-deluded father leaves the stage and Edmund mocks his superstitious empiricism:

> My father compounded with my mother under the Dragon's tail and my nativity was under Ursa Major, so that it follows I am rough and lecherous. Fut, I should have been that I am, had the maidenliest star in the firmament twinkled on my bastardizing. Edgar—[s.d. *Enter Edgar*].

Precisely as the subject turns to Edmund's bastardizing, pat he comes, Edgar the true son and heir, as if summoned up as the bodily proof of Edmund's bastardy and as the model of what Edmund would be. The deepest irony in this scene now follows, in the full text of Edmund's aside on Edgar's entrance: "Edgar—and pat he comes like the catastrophe of the old comedy. My cue is villainous melancholy, with a sigh like Tom o'Bedlam. O, these eclipses do portend these divisions! Fa, sol, la, mi" (1.2.131–40). Edmund thus names, by first impersonating, the theatrical role into which Edgar will be cast, displaced from old comedy to new tragedy, his biological identity subverted into a marginal fiction.[2] Himself speaking *as* Tom o'Bedlam, Edmund sees his own way to "eclipse" the *sol*, the true son, reversing sides of the biological distinction between them. Edmund has therefore *named* both the true son and heir—"Legitimate Edgar"—and his antithetical displacement, the pathetic figure of exile—"Tom o'Bedlam"—whose name is not a unique name but a generic label, because Poor Tom is all that is left over when "Legitimate Edgar" vanishes. Indeed, the change in epithets—from "legitimate" to "poor"—signals how Edgar falls from hierarchical privilege to marginality.

Edmund's forgeries quickly work their way on Gloucester, who asks of Edgar incredulously, "Would he deny his letter[?]" He doesn't wait for Edmund to reassure him, but rushes to the awful conclusion, "I never got him" (2.1.78). Edgar's biological identity as son—the fact that he was "got" by Gloucester— is renounced, as Lear does his bond to Cordelia, as if it were merely an arbitrary convenience, a matter of the "letter" rather than of blood, and so Edmund becomes the son and heir now. Edmund has indeed produced Edgar's very "character" (1.2.63), taken over his voice, his role, his name, and now his place in his father's

---

[2] The Quarto here reads "them of Bedlam" rather than the "*Tom* o'Bedlam" of the Folio; if "them" is not simply a compositor's misreading, this revision may suggest an attempt to equate Edmund's assumed voice and Edgar's enforced role even more closely. Edmund's own heritage as a Vice figure and the tradition of the Vice's histrionic powers are fully outlined in Spivack.

eyes; that is one reason why Gloucester will have to lose them. When Edmund gains "no less than all" (3.3.24), his brother and his father are left with no more than nothing.

Edmund's sudden hierarchical rise represents a triumph over his earlier obsession with merely biological reproduction. In forging Edgar's "character," Edmund forces his father to renounce what is natural and to engage in a kind of social reproduction instead—to *name* his (other) son *as heir*. Legitimacy has now been decoupled from the natural body, the "order of law" set aside as arbitrary. It is at precisely this point, however, that we may ask what, exactly, does Edmund gain at the moment of his triumph? The answer is that *Edmund* gains "nothing." He has become at best a ventriloquist, speaking someone else's words, bearing someone else's name. He succeeds (in all senses of the term) only *as* Edgar. Moreover his accession to this particular form of power stems from a violent deviation from the very system that mediates this power. Edmund's project is doomed by self-annihilating contradictions from its inception. Edgar, on the other hand, falls from his status as the son "by order of law" to that of an outlaw exposed to "the winds and persecutions of the sky" (2.3.12), from privilege to persecution.[3] When the legitimate body of the son and heir is displaced, the play reveals its translation into man as mere body, as Poor Tom.

Long before we see Poor Tom's naked, suffering body, the play has emphasized the ways in which the physical body functions as a contradictory signifier. The play opens with Gloucester displaying Edmund— the body that is both the result of, the public sign of, and the eventual punishment of Gloucester's physical and spiritual sin. But the physical results here are deceiving, already decoupled from the moral, for Edmund is handsome (Kent: "the issue of it being so proper," 1.1.17–18). Edmund will in fact employ the appearance of his body as proof of his fitness to be true son and heir, using nature, as it were, to justify or determine the order of law:

> Why bastard? Wherefore base?
> When my dimensions are as well compact,
> My mind as generous, and my shape as true,
> As honest madam's issue?

$$(1.2.6-9)$$

---

[3] The play links Gloucester's and Edgar's descents in several ways, and their roles as reflectors of Lear's suffering have been frequently documented. See, for example, Bradley (215–16), Mack (71–73), and Burckhardt (238).

Indeed, he argues, he is superior to the "whole tribe of fops" who are "legitimate" because he was created "in the lusty stealth of nature" and therefore takes "more composition and fierce quality" than those conceived legitimately (lines 14, 11).

Throughout the play, Edmund will rely on his body—and particularly its sexual attractiveness, its "fierce quality"—as much as his wit to advance him. Goneril and Regan feud over him, each worrying whether he has found the "way / To the forfended place" (5.1.10–11) with the other, each claiming him before the other in a public scene. Edmund then reenacts with them the same fatal quantification and attempted division of love—though now in a grotesque physical mockery—which he has himself suffered, and which Lear has already perpetrated in the opening scene:

> To both these sisters have I sworn my love,
> Each jealous of the other as the stung
> Are of the adder. Which of them shall I take?
> Both? One? Or neither? Neither can be enjoyed
> If both remain alive.
>
> (5.1.58–62)

Edmund would have to give each half his "love," but the play keeps showing, as even he realizes, that love, by whatever name, cannot be divided. Edmund's method destabilizes the relation between the natural and the social, between his body and its place in a social hierarchy.

When Edmund has been fatally wounded by Edgar, and the news brought that Goneril and Regan are dead, there follows what is sometimes felt to be an awkward piece of Shakespearean staging, Albany's command to "Produce the bodies, be they alive or dead" (5.3.234); Goneril's and Regan's corpses are brought onstage several lines later. This staging can be defended as necessary to produce a terrible symmetry between the opening and the final scenes of the play—all three of the daughters onstage together again, with all the horrible ironies associated. I find this argument persuasive, but I would argue as well that it is the presence of the *body* that is essential here, the physical fact that drives home the point. Moreover, Albany offers the further command to "Cover their faces" (line 247), so that only their bodies remain visible. When Cordelia's body is brought on stage, by contrast, her face is *not* covered, for we always need to see Cordelia's lips, and she always represents more than simply her body: her words are all. With Goneril and Regan, however, we are left with the bodies *qua* bodies, for that is all they were and are. Edmund's body, moreover, is borne off the stage just as Cordelia's is brought on. His offstage death befits the disappearance of his role; no longer the Earl of Gloucester, his identity as son and heir taken back by Edgar, his body simply vanishes. His death is like his marginal social status, "but a trifle" (line 301).

The play's emphasis on the bodies of Edmund, Gloucester, Goneril, and Regan—to nature in its basest form—leads us inevitably to the body of Edgar as well: as the outcast beggar, he incarnates everything anti-thetical to the "order of law" represented in his initial identity. The name of loss and exile, of suffering and abasement, is Poor Tom. When Edmund becomes the son and heir, Edgar is left with nothing but his own body—the residue remaining once all the "bonds" of life and social order have been stripped away. Caroline Spurgeon long ago noted that perhaps the key recurring image in *King Lear* was that "of a human body in anguished movement, tugged, wrenched, beaten, pierced, stung, scourged, dislocated, flayed, gashed, scalded, tortured and finally broken on the rack" (339). Such a body is quite literally before us in the middle of the play in the figure of Poor Tom.

Much recent commentary has been very critical of Edgar's actions while in the disguise of Poor Tom, though there are still strong defenders of Edgar's essential goodness throughout.[4] Still, even those who find fault with Edgar have tended to sentimentalize or even ignore the meaning of the disguise as Poor Tom. I would emphasize, however, how nasty and repulsive Tom o'Bedlam might have seemed to Shakespeare's audience, and suggest at least one reason why Shakespeare chose this particular disguise for Edgar rather than some other. Most accounts of Poor Tom take the connection (or lack of it) between Edgar and Poor Tom as their subject,[5] but it might be useful to think of Poor Tom by himself for a moment. For most of Shakespeare's audience, Tom o'Bedlam would not

---

[4] A representative negative view of Edgar may be found in Rosenberg, who questions Edgar's stated motives throughout while arguing for the presence of "motives of revenge and punishment" (266); "Edgar," he says, "hates well" (245). To Goldberg, Edgar "is the most lethal character in the play" (121). For Cavell, "Edgar's capacity for cruelty" is "the *same* cruelty as that of the evil characters" (283). The sentimentalizing tradition of the ideal Edgar is of much longer standing but equally one-sided. To Peers, "Edgar is Shakespeare at his best and truest—he rings true—we may even say that he stands for Truth itself" (173). Granville-Barker concludes that Edgar became "a man of character indeed, modest, of a discerning mind, and, in this pagan play, a very Christian gentle-man" (213). Two other essays, by Adelman (1978) and Berger, have presented a more complex and, to me, a more persuasive view of Edgar.

[5] Adelman: "Despite Edgar's attempt to keep himself separate from Poor Tom, the likeness between Edgar and Poor Tom is finally as striking as the difference" (1978: 15).

be a figure to pity, but one to flee; not just a Dickensian figure reduced in circumstances by an unjust social order, but also something of a charlatan. That Tom *becomes* pitiable and a figure eliciting our sympathy is more the result of our seeing Edgar *within* Tom; on the surface, Tom o'Bedlam is a figure of disturbing deformity. As Michael Goldman has noted, Edgar is the kind of beggar "that you pay . . . to go away . . . and certainly not the decent young man down on his luck that actors frequently portray him to be. He is the kind that sticks his stump in your face" (97–98).[6] If we can overcome the terror of the body that Tom represents, and even care for his welfare, as Lear learns to do, so much greater the triumph.

Poor Tom is a lunatic beggar, supposedly an escaped or released inmate of Bedlam Hospital, as we have seen (Fig. 9). For many Elizabethans he was thus also a stereotype of the con-man. As an Abraham Man, he was described as one who "faineth him selfe mad" (Awdeley: 3). Or, as Harman put it, Abraham Men "faine themselves to have beene mad, and have bene kept either in Bethelem or in some other prison a good time, and not one amongst twenty that ever came in prison for any such cause" (47).

In many contemporary accounts, these men are a species of actor—costumes, rhetoric, feigned gestures, and familiar street plots remain the same within the individual variation.[7] "Every one of these *Abr'ams* hath a several gesture in playing his part," Dekker reports in *O per se O*. "Some make an horrid noise hollowly sounding, some whoop, some holler, some show only a kind of wild distracted ugly look." The cumulative effect, Dekker says, is that these men "walking up and down the country are more terrible to women and children than the name of Raw-head and Bloody-bones, Robin Goodfellow or any other hobgoblin. Crackers tied to a dog's tail make not the poor cur run faster than these Abr'am ninnies do the silly villages of the country, so that when they come to any door a-begging, nothing is denied them" (Pendry 1968: 292, 291).

Peck: "Edgar capitalizes on this mad role of the sin-infected man to make of his 'Poor Tom of Bedlam' identity a kind of scapegoat" (228).

[6] Goldman insists that on the stage "Edgar must be filthy, grotesque, very nearly naked, and bear on his body evidence of horrible mutilation" (97). Cf. Rosenberg on the theatrical necessity of Edgar's nakedness: "The visible, anguished, animal body enduring physical pain is again central to the ritual design, though its caperings and language may be grotesquely comic" (217).

[7] Dekker describes the costume: "He goes without breeches; a cut jerkin with hanging sleeves in imitation of our gallants—but no satin or camlet elbows, for both his legs and arms are bare . . . a face staring like a Saracen; his hair long and filthily knotted . . . a good . . . 'staff' of grown ash or else hazel in his . . . 'hand' " (Pendry 1968: 290–91).

Figure 9. Poor Tom of Bedlam. C20f7, Roxburghe Ballads, Ballad 352. By permission of the British Library.

Both the rogue pamphlets and official documents frequently mention the mutilated bodies of these Bedlamites and warn against their fraud. Thus in *The Bel-Man of London*, Dekker describes one of them who

> sweares he hath bin in bedlam, and will talke frantickly of purpose; you see pinnes stuck in sundry places of his naked flesh, especially in his armes, which paine hee gladly puts himselfe to . . . onely to make you beleeve he is out of his wits: he calls himselfe by the name of *Poore Tom* and comming neere any body, *cryes* out, *Poore Tom* is a cold. (1963: 3.101)

Some contemporaries even provided, in a debunking if voyeuristic spirit, recipes and advice on temporary self-mutilation. Harrison describes the "making of corosives, and applieng the same to the more fleshie parts of their bodies: and also laieng of ratsbane, sperewort, crowfoot, and such like unto their whole members, thereby to raise pitifull and odious sores, and moove the harts of the goers by such places where they lie, to yerne at their miserie, and thereupon bestow large almesse upon them" (Holinshed: 1.308). In *O per se O*, Dekker observes that some of them

> have the letters E and R upon their arms; some have crosses and some other mark, all of them carrying a blue colour. . . . Which marks are printed upon their flesh by tying their arm hard with two strings three or four inches asunder and then with a sharp awl pricking or razing the skin to such a figure or print as they best fancy. They rub that place with burnt paper, piss and gunpowder which, being hard rubbed in and suffered to dry, sticks in the flesh a long time after. When these marks fail they renew them at pleasure. If you examine them, how these letters or figures are printed upon their arms, they will tell you it is the mark of Bedlam, but the truth is they are made as I have reported. (Pendry 1968: 291–92)

The self-mutilations of these fraudulent beggars are deeply ironic, for these marks become the self-confirming stigmata of those excluded from society; they write their humiliation at large on their skins as an acceptance of what the social order has already inscribed them to be. Moreover, those beggars with the letters *E* and *R*—presumably for "Elizabeth Regina"—mock their "natural" subjection to sovereignty by counterfeiting it.

Two points stand out in this strange eventful social history. First, Poor Tom of Bedlam, as we saw here as well as in chapter 3, was a widely known figure, a social stereotype of the underclass; he is described, and reviled, in both popular and legal literature from the mid-sixteenth century on. If he later becomes sentimentalized (the "Loving Mad Tom" of the ballads), there is no doubt that he began life primarily as a fraud.[8] Rather than eliciting pity, this particular type of vagabond seemed to excite something more in the way of amusement, fear, and contempt. It would not be too much to say, in the end, that the role of Poor Tom was usually conceived of by the culture at large as a theatrical fiction.[9]

The second point that stands out in the history of Poor Tom, and which takes on the utmost importance in *King Lear*, is the emphasis, through Tom, on the body. Poor Tom of Bedlam is, after all, allegedly someone who has lost his mind, and so has only his body left, his language fractured into disordered fragments. The mutilations of his body reflect this disorder and monstrosity. Above all, Poor Tom *used* his body as a means of forcing his will on the populace, by assaulting men's senses: people give them money partly out of sympathy, but mostly "for feare . . . largely to be rid of theim," Harman notes (47); "when they come to any door a-begging," Dekker concurs, "nothing is denied them."

Nothing is denied them: no wonder Edgar, who has become nothing by being denied, finds Poor Tom such an appropriate disguise. Against these contemporary accounts of Poor Tom, let me now quote Edgar's soliloquy as he turns himself into a Shakespearean Poor Tom:

> Whiles I may scape
> I will preserve myself, and am bethought
> To take the basest and most poorest shape
> That ever penury, in contempt of man,
> Brought near to beast. My face I'll grime with filth,
> Blanket my loins, elf all my hairs in knots,
> And with presented nakedness outface

---

[8] See the remarkable collection, *Loving Mad Tom: Bedlamite Verses of the XVI and XVII Centuries*. All of these songs are later than 1605; even Edgar/Poor Tom's cries of pain were sentimentalized, showing up in comedies and entertainments in the later seventeenth and eighteenth centuries. Isaac D'Israeli noted that "Poems composed in the character of a Tom-o'-Bedlam appear to have formed a fashionable class of poetry among the wits; they seem to have held together their poetical contests, and some of these writers became celebrated for their successful efforts." In *The Compleat Angler*, he notes, Izaak Walton refers to "Mr William Basse as one who has made the songs of the *Hunter in his Career*, and of *Tom-o'-Bedlam*, and many others of note" (Logan: 173).

[9] Approaching the play from his analysis of Harsnett and the fraudulent Catholic exorcisms of 1585–86, Greenblatt notes that "Shakespeare appropriates for Edgar a documented fraud," a model of "inauthenticity" (1988: 117). After reviewing archival and historical documents, on the other hand, Beier cautions that "such contradictory evidence suggests that it would be unwise to accept the literary portrayal of all Tom O'Bedlam men as impostors" (1985: 117).

> The winds and persecutions of the sky.
> The country gives me proof and precedent
> Of Bedlam beggars who with roaring voices
> Strike in their numbed and mortified arms
> Pins, wooden pricks, nails, sprigs of rosemary;
> And with this horrible object, from low farms,
> Poor pelting villages, sheepcotes, and mills,
> Sometimes with lunatic bans, sometimes with prayers,
> Enforce their charity. Poor Turlygod! Poor Tom!
> That's something yet. Edgar I nothing am.
>
> (*King Lear* 2.3.5–21)

Edgar's self-description follows the tradition closely, as he takes on the part with all its theatrical implications—grimed face, presented nakedness, roaring voice—and disappears into "nothing," into Tom's body. The gap between Tom's "basest and most poorest shape" (1.7) and Edmund's "shape as true, / As honest madam's issue" (1.2.8–9) seems absolute.

During the heath scene, Lear says to, or of, Tom, "Thou wert better in a grave than to answer with thy uncovered body this extremity of the skies" (3.4.100–102). For Lear, though not for those aware of who Tom is, the beggar's shivering, near-naked body is "the thing itself; unaccommodated man is no more but such a poor, bare, forked animal as thou art" (3.4.105–7). Lear's vision is powerful but incomplete: when he asks of Tom, "Is man no more than this?" (lines 101–2), we want to reply "Yes, much more," for the entire role of Poor Tom, as we have seen, is a complicated fiction. Tom is *always* "more than this," because he is always Edgar-as-Tom, and Edgar-as-Tom's suffering is in part a *performance* of marginality, exclusion, and dispossession. What seems to be the basest shape of nature is also seen by the audience to be a social construct: a stereotypical beggar's role fantastically performed by an Edgar who far out-tops even his brother's histrionic genius.

Yet "sophisticated" as he is, Edgar nevertheless still feels, in all its real pain, the role he performs. The burden of both playing and being such a creature as Poor Tom is very heavy for Edgar, the more so because Edgar's impersonation of Poor Tom is a particularly graphic and horrifying instance. "What are you there?" Gloucester asks, and Edgar tells him, with a vengeance:

> Poor Tom, that eats the swimming frog, the toad, the tadpole, the wall
> newt and the water; that in the fury of his heart, when the foul fiend

rages, eats cow dung for salads, swallows the old rat and the ditch-dog,
drinks the green mantle of the standing pool; who is whipped from tithing to tithing and stock-punished, and imprisoned; who hath had three
suits to his back, six shirts to his body,

> Horse to ride, and weapon to wear;
> But mice and rats and such small deer
> Have been Tom's food for seven long year.

(3.4.128–38)[10]

Tom seems little more than an embodied mouth here, a paradigm of
mere appetite which eats and drinks the scum of nature. This relentless
emphasis on the physical body—what it ingests, how it is punished, what
it wears—marks Tom's complete fall to the bottom of the lake of darkness, making Lear's belief that "our basest beggars / Are in the poorest
thing superfluous" (2.4.266–67) seem optimistic by comparison. To be
Tom at all is to feign *and* to endure grotesque physical torment.

The play's insistence on the suffering of the body is not confined to
the Gloucester plot, to be sure, but it is represented most intensely there.
Certainly Lear, Kent, and Cordelia endure their own physical tortures.
As terrible as it is to shut an old man out in a storm, however, Lear's
greatest punishments, in keeping with the nature of his transgression, are
suffered in the heart. "We are not ourselves," he says, "when nature,
being oppressed, commands the mind / To suffer with the body"
(2.4.105–7). When an image of bodily torture is used with respect to
Lear, such as the "rack," it is the rack "of this tough world" (5.3.320),
but it is Gloucester who is physically bound, tormented, and blinded.
When Lear feels as if he is "bound / Upon a wheel of fire, that mine
own tears / Do scald like molten lead" (4.7.47–49), his suffering is in-
ternalized, the image figurative, though no less powerful or "real." And
when Lear is cut, he is "cut to th' brains" (4.6.193), in an exquisite
agony of suffering and despair, but it is Poor Tom who would actually
lacerate his "numbed and mortified arms," and Edmund who will enact
the "queasy question" (2.1.17) by cutting his own arm while claiming
that Edgar "with his prepared sword he charges home / My unprovided
body, latched mine arm" (2.1.50–51). For Edgar, Lear's insight that
"when the mind's free, / The body's delicate" (3.4.11–12) is transformed into overwhelming bodily pain as a cause, consequence, and sign
of mental suffering.

---

[10] The verbal links to other characters in the play—Kent is also "stock-punished" in
2.2, Oswald is called "three-suited" at 2.2.15—again make Edgar's experience refract
that of others.

The great irony of the figure of Poor Tom is that while it is his body that endures mutilation and deprivation, it is Edgar's spirit that is trapped within, and Edgar—who would "the pain of death . . . hourly die / Rather than die at once" (5.3.189–90)—suffers spiritually. Many readers have always seen Tom as the embodiment of Edgar's suffering even as he is also a way of escaping it,[11] but we should also recognize how Poor Tom is in a sense the *cause* of Edgar's suffering. Edgar's suffering is both released and caused by his performance of Tom's suffering.

To be Poor Tom is Edgar's trial. And in becoming as it were all body, subjected to nature, Edgar is forced to live out a grotesque version of what it must be like to be Edmund. Poor Tom's sufferings are therefore not only Edgar's—it is clear how his own personal pain is transmitted through this hideous disguise—but they are Edmund's as well. Displacement links them together, as does their fate to be nothing more than natural bodies, forbidden by law or culture from any place in the social hierarchy; Edmund's bastardy and Edgar's vagrancy are mirrored forms of arbitrary social exclusion. The link between Edmund and Poor Tom is thus both implicit—Poor Tom appears only when Edmund has displaced Edgar and disappears when the son and heir is reunited with his father—and explicit, since Edmund first performs the voice of Poor Tom. Facing yet another banishment by his father—"He hath been out nine years, and away he shall again" (1.1.32–33)—Edmund has carefully engineered his plot so that he and his brother will be forced to exchange places: the category of "sonne and heir" and social outcast will be reversed; "the base / Shall top th'legitimate" (1.2.20–21) only to replace it. Edgar has not chosen this enforced role—no explicit motive is articulated for him—but it fits him perfectly.

The place where Edgar is freed and Poor Tom vanishes is Dover Cliff. Poor Tom of Bedlam is both "some fiend," as Edgar says (4.6.72), and "a poor unfortunate beggar" (line 68), as Gloucester says, and in 4.6 Edgar is released from the "fiend." The process begins with Gloucester's unexpected tenderness, when he asks the Old Man leading him to "bring some covering for this naked soul, / Which I'll entreat to lead me" (4.1.44–45). The significance of the clothing theme, as R. B. Heilman (67–87) and others have shown, is reflected on several interpretive levels,

---

[11] Adelman argues that Edgar "tries more insistently than any other character to gain some distance on suffering, and hence relief from it" (1978: 3), and that "Edgar's disguises throughout are emblematic partly of Edgar's own distance from what he can recognize as himself" (19).

but I am interested in it here on the most literal of levels: the "naked soul" will be clothed, the body veiled.

Although he continues on as Poor Tom through 4.6, Edgar almost immediately, upon Gloucester's request to the Old Man in 4.1, begins to emerge from the body of Poor Tom. It is not Tom the "fiend" but the poor unfortunate beggar "whom the heavens' plagues / Have humbled to all strokes" (4.1.63–64) who stands in Gloucester's imagination, a Poor Tom whom the devils have released and who therefore has begun the process of turning back into Edgar. That process of self-return is dramatically accelerated in 4.6, beginning with Edgar's entrance wearing clothes. To Gloucester's sense that Edgar's "voice is altered," he deviously and ambiguously replies, "You're much deceived. In nothing am I changed / But in my garments" (4.6.7–10).

Most discussions of the Dover Cliff scene have focused either on the nature of Edgar's motivation toward his father—"Why I do trifle thus with his despair / Is done to cure it" (4.6.33–34), he says—or on the staging of the scene and its illusory quality.[12] I would like to consider the scene also as a "cure" or final exorcism of Poor Tom. In one way, the cure has already occurred: Tom has spoken of the five fiends once in his body, now apparently gone, and he entered 4.6 with new clothing and altered speech. The famous image that Edgar creates of the view from the cliff ("the crows and choughs that wing the midway air / Show scarce so gross as beetles") contains perhaps more detail than even Gloucester needs to convince him of where he stands (he has condemned his true son on less). The perspective Edgar imagines which makes a man seem "no bigger than his head" and the "fishermen that walk upon the beach / Appear like mice" (lines 16–18) is created, I think, as much for Edgar's own sake as it is for Gloucester's. This view of man "brought near to beast," in which there is no sign of a human figure but only crows, choughs, beetles, and mice, represents both Gloucester's view of the world as he prepares to attempt suicide and Edgar's experience as Poor Tom. When Edgar says, "I'll look no more, / Lest my brain turn, and the deficient sight / Topple down headlong" (lines 22–24), he is not only trying to convince Gloucester that they are "within a foot / Of th'extreme verge" (lines 25–26), but speaking for himself as he turns away from the role of Tom.

---

[12] On the staging, see among others Levin, Kernan, Rosenberg (264–65), Dessen, and Peat. On the cliff scene's iconoclastic nature, see the stimulating discussion by Siemon (1985: 269–73).

After Gloucester's dramatic "fall," Edgar asks his father the same question ("What are you, sir?" 4.6.48) that his father had directed at him when he was Poor Tom ("What are you there? Your names?" 3.4.127). The fall from top to bottom, "so many fathom down" (4.6.50), is also a refraction of Edgar's fall, who as Poor Tom was "fathom and half" down. For Edgar, the fall as Poor Tom is over, his life also a miracle. When Edgar describes to his father the figure he was, standing at the top of the cliff, he turns out to have been a kind of cosmological monster:

> As I stood here below, methought his eyes
> Were two full moons; he had a thousand noses,
> Horns whelked and waved like the enridged sea.
> It was some fiend.
>
> (4.6.69–72)

As a paradigm of a demonized beggar, Poor Tom's was the body of a nightmare. But the "fiend" left behind on the cliff is gone forever. When Gloucester returns the iterated question of identity back on Edgar later in the scene—"Now, good sir, what are you?" (4.6.223)—Edgar's response completes the full transition from the fiend to a more sympathetic portrait of human suffering. His reply is evocative of both his father's and of Lear's new-found capacities to *feel*: "A most poor man, made lame by fortune's blows, / Who, by the art of known and feeling sorrows, / Am pregnant to good pity" (4.6.224–26).[13]

Edgar's transition from the role of suffering madman to his father's active guide receives an immediate test in the challenge of Oswald, who enters the scene exactly at the moment that Edgar's identity has shifted: pat he comes like the catastrophe of the old morality. Now Edgar plays a "bold peasant" (4.6.234) to Oswald and adopts a country dialect. He has risen on the social scale above the level of beast and beggar, but he remains "a most poor man," displaced from the court, where he was heir to an earl. "Good gentleman," he humbly asks Oswald, "let poor volk pass" (4.6.239–40), but the poor have no rights of passage in this play. Edgar's judgment upon Oswald, whom he easily kills, is that he was "a serviceable villain" (255)—the adjective of course linking Oswald with Edmund. Throughout the play Oswald has represented one of the deepest perversions of human bonds, the destruction of "service" in its widest

---

[13] I prefer the Quarto's "lame by" to the Folio's "tame to" because it reinforces the subplot's emphasis on the physical body, and because the "poor man" who is "lame" is a standard beggar type.

sense, and Poor Tom described his own history in terms that recall Oswald and Edmund in particular:

> A servingman, proud in heart and mind, that curled my hair, wore gloves in my cap, served the lust of my mistress' heart, and did the act of darkness with her; swore as many oaths as I spake words, and broke them in the sweet face of heaven. One that slept in the contriving of lust and waked to do it. Wine loved I deeply, dice dearly, and in woman outparamoured the Turk. False of heart, light of ear, bloody of hand; hog in sloth, fox in stealth, wolf in greediness, dog in madness, lion in prey.
> (3.4.84–93)

Poor Tom's self-description emphasizes the body in all ways—the vanity of physical appearance, the urgings of the sensual appetite, the bestial identification. He describes his life as a fall: from serving-man to beggar, from the court to the heath, from vanity to madness, from a place in the hierarchy to the level of the beasts.[14] Edgar-as-Tom's description of his earlier life as son and heir transforms it into its opposite, that of a "servingman," his former position of hierarchical privilege now seen to be really one of subservience. In slaying Oswald, Edgar destroys yet another parodic alter ego of Edmund.

The final confrontation between the true son and heir and the new son and heir occurs in a scene of ritual combat; as in any doppelganger tale, one must be vanquished. Summoned by the third sound of the trumpet, Edgar appears as an unknown but noble soldier. As we might expect, only his body can be seen, for his face is covered, his anonymity and facelessness a reflection of Edmund's own marginality and emptiness. Edmund knows better than to trust a fair shape, but does so anyway, seeming to find something naturally noble in the figure before him:

> In wisdom I should ask thy name.
> But since thy outside looks so fair and warlike,
> And that thy tongue some say of breeding breathes,
> What safe and nicely I might well delay
> By rule of knighthood, I disdain and spurn.
>
> (5.3.144–48)

---

[14] As several readers have noticed, Kent's verbal attack on Oswald in 2.2 corresponds closely to Tom's self-description; see for example Kirschbaum (15).

Had Edmund indeed asked him his name, it would have done little good. Edgar's response to the Herald's now familiar question of identity, "What are you? / Your name, your quality[?]" is necessarily cryptic, reflecting his still indeterminate place in any hierarchy:

> Know my name is lost,
> By treason's tooth bare-gnawn and canker-bit.
> Yet am I noble as the adversary
> I come to cope.
>
> (5.3.122–27)

The distinction made between his name and the knowledge of his own nobility is not merely paradoxical, for now his name "by order of law"—with his father dead off-stage—*is* the Earl of Gloucester, a name however now appropriated by Edmund. Moreover, his name is clearly something separable from his body: it can be "lost," and found again. When Edmund forgives his still unknown assailant after their battle and pronounces his own death, Edgar is at last allowed to reclaim his status as the son and heir:

> Let's exchange charity.
> I am no less in blood than thou art, Edmund;
> If more, the more th'hast wronged me.
> My name is Edgar, and thy father's son.
>
> (5.3.169–72)

But if Edgar is "no less in blood" than his brother, then there is a kind of equality between them, and Edmund's chief motive for doing evil has been a colossal mistake. Of course Edgar is "more" in blood, in the sense of nature, yet he speaks here as if he might be less—as if he were Edmund. He speaks, then, no longer from a privileged but from a marginal position, reclaiming his name as if it were only a piece of missing property—we might recall, for contrast, Hamlet's more forceful, "This is I, / Hamlet the Dane" (*Hamlet* 5.1.257–58).

The uniqueness of Edgar's proper name—already compromised in the repetition of the "Ed" sound in Edmund's—is further diluted by the odd grammar of his speech, so that his *full* name is really two things: "Edgar and thy father's son." In this formulation, the uniqueness of "Edgar" is subverted by the ambiguity of "thy father's son," since Edmund himself fulfills that category as well. Edgar's claim, moreover, is expressed in the most indirect way possible: he tells Edmund that he,

Edgar, is "thy father's son." While this establishes a human and fraternal bond with Edmund, it is also a displacement of his identity, through the father and the half-brother, elevating Edmund to co-equal status and implying that Gloucester was first Edmund's father. Again, it sounds as if it is the claim Edmund would make, as Edgar seems to give away the very principles that made him son and heir. It is as if Edgar has realized the arbitrariness within the system of social privilege and can no longer claim his body as an absolute against which the social order must be measured; rather the reverse seems the case now. He has *been* Poor Tom long enough to know the pain of dispossession, and in returning as Edgar he seems vastly more tentative now. The apparent allegorical clarity of the ritual battle with Edmund is soon complicated by Edmund's change of heart, and by Edgar's ineffectualness at the end of the play.

Edgar's self-denial does not extend much further, however. His experience of dispossession has perhaps allowed him a deeper vision of the world, but his moral judgment on Edmund and Gloucester is harsh indeed:

> The gods are just, and of our pleasant vices
> Make instruments to plague us.
> The dark and vicious place where thee he got
> Cost him his eyes.
>
> (5.3.173–76)

Edmund's ready agreement—"Th'hast spoken right. 'Tis true"—may surprise more liberal modern audiences, but by this point we should really expect that the subplot will insist on an unforgiving economy of the body, in which a bodily sin redounds upon the body, one dark place leading to another.

Edgar is our guide to one kind of suffering throughout the play—the pain of the body—his body as Poor Tom not just an instance of but also an enforced performance of extreme pain and deprivation. There is nothing at all ironic in this role, and yet the nature of Poor Tom has reflected ironically on Lear. Poor Tom's only function is to beg, but more than that, to use the horror of his deformity and degradation to make us feel guilty, to make us question the integrity of our own bodies; such beggars, Edgar said, would "enforce their charity" (2.3.20). This formulation presents undoubtedly the most powerful oxymoron in the play—the idea that anyone could "enforce" charity.[15]

---

[15] The word "charity" is used only in the subplot, where it refracts the failure of love so evident in the main plot: Tom bids us, "Do poor Tom some charity" (3.4.59), Gloucester wishes that "my charity be not of him perceived" (3.3.16), and Edgar, after he has

As Poor Tom, Edgar *performed* the role of suffering and marginalization, but also profoundly experienced it, just as the counterfeit madmen of the period may have feigned self-mutilations that were essentially indistinguishable from the real thing. This disguise is an escape for Edgar, because it saves his life; it is a release for him, because it allows his own bitter fury to be anonymously released through the madman's voice; it is a deep necessity, because through it he can beg for the love that has been denied him; and finally it is a torment to him, as much the cause as the relief of his suffering. To be dispossessed, to be stripped of all social bonds, to be reduced to the basest and most poorest shape, to surrender one's body to the winds and persecutions of the sky—this experience of alienation forces Edgar to feel what it must, in part, be like to be his bastard brother Edmund. These half-brothers exchange the voice of dispossession in the course of the play: as Edgar disappears into Tom when Edmund becomes Earl of Gloucester, so Edmund disappears altogether when Edgar becomes Earl of Gloucester.

At the very end, the biological order of succession has been shattered, and the legal order of succession is abrogated. No one looks much like a king: Lear is dead, Kent dying, Albany ineffectual and blind, Edgar mostly a bystander and, presumably, succeeding to the throne only through catastrophe.[16] Nevertheless, through his suffering Edgar can be said to have earned it; the way down, through Poor Tom, has been the way up. The wonder is he hath endured so long.

By the time Lear falls to his knees in prayer for the "houseless poverty" in 3.2, Shakespeare has made him experience "Necessity's sharp pinch" (2.4.212) in a number of cruelly appropriate ways. The primitive grandeur of the court in the opening scene has quickly given way to a savage subtraction of everything Lear had ever possessed. In giving away his land as king, Lear discovers, as Richard Halpern notes, that "he has given away all, for the kingship is nothing more than the power that accrued to him from owning the kingdom" (222).[17] Without land, then, the king

---

mortally wounded Edmund and in response to Edmund's forgiveness, says "Let's exchange charity" (5.3.169). To "enforce" charity seems to be a continuing concern in the subplot. Saltonstall (1631) says of the "wandring Rogue" (not a specifically Bedlam beggar) that he "extorts a benevolence rather for feare than charity" (39).

[16] Clearly, I accept the Folio's attribution of the final four lines to Edgar rather than the Quarto's attribution of them to Albany.

[17] Halpern argues further that "*Lear* is perhaps the most demystifying, indeed materialist, of Shakespeare's meditations on kingship . . . kingly authority is not only legitimated but constituted by landownership" (222). Halpern also notes that "Tom and the heath form an ideological couplet, the personification and landscape of dearth, the zero

is "nothing": this is the same equation that Edgar, whose very identity seems constituted by his property, discovers so quickly. For Lear, though, the process of this discovery is much more drawn-out and painful. The storm begins after Goneril completes the stripping away of the hundred knights. They have become the remaining substance and the material sign of Lear's royal authority and wealth, and when they vanish Lear will possess, and nearly become, nothing himself. It is at this point that Lear summons up his inverted image, fast becoming his double: "Our basest beggars / Are in the poorest thing superfluous" (2.4.266–67).

Shakespeare engineers the action of the play so that Lear falls into actual, not just figurative, madness at the precise moment that he hears Poor Tom's voice answering his prayer in 3.4. In almost every production of the play, Marvin Rosenberg notes, this is the point at which "Lear is visualized slipping—or breaking—into madness, and the reason is not only that Poor Tom appears, but how" (205).[18] I would shift the emphasis here, however, from the implication that Poor Tom somehow *causes* Lear's madness by his voice and/or appearance to the symbolic inevitability of this confrontation of king and beggar—no longer opposites but now equals, yet neither quite what he seems to be. Edgar's survival in madman's rags, "a semblance / That very dogs disdained" (5.3.191–92), finds an equivalent in Lear's vision of "the little dogs and all, / Tray, Blanch, and Sweetheart, see, they bark at me" (3.6.61–62). Lear now sees in a mirror, darkly, as he asks of Poor Tom, "Didst thou give all to thy daughters? And art thou come to this? . . . Couldst thou save nothing[?]" (3.4.48–49, 62). But of course "nothing" is the only thing that can remain once one "give[s] 'em all" (line 63). For Lear, Poor Tom becomes himself, the rejected father, as well as a "philosopher" and "learned Theban" (lines 152, 155), and eventually a "most learned justicer" (3.6.21). These inversions of patriarchal and monarchical authority serve, among other ends, to fill up or write over the awful nothingness of the "lake of darkness" (3.6.7), the nothing that Lear has become.

As Lear and Gloucester wander the heath, the image or presence of Edgar-as-Poor Tom links them together. So Gloucester's parallel prayer

---

sum reduced to the zero degree. At least, so Lear reads Tom" (261). Halpern's entire chapter on *King Lear* is relevant to my argument.

[18] Rosenberg continues: "Actors who begin Lear as sane . . . invariably begin to shatter at Tom's entrance. This is a cataclysmic moment. . . . In the theatre, particularly to naive spectators, the scene becomes genuinely terrifying" (215). Neely also finds that this specific moment "manifests one of the places where the boundary between sanity and madness was defined and crossed" (333n.).

scene, in 4.1, responds to Poor Tom not so much as an image of madness as of spiritual despair:

> Here, take this purse, thou whom the heavens' plagues
> Have humbled to all strokes. That I am wretched
> Makes thee the happier. Heavens, deal so still!
> Let the superfluous and lust-dieted man,
> That slaves your ordinance, that will not see
> Because he does not feel, feel your pow'r quickly!
> So distribution should undo excess
> And each man have enough.
>
> (4.1.63–70)

Gloucester's prayer offers an even more radical critique of the extremes of wealth and poverty, in which the fat man, "superfluous and lust-dieted," is made to pay for his lack of charity. Gloucester may even be imagining a "distribution" that could level all distinction by undoing "excess"—by unmaking the social and economic hierarchy.[19] Yet Gloucester, still blind in many ways, never sees how he himself is implicated in this system, both at the top, as Earl of Gloucester, and now at the bottom, displaced by Edmund, confirmed as the new earl in the previous scene. Gloucester's prayer, moreover, is only the prelude for his journey to suicide at Dover.

If Gloucester can only "feel" injustice and "excess," Lear can now see it, even if only as a hallucination, when he summons the "yokefellow of equity" to join with his "robed man of justice" (3.6.37, 36). To re-establish "equity" in the world would require even more miracles than the Fool's prophecy imagines, but Lear at least begins to see and to recognize that the "order of law" and his own place in it have been subverted by his own actions. He responds to Gloucester's "I see it [how the world goes] feelingly" with a piercing analysis of the severance of power from moral and natural "right."

> A man may see how this world goes with no eyes. Look with thine ears.
> See how yond justice rails upon yond simple thief. Hark in thine ear:

---

[19] See Heinemann's account of the play's enactment of the "world turned upside down" trope. See also Kronenfeld's correction to current interpretations of the "radical" nature of Gloucester's "distribution should undo excess." She links the word "distribution" with traditions of alms giving rather than a prophetic communism taking private property for all. Her survey of contemporary attitudes toward charity is highly relevant.

change places and, handy-dandy, which is the justice, which is the thief?
Thou hast seen a farmer's dog bark at a beggar? . . . And the creature
run from the cur? There thou mightst behold the great image of authority: a dog's obeyed in office. (4.6.150–57)

No matter who holds the place of "authority," then, he will be obeyed;
the interchangeability of justice and thief rests on a conception of
"place"—of social position—as arbitrary, not natural. Yet no matter who
is in office the beggar's place is only to obey; nothing is beneath him.

Lear continues his analysis with a terrifying hallucination that modu-
lates into a cynical, though at the moment undeniable, perception of the
nature of justice and power.

> Thou rascal beadle, hold thy bloody hand!
> Why dost thou lash that whore? Strip thine own back;
> Thou hotly lusts to use her in that kind
> For which thou whipp'st her. The usurer hangs the cozener.
> Through tattered clothes small vices do appear;
> Robes and furred gowns hide all. Plate sin with gold,
> And the strong lance of justice hurtless breaks;
> Arm it in rags, a pygmy's straw does pierce it.
>
> (4.6.158–67)

In London it was chiefly in Bridewell, of course, that beadles regularly
whipped whores. Just as the justice and the thief might "change places,"
so now (in a gender reversal as well) might the beadle and the whore.
Justice itself has become a function of histrionic power: "Robes and
furred gowns hide all." Tudor sumptuary laws—whose authorizing statutes had lapsed in the year before *Lear* was written—were designed to
define and confirm, indeed to fix immutably, the exact signifying cor-
respondences between the representations of clothing and socioeconomic status; for example, no man under the degree of baron was
permitted to use any cloth of gold, cloth of silver, and so on. *King Lear*
exposes the arbitrariness of these signifiers in several ways, not only in
the inversion and critique of "robes and furred gowns," but also in the
beggar's very nakedness, for the beggar, as John Webster ironically notes,
"offends not the Statute against the excesse of apparell, for hee will goe
naked, and counts it a voluntary penance" (4.41).

Poor Tom vanishes from the play at the end of the fourth act, at the
same time that Lear's madness vanishes. Lear, Cordelia reports, was
"fain, poor Father, / To hovel thee with swine and rogues forlorn / In

short and musty straw" (4.7.39–41), but now awakes, as if in a dream, to hear himself addressed by his daughter as "royal lord . . . Your Majesty" (4.7.45). The "rogues forlorn," the vagabonds of the kingdom with whom Lear has slept, are transmuted in the final scene of the play to the "poor rogues [who] / Talk of court news" (5.3.13–14), not vagabonds now but men no less despicable and marginal from Lear's perspective. The difference between "packs and sects of great ones" (5.3.18) and Lear himself is now enormous. The confrontation with the lean beggar reveals many things about this old king, and suggests that, if nothing else, Lear learns that "the art of our necessities is strange, / And can make vile things precious" (3.2.70–71).

CHAPTER SEVEN

"Is Poverty a Vice?":
The Disguise of Beggary

Most "beggars" on the English Renaissance stage are not beggars at all, but gentry or noblemen in disguise, like Edgar in *King Lear*. But one difference between Edgar and the others is the signal lack of suffering on the part of the non-Shakespearean exemplars and even, in some cases, the presence of a positive merriment. Poverty is often merely a thematic, not a painfully felt deprivation. In Henry Chettle and John Day's *The Blind Beggar of Bednall Green* (c. 1600), a complex example of a romanticized counterfeit beggar may be seen in the virtuous Momford, who must return from the wars in France in disguise in order to penetrate and reveal the conspiracy against him. His plan is a familiar one, and it anticipates Edgar's disguise in *King Lear* in curious ways.

> I am exil'd, Yet I will England see,
> And live in England 'spight of my infamy.
> In some disguise I'll live, perhaps I'll turn
> A Beggar, for a Beggars life is best,
> His Diet is in each mans Kitchin drest.
>
> (lines 256–260)

An "expert in shapes," Momford deceives even his daughter Bess in his disguise. In a scene that is a mirror image reversal of Edgar's first encounter with his blind father Gloucester (who must be saved from "despair"), the father here feigns blindness and must save his child from despair:

> [Aside] My Daughter in dispair, then play thy part,
> Prevent her ills that did procure her smart,
> Alas where am I? how shall I return
> Unto my homely Cabbin? where's my boy?
> I prethee do not leave me gentle wag,
> Take pity of my miserable state.
>
> (lines 903–8)

Still, for Momford the role of the beggar is more than acceptable, because "a Beggars life is best" (line 259). In George Chapman's *The Blind Beggar of Alexandria* (c. 1596), the blind beggar Irus, who is said to be "most rich . . . in his povertie" and "in this barrennesse . . . most renound" (Sc. 1.87, 84), is really Duke Cleanthes in disguise (he plays several other roles as well), who has been banished for offering love to Aegiale, the queen of Egypt. The play concludes with his "happie end" (Sc. 10.176). In Francis Beaumont and John Fletcher's *The Captain* (c. 1610), the beggar is Lelia's father in disguise, looking like "another winde-fall of the warrs" (2.1.124). Scorned for his age and poverty ("Two sinnes that ever do out grow compassion," 1.3.93), the father disguises himself and triumphs over all, revealing himself in the final scene.

So too in Fletcher and Massinger's *Beggars' Bush*, the beggar Clause is the disguised "Gerrard, nobleman of Flanders" and two other noblemen, Ferret and Gynkes, also disguise themselves as beggars.[1] In this play, however, there are also real beggars, of the happy variety: Higgen, Prig, and Snap. The song of the beggars' holiday pronounces their freedom: "Here at liberty we are, / And enjoy our ease and rest; To the fields we are not prest; / Nor are call'd into the Towne, to be troubled with the Gowne" (2.1.146–48). Revealing himself at the end, Gerrard offers to help his low friends "finde / Some manly, and more profitable course / To fit them, as a part of the Republique" (5.2.204–6), but this token offer is rejected by the beggars. Higgen even suspects that something like Bridewell awaits them: "Yes, to beat hemp, and be whipt twice a weeke, / Or turne the wheele, for Crab the Rope-maker" (5.2.210–11). In Thomas Middleton's *The Spanish Gypsy* (1623), the old lord Alvarez de Castilla is disguised as the "captain" (2.1.23) of the gypsies, but these are nobler vagabonds than English ones, it is said, for they have renounced "filching, foisting, nimming, jilting," and crime in general (2.1.14–15).

---

[1] The date of this play is controversial. Bowers argues for a date c. 1612 (Beaumont and Fletcher: 3.227–45), while in his edition, Dorenkamp argues for a "late date" between 1613 and 22 December 1622, because he links the play to Massinger rather than Beaumont (Fletcher and Massinger: 38).

Among the other gentles in disguise are Constanza, Christiana, and Guia-mara, Alvarez's wife and known as the mother of the gypsies. At the end, Alvarez reveals himself to his enemy Louis, whose father he had killed; Louis, of course, is conquered by Alvarez's nobleness. In Jonson's *The Staple of News* (1626), the old "canter" is Frank Pennyboy in disguise (he has pretended to die), the father of the prodigal Pennyboy Junior. Eventually Frank reveals himself to his spendthrift son, and after Pennyboy Junior's repentance, father and son happily reunite. And in Jonson's *The New Inn*, the Host of the Inn is himself Lord Frampul in disguise, who has in his exile observed

> those wilder nations
> Of people in the *Peake*, and *Lancashire*
> Their Pipers, Fidlers, Rushers, Puppet-masters,
> Juglers, and Gipseys, all the sorts of Canters,
> And Colonies of beggars, Tumblers, Ape-carriers,
> For to these savages I was addicted,
> To search their natures, and make odde discoveries!
>
> (5.5.94–100)

The Host's fascination with the lower, marginally criminal orders was shared by many readers in early modern England. The "wilder nations / Of people" served as fodder for both fantasy and demonization in works ranging from the rogue pamphlets to governmental edicts.

One of the last—indeed, perhaps the *very* last (Brome: xi–xii)—plays acted before the closing of the theaters in 1642, Richard Brome's *A Jovial Crew*, transports a number of gentles into the disguise of beggary—Vincent, Hilliard, Rachel, and Meriel—but also includes a variety of supposedly "real" beggars, some with such generic names as "Autem-Mort" and "Patrico,"[2] though in most cases, they are merely fallen from a higher social position: one is a "decay'd poet," another formerly an "attorney," still another "a courtier born [who] begs on pleasure" (1.1.377, 383, 402). Eight decades after Awdeley and Harman first represented the beggars as various hypocritical types, Brome has his beggars sing merrily,

> From hunger and cold, who lives more free,
> Or who more richly clad than we?

---

[2] A "Patrico," according to Harman, "is a [counterfeit] priest that should make mariages till death did depart" (60); an "Autem-Mort" is "a wife maried at the Church, and they be as chaste as a Cowe I have, that goeth to Bull every moone" (67).

> Our bellies are full; our flesh is warm;
> And, against pride, our rags are a charm.
>
> (1.1.339–42)

These beggars "obey no governor, use no religion," yet, most important, they "are no rebels" (2.1.174–76). Although "now the countries swarm with 'em under every hedge, as if an innumerable army of 'em were lately disbanded without pay" (5.1.74–76), as one character notes, the play never investigates their real suffering in any way. At the end, all the beggars are given Justice Clack's "free pass, without all manner of correction!" (5.1.487–88). This fantasy of juridical forgiveness and good-willed unity certainly found no correlation at all in official discourse or governmental action in this period.[3]

The trope of the "noble disguised as beggar" led to familiar, recurring plot situations—joining a band of merry, even noble vagabonds; righting, through this disguise, some injustice or misfortune; a dramatic revelation scene; the restoration of the disguised figures to their "natural" and of course higher places in the social hierarchy.[4] Like *any* disguise in a romance plot, poverty is simply tossed aside at the end. The "real" beggars encountered, moreover, invariably reflect the paradigm of the rigidly organized hierarchy seen in the rogue pamphlets decades earlier. In *The Spanish Gypsy*, Alvarez is "your major-domo, your teniente [lieutenant], / Your captain, your commander" (2.1.22–23). Gerrard, as Clause in *Beggars' Bush*, is chosen as king of the beggars. Higgen, the Orator (his beggar type is, ironically, the speechless "Dommerer," 2.1.9), heralds Clause as "our King and Soveraign; Monarch o'th Maunders" (2.1.76), whose regal appearance signaled his worthiness when Higgen once saw him "gravely leaning on one Crutch, / Lift the other like a Scepter at my head" (2.1.87–88). The protection of Clause's bushy beard will usher in a rural utopia for the beggars:

> No impositions, taxes, grievances,
> Knots in a State, and whips unto a Subject,
> . . .
>   . . . under him
> Each man shall eate his own stolne eggs, and butter,

[3] *A Jovial Crew* is, to be sure, a more complex play than I have been able to indicate here. For an excellent analysis of its ideological ambivalence in the context of the 1640s, see Butler.

[4] Gaby examines the idea of a "beggars' commonwealth" in *Beggars' Bush, A Jovial Crew*, and Shirley's *The Sisters* (which has bandits rather than beggars).

> In his owne shade, or sun-shine, and enjoy
> His owne deare Dell, Doxy, or Mort, at night
> In his own straw, with his owne shirt, or sheet,
> That he hath filch'd that day.
>
> (2.1.105–6, 114–18)

This dream of political, sexual, and gustatory freedom is clearly preferable to the tyranny Prig promises "if e're I come to reigne" (2.1.17): he would straight "seize on all your Priviledges, / Places, revenues, offices as forfeit" (lines 24–25), take all their food, and deflower "all your daintiest dells too" (line 34). Beyond Prig's promise to be a "very tyrant" and Ferret's to be a "mercifull mild Prince" (lines 16, 15), or the prospect of "good King *Clause*" (line 139), however, the beggars can only imagine *some* form of sovereignty still over them; the "freedom" they seek remains an accidental of their essential powerlessness. The "Common-wealth" (1.3.164) of beggars is morally superior to the legitimate "official" one under the control of the usurper Woolfort, but Gerrard and the others automatically return to the official order at the end, once Woolfort has been exposed, and abandon the alternative commonwealth of the beggars, who will move on, they say, to take up residence in England.

In *A Jovial Crew*, Springlove praises the freedom of the state of beggary, only to be hailed by his unnamed jovial crew:

> *3 Beggar.* Will you make us happy in serving you? Have you any enemies?
>   Shall we fight under you? Will you be our captain?
> *2 Beggar.* Nay, our king.
> *3 Beggar.* Command us something, sir.
>
> (1.1.465–68)

The threat of social and political disorder represented in the beggars and vagabonds is thus refracted in the discourse of poverty into two quite different, but related, directions. On the one hand, such vagabonds reject, some quite consciously, the established order and so undermine hierarchical order in their quest for "freedom"; on the other hand, early modern writers can rarely imagine the beggars themselves as anything other than inverted images of themselves—organized by rank and gradation, the freedom they seek not really chaos but a new form of subjection. The thirst for subjection, it seems, is never slaked. The beggar may be a king in his own realm, but he still seeks a king over himself.

The hunger of the poor is similarly turned inside out in many texts, so that the beggars are observed indulging themselves at feasts and banquets. Dekker, as we saw in chapter 1, described one of the beggars' "Quarter-dinners" in *The Bel-Man of London*. Lelia offers a "banquet" to her disguised father in *The Captain* (4.4.63), as part of her planned seduction of him. In *A Jovial Crew*, the stage direction at 2.2.166 reveals "*The* Beggars *discovered at their feast. After they have scrambled awhile at their victuals,*" they sing of the "peck . . . pannum . . . lap, and good poplars of yarrum" (that is, meat, bread, buttermilk, and milk pottage) which "comfort[s] the quarron [body]" (lines 167–70). Festivities frequently get out of hand—these are only beggars, after all, as we saw in chapter 6, where Dekker, in *O per se O*, described the drunken rout concluding the Deerhurst Fair. The stage directions in Dekker's *Patient Grissil* (1603) tell the usual story: "*Enter* Rice *with a company of beggars: a Table is set with meate . . . A drunken feast, they quarrel and grow drunke, and pocket up the meate, the dealing of Cannes like a set at Mawe*" (4.3.11s.d., 38s.d.). Hunger and deprivation are thus rewritten as gluttony, drunkenness, and excess. One of the extremely rare exceptions to these romanticized inversions can be seen in Thomas Lodge and Robert Greene's *A Looking Glass for London and England* (c. 1590), when Samia and her son Clesiphon are shown near starvation ("Mother, some meat or else I die for want," Lodge: 4.33). When Samia appeals to her other son, Radagon, who has risen far in the world—"Behold thy brother almost dead for foode" (4.34)—her appeal is cruelly rejected, but, after an appropriate curse is uttered, "*a flame of fire appeareth from beneath, and* Radagon *is swallowed* (4.37). Thus he who denies food, becomes food.

When the poor Nurse in Jonson's *New Inn* asks in indignation, "Is poverty a vice?" and is answered, "Th'age counts it so," she mounts a stirring defense:

> God blesse them all,
> And helpe the number o'the vertuous,
> If poverty be a crime. You may object
> Our beggery to us, as an accident,
> But never deeper, no inherent basenesse.

> (5.5.58–62)

But the Nurse, as we might expect, is actually someone else: "A poor chare-woman in the Inne; with one eye, that tends the boy, is thought the Irish begger that sold him, but is truly the Lady Frampul, who left her home melancholique, and jealous that her Lord lov'd her not, because she brought him none but daughters, and lives, unknowne to her husband, as he to her" ("Persons of the Play"). *She* of course is not inherently base and can make this defense precisely because she is not a beggar. The available historical evidence in fact suggests that poverty was indeed counted a "vice," a moral failing more than an economic or systemic one. As John Earle observed (1628), even for an honest poor man, much less a beggar,

> the bitterest thing he suffers is his neighbours. All men put on to him a kind of churlisher fashion, and even more plausible natures are churlish to him, as who are nothing advantaged by his opinion. Whom men fall out with before-hand to prevent friendship, and his friends too to prevent engagements, or if they own him 'tis in private and a by-room, and on condition not to know them before company. All vice put together is not half so scandalous, nor sets off our acquaintance farther. . . . The least courtesies are upbraided to him, and himself thanked for none, but his best services suspected as handsome sharking and tricks to get money. (203–4)

The poor man, Nicholas Breton said, "is a stranger in the world, for no man craves his acquaintance, and his funeral is without ceremony, when there is no mourning for the miss of him" (33). The rich and the poor, the fat and the lean, are actually fused together in the fantasies of the "gentleman disguised as beggar" trope, in which poverty can be magically transformed into wealth, sickness into health, and baseness into nobility, through a revelation scene. But such revelations were not available outside of the theaters, for the rich "shunned like infection" (Breton: 33) their inverted images, and poverty and hunger remained ineradicable.

The courtiers of the Jacobean court appear to have badly miscalculated, on one occasion, how the representation of the low could trouble the high. I have already referred, in chapter 3, to the performance on 9 January 1618 of an entire "Play . . . of Tom of Bedlam, the Tincker and such other mad stuffe" (McClure: 2.129), as noted by John Chamberlain. Details of the performance are not available, but a week later, on the seventeenth, Chamberlain wrote an account of the play's reception: "The play or enterlude did not *riuscire* to the expectation, but rather fell out the wronge way, specially by reason of a certain song sunge by Sir John Finet, (wherin the rest bare the bourdon) of such scurrilous and base stuffe that it put the King out of his goode humor, and all the rest that heard it." The antics of this noble disguised as beggar not only did not amuse the monarch but apparently offended the entire court. The promoters should have known better, for the beggar is always a principle of scandal, scurrilous and base by definition. Chamberlain understood that confrontations of monarch and beggar could take place only *within* a play, and not on a stage at court where the royal audience would be implicated: "I marvaile the more that among so many none had the judgement to see how unfit it was to bring such beastly geare in publike before a Prince" (McClure: 2.131). Poor Tom was always "unfit" to be placed in confrontation with a prince.

Shakespeare clearly understood the "nobleman as beggar" trope well, employing it in *King Lear* and *The Winter's Tale*, and even in Cade's absurd claim of noble descent. But the substantial differences between Edgar and, say, Gerrard in *Beggars' Bush* or Momford in *The Blind Beggar of Bednall Green*, are clear enough. Even in the cases of his own "merry" beggars, Sly and Autolycus, Shakespeare's employment of the type raises questions about the very categories of class and gender that define them as vagrants. Moreover, Shakespeare continually maneuvers his plots so as to construct confrontations between nobility, especially kings, and beggars. The power that authorizes kings and dukes is inverted, exposed, and thereby questioned. Shakespeare may not have quoted his knowledge of vagrant types, their canting language, and their seamy habits, as frequently as some playwrights, and he seems to have known less about beggars and vagabonds than Dekker did, but that was true of virtually everyone at the time.[5] What Shakespeare does understand, perhaps better than the others—and certainly better than the Jacobean courtiers of January 1618—is the necessary political and social bond between high and low, fat king and lean beggar—two dishes, but to one table.

In Poor Tom, above all, the complex cultural tradition of the sturdy beggar is subject to the most profound Shakespearean interrogation. This representation is a powerful intervention in the Tudor-Stuart discourse of poverty in general, and in particular it is a response to the divided dramatic heritage by which beggars were represented either as devious counterfeitors or as romanticized quasi-pastoral figures. In modifying this tradition—in fusing the histrionic with the genuine voice of dispossession—and in rejecting idealization, Shakespeare represents in Edgar/Poor Tom an acute questioning of the beggar's cultural status. In giving this marginalized figure so rich and painful a subjectivity, Shakespeare created a voice unique in early modern drama.

[5] Shakespeare did not fail to bequeath ten pounds "unto the Poore of Stratford" in his will (David Thomas: 31).

WORKS CITED

Acts of the Privy Council, ed. J. R. Dasent. London, 1890–1964.

Adams, Thomas. *The Devills Banket.* London, 1614.

———. *Diseases of the Soule.* London, 1616.

———. *Mystical Bedlam, or the World of Mad-Men.* London, 1615.

———. *The White Devil, or the Hypocrite Uncased.* London, 1613.

Adelman, Janet. " 'Anger's My Meat': Feeding, Dependency, and Aggression in *Coriolanus*." In *Representing Shakespeare*, ed. Murray M. Schwartz and Coppelia Kahn. Baltimore: Johns Hopkins University Press, 1980.

———. "Introduction" to *Twentieth Century Interpretations of King Lear.* Englewood Cliffs, N.J.: Prentice-Hall, 1978.

Agnew, Jean-Christophe. *Worlds Apart: The Market and the Theater in Anglo-American Thought, 1550–1750.* Cambridge: Cambridge University Press, 1986.

Allderidge, Patricia. "Bedlam: Fact or Fantasy?" In *The Anatomy of Madness: Essays in the History of Psychiatry*, 2 vols., ed. W. F. Bynum, Roy Porter, and Michael Shepherd. London: Tavistock, 1985.

———. "Management and Mismanagement at Bedlam, 1547–1633." In *Health, Medicine, and Mortality in the Sixteenth Century*, ed. Charles Webster. Cambridge: Cambridge University Press, 1979.

Allen, Robert. *A Treatise of Christian Beneficence.* London, 1600.

Archer, Ian. *The Pursuit of Stability: Social Relations in Elizabethan London.* New York: Cambridge University Press, 1991.

Armin, Robert. *Collected Works*, ed. J. P. Feather. London: Johnson Reprints, 1972.

Awdeley, John. *The Fraternity of Vacabondes.* In *The Rogues and Vagabonds of Shakspere's Youth*, ed. Edward Viles and F. J. Furnivall. London, 1880.

Aydelotte, Frank. *Elizabethan Rogues and Vagabonds.* 1913; reprint New York: Barnes & Noble, 1967.

Babcock, Barbara, ed. *The Reversible World: Symbolic Inversion in Art and Society.* Ithaca: Cornell University Press, 1978.

Bacon, Francis. *The Works of Francis Bacon*, ed. James Spedding et al. London: Longmans, 1857–74.

Bakhtin, Mikhail. *Rabelais and His World.* Cambridge: MIT Press, 1968.

Bald, R. C. *John Donne: A Life.* Oxford: Oxford University Press, 1970.

Barclay, Alexander, trans. *The Ship of Fools.* 1874; reprint New York: AMS Press, 1966.

Barroll, J. Leeds. *Politics, Plague, and Shakespeare's Theater: The Stuart Years.* Ithaca: Cornell University Press, 1991.

Baudrillard, Jean. *Simulations.* New York: Semiotext(e), 1983.

Baxter, Stephen B., ed. *Basic Documents of English History.* Boston: Houghton Mifflin, 1968.

Beaumont, Francis, and John Fletcher. *The Dramatic Works in the Beaumont and Fletcher Canon,* ed. Fredson Bowers. New York: Cambridge University Press, 1985.

Beier, A. L. "The Canting Lexicon in Early Modern England: Antilanguage or Jargon?" In *The Social History of Language: Language and Jargon,* vol. 3, ed. Peter Burke and Roy S. Porter. London: Polity Press, 1995.

——. *Masterless Men: The Vagrancy Problem in England 1560–1640.* London: Methuen, 1985.

——. *The Problem of the Poor in Tudor and Early Stuart England.* London: Methuen, 1983.

Beier, A. L., and Roger Finlay, eds. *London 1500–1700: The Making of the Metropolis.* London: Longman, 1986.

Bellamy, John G. *Crime and Public Order in England in the Late Middle Ages.* London: Routledge, 1973.

——. *The Tudor Law of Treason.* London: Routledge, 1979.

Berger, Harry, Jr. "Text against Performance: The Gloucester Family Romance." In *Shakespeare's "Rough Magic": Renaissance Essays in Honor of C. L. Barber,* ed. Peter Erickson and Coppelia Kahn. Newark: University of Delaware Press, 1985.

Bergeron, David. *English Civic Pageantry, 1558–1642.* Columbia: University of South Carolina Press, 1971.

——. "Jack Straw in Drama and Pageant." *The Guildhall Miscellany* 2, no. 10 (1968): 459–63.

Berlin, Normand. *The Base String: The Underworld in Elizabethan Drama.* Rutherford, N.J.: Fairleigh Dickinson University Press, 1968.

Bernthal, Craig A. "Treason in the Family: The Trial of Thumpe v. Horner." *SQ* 42 (1991): 44–54.

Bevington, David. *Tudor Drama and Politics.* Cambridge: Harvard University Press, 1968.

Birch, Thomas. *The Court and Times of James the First.* London: Henry Colburn, 1849.

Blayney, Peter. *The Texts of King Lear and Their Origins.* Cambridge: Cambridge University Press, 1982.

Book of Sir Thomas More, The. 1911; reprint Oxford: Oxford University Press, 1961.

Boose, Lynda E. "*The Taming of the Shrew,* Good Husbandry, and Enclosure." In *Shakespeare Reread,* ed. Russ McDonald. Ithaca: Cornell University Press, 1994.

Born, Hanspeter. "The Date of *2,3 Henry VI.*" *SQ* 25 (1974): 323–34.

Bowen, Thomas. *Extracts from the Records and Court Books of Bridewell Hospital.* London, 1798.

——. *An Historical Account of the Origin, Progress, and Present State of Bethlem Hospital.* London, 1783.

Bradley, A. C. *Shakespearean Tragedy.* 1904; reprint New York: Fawcett, 1968.

Breen, Timothy H. "The Non-Existent Controversy: Puritan and Anglican Attitudes on Work and Wealth, 1600–1640." *Church History* 35 (1966): 273–87.

Breight, Curt. "Duelling Ceremonies: The Strange Case of William Hacket, Elizabethan Messiah." *JMRS* 19 (1989): 35–67.

——. " 'Treason Doth Never Prosper': *The Tempest* and the Discourse of Treason." *SQ* 41 (1990): 1–28.

Brenner, Robert. *Merchants and Revolution: Commercial Change, Political Conflict, and London's Overseas Traders, 1550–1653.* Princeton: Princeton University Press, 1993.

Breton, Nicholas. *The Good and the Bad; or, Descriptions of the Worthies and Unworthies of this Age.* London, 1616.

Bristol, Michael D. *Carnival and Theater: Plebeian Culture and The Structure of Authority in Renaissance England.* New York: Methuen, 1985.

——. "In Search of the Bear: Spatiotemporal Form and the Heterogeneity of Economies in *The Winter's Tale.*" *SQ* 42 (1991): 145–67.

Brome, Richard. *A Jovial Crew,* ed. Ann Haaker. Lincoln: University of Nebraska Press, 1968.

Brown, Stephen J. "Shakespeare's King and Beggar." *YR* 64 (1975): 370–95.

Bullough, Geoffrey, ed. *Narrative and Dramatic Sources of Shakespeare.* New York: Columbia University Press, 1975.

Bulow, G. von, ed. "Diary of the Journey of Philip Julius, Duke of Stettin-Pomerania, through England in the Year 1602." *TRHS* ns. 6 (1892): 1–67.

——, ed. "A Journey through England and Scotland made by Lupold von Wedel in the Years 1584 and 1585." *TRHS* n.s. 9 (1895): 223–70.

Bunyan, John. *Grace Abounding to the Chief of Sinners and The Pilgrim's Progress,* ed. Roger Sharrock. London: Oxford University Press, 1966.

Burckhardt, Sigurd. *Shakespearean Meanings.* Princeton: Princeton University Press, 1968.

Burt, Richard, and John Michael Archer, eds. *Enclosure Acts: Sexuality, Property, and Culture in Early Modern England.* Ithaca: Cornell University Press, 1994.

Burton, Robert. *The Anatomy of Melancholy,* ed. Holbrook Jackson. New York: Vintage Books, 1977.

Butler, Martin. *Theatre and Crisis, 1632–1642.* Cambridge: Cambridge University Press, 1984.

Canny, Nicholas. "The Permissive Frontier: The Problem of Social Control in English Settlements in Ireland and Virginia 1550–1650." In *The Westward Enterprise,* ed. K. R. Andrews, N. P. Canny, and P. E. H. Hair. Liverpool: Liverpool University Press, 1978.

Carroll, William C. " 'The Base Shall Top th'Legitimate': The Bedlam Beggar and the Role of Edgar in *King Lear.*" *SQ* 38 (1987): 426–41.

——. "Language, Politics, and Poverty in Shakespearian Drama." *ShS* 44 (1992): 17–24.

——. *The Metamorphoses of Shakespearean Comedy.* Princeton: Princeton University Press, 1985.

——. "New Plays vs. Old Readings: *The Division of the Kingdoms* and Folio Deletions in *King Lear.*" *SP* 85 (1988): 225–44.

Cartelli, Thomas. "Jack Cade in the Garden: Class Consciousness and Class Conflict in *2 Henry VI.*" In Burt and Archer.

Cater-Character, A, Throwne out of a Boxe by an Experienced Gamester (1631), ed. James O. Halliwell. London: Thomas Richards, 1859.

Cavell, Stanley. *Must We Mean What We Say?* New York: Scribner's, 1969.

Chambers, E. K. *William Shakespeare: A Study of Facts and Problems.* Oxford: Clarendon, 1930.

Chandler, Frank W. *The Literature of Roguery.* New York, 1907.

Chapman, George. *The Plays of George Chapman*, ed. Allan Holaday. Urbana: University of Illinois Press, 1970.

Chettle, Henry. *Kind-Hartes Dreame (1592)*, ed. G. B. Harrison. London, 1923.

Chettle, Henry, and John Day. *The Blind Beggar of Bednall Green*, ed. W. Bang. Louvain: Uystpruyst, 1902.

Chew, Samuel C. *The Pilgrimage of Life*. New Haven: Yale University Press, 1962.

Clark, Alice. *Working Life of Women in the Seventeenth Century*. New York: Harcourt, Brace & Howe, 1920.

Clark, Peter. "Popular Protest and Disturbance in Kent, 1558–1640." *EcHR* 29 (1976): 365–82.

———, ed. *The European Crisis of the 1590s*. London: 1985.

Clark, Peter, and Paul Slack, eds. *Crisis and Order in English Towns 1500–1700*. London: Routledge & Kegan Paul, 1972.

Clark, Stuart. "Inversion, Misrule and the Meaning of Witchcraft." *P&P* 87 (1980): 98–127.

Clay, C. G. A. *Economic Expansion and Social Change: England 1500–1700*. Cambridge: Cambridge University Press, 1984.

Clowes, William. *A Short and profitable Treatise touching the cure of the disease called (Morbus Gallicus) by Unctions*. London, 1579.

Cockburn, J. S., ed. *Calendar of Assize Records, Kent Indictments, Elizabeth I*. London, 1979.

———, ed. *Crime in England 1550–1800*. Princeton: Princeton University Press, 1977.

Coleman, D. C. "Labour in the English Economy of the Seventeenth Century." *Economic History Review* ser. 2, 8 (1956): 280–95.

Colie, Rosalie. *Paradoxia Epidemica: The Renaissance Tradition of Paradox*. Princeton: Princeton University Press, 1966.

Collections Part I. The Malone Society. Oxford: Oxford University Press, 1907.

Comedy of George A Green 1599, The. New York: AMS Press, 1985.

Cook, Ann Jennalie. *The Privileged Playgoers of Shakespeare's London, 1576–1642*. Princeton: Princeton University Press, 1981.

Copeland, Alfred J. *Bridewell Royal Hospital: Past and Present*. London, 1888.

Copland, Robert. *The Highway to the Spital-House*. Reprinted in Judges.

Cosin, Richard. *Conspiracie, for Pretended Reformation*. London, 1592.

Cox, Lee Sheridan. "The Role of Autolycus in *The Winter's Tale*." *SEL* 9 (1969): 283–301.

Crowley, Robert. *The Select Works of Robert Crowley*, ed. J. M. Cowper. London, 1872.

Crump, C. G., ed. *The History of the Life of Thomas Ellwood*. London: Methuen, 1900.

Curtis, T. C., and F. M. Hale. "English Thinking about Crime, 1530–1620." In *Crime and Criminal Justice in Europe and Canada*, ed. Louis A. Knafla. Waterloo: Wilfrid Laurier University Press, 1981.

Davies, C. S. L. "Slavery and Protector Somerset; the Vagrancy Act of 1547." *Economic History Review* 19 (1966): 533–49.

Davis, Natalie Zemon. *Society and Culture in Early Modern France*. Stanford: Stanford University Press, 1975.

Dekker, Thomas. *The Dramatic Works of Thomas Dekker*, ed. Fredson Bowers. Cambridge: Cambridge University Press, 1955.

———. *The Non-Dramatic Works of Thomas Dekker*, ed. A. B. Grosart. 1885; reprint New York: Russell & Russell, 1963.

Dessen, Alan C. "Two Falls and a Trap: Shakespeare and the Spectacles of Realism." *ELR* 5 (1975): 291–307.

Donne, John. *The Sermons of John Donne*, ed. Evelyn M. Simpson and George R. Potter. Berkeley: University of California Press, 1953.

Downame, John. *The Plea of the Poore, or a Treatise of Beneficence and Almes-Deeds: teaching how these Christian duties are rightly to be performed, and perswading to the frequent doing of them.* London, 1616.

Dubrow, Heather, and Frances E. Dolan. "The Term *Early Modern*" and "Reply." *PMLA* 109 (1994): 1025–27.

Earle, John. *Microcosmography; or A Piece of the World discovered.* In *Essays and Characters*, ed. Philip Bliss. London, 1811.

Ellis, Sir Henry, ed. *Three Books of Polydore Vergil's English History.* London: Camden Society, 1844.

"Extracts from the Old Court Books at Bridewell Hospital from 1559–1634." In *Under the Dome: The Quarterly Magazine of Bethlem Royal Hospital*, vols. 10, 11, 12 (1901–3).

Farnham, Willard. *The Medieval Heritage of Elizabethan Tragedy.* Oxford: Blackwell, 1936.

Feinberg, Anat. "The Representation of the Poor in Elizabethan and Stuart Drama." *L&H* 12 (1986): 152–63.

Felperin, Howard. *Shakespearean Romance.* Princeton: Princeton University Press, 1972.

Finlay, Roger, and Beatrice Shearer. "Population Growth and Suburban Expansion." In Beier and Finlay.

Fish, Simon. *A Supplicacyon for the Beggers*, ed. J. M. Cowper. London: EETS, 1871.

Fisher, F. J. *London and the English Economy, 1500–1700*, ed. P.J. Corfield and N. B. Harte. London: Hambledon, 1990.

Fletcher, Anthony, ed. *Tudor Rebellions.* London: Longmans, 1968.

Fletcher, John. *The Dramatic Works in the Beaumont and Fletcher Canon*, ed. Fredson Bowers. New York: Cambridge University Press, 1985.

Fletcher, John, and Philip Massinger. *Beggars' Bush*, ed. John H. Dorenkamp. The Hague: Mouton, 1967.

Ford, John. *The Lover's Melancholy*, ed. R. F. Hill. Glasgow: Manchester University Press, 1985.

———. *Perkin Warbeck*, ed. Donald K. Anderson, Jr. Lincoln: University of Nebraska Press, 1965.

Foucault, Michel. *Discipline and Punish: The Birth of the Prison.* New York: Vintage, 1979.

Frey, Charles. *Shakespeare's Vast Romance: A Study of "The Winter's Tale."* Columbia: University of Missouri Press, 1980.

Gabrieli, Vittorio, and Giorgio Melchiori, eds. *Sir Thomas More.* Manchester: Manchester University Press, 1990.

Gaby, Rosemary. "Of Vagabonds and Commonwealths: *Beggars' Bush, A Jovial Crew*, and *The Sisters.*" *SEL* 34 (1994): 401–24.

Gadd, Derek, and Alan Thompson. "Bridewell Palace." *The London Archaeologist* 3 (1979): 255–60.

Gerard, John. *The Autobiography of a Hunted Priest*, trans. Philip Caraman. New York: Pellegrini & Cudahy, 1952.

Goldberg, S. L. *An Essay on "King Lear."* Cambridge: Cambridge University Press, 1974.

Goldman, Michael. *Shakespeare and the Energies of Drama.* Princeton: Princeton University Press, 1972.

Granville-Barker, Harley. *Prefaces to Shakespeare, First Series.* London: Sidgwick and Jackson, 1927.

Greenblatt, Stephen. "Murdering Peasants: Status, Genre, and the Representation of Rebellion." *Representations* 1 (1983): 1–29.

——. *Shakespearean Negotiations.* Berkeley and Los Angeles: University of California Press, 1988.

Greevous Grones for the Poore. Done by a Well-willer, who wisheth, That the poore of England might be so provided for, as none should neede to go a begging within this Realm. London, 1621.

Griffiths, Paul. "The Structure of Prostitution in Elizabethan London." *Continuity and Change* 8 (1993): 39–63.

Gurr, Andrew. *Playgoing in Shakespeare's London.* Cambridge: Cambridge University Press, 1987.

Hager, Alan. *Shakespeare's Political Animal: Schema and Schemata in the Canon.* Newark: University of Delaware Press, 1990.

Halliday, M. A. K. "Antilanguage." In *Language as a Social Semiotic: The Social Interpretation of Language and Meaning.* London: Arnold, 1978.

Halpern, Richard. *The Poetics of Primitive Accumulation: English Renaissance Culture and the Genealogy of Capital.* Ithaca: Cornell University Press, 1991.

Hamilton, Donna B. *"The Winter's Tale* and the Language of Union, 1604–1610." *ShakS* 21 (1993): 228–50.

Hanson, Elizabeth. "Torture and Truth in Renaissance England." *Representations* 34 (1991): 53–84.

Harman, Thomas. *A Caveat or Warening for Commen Cursetors Vulgarely Called Vagabones.* In *The Rogues and Vagabonds of Shakspere's Youth,* ed. Edward Viles and F. J. Furnivall. London, 1880.

Hattaway, Michael. "Rebellion, Class Consciousness, and Shakespeare's 2 *Henry VI.*" *CE* 33 (1988): 13–22.

Hawkes, Terence. *That Shakespeherian Rag: Essays on a Critical Process.* London: Methuen, 1986.

Haynes, Jonathan. *The Social Relations of Jonson's Theater.* Cambridge: Cambridge University Press, 1992.

Heilman, R. B. *This Great Stage.* 1948; reprint Seattle: University of Washington Press, 1963.

Heinemann, Margot. " 'Demystifying the Mystery of State': *King Lear* and the World Upside Down." *ShS* 44 (1992): 75–83.

Heywood, John. *The Plays of John Heywood,* ed. Richard Axton and Peter Happe. Cambridge: D. S. Brewer, 1991.

Heywood, Thomas. *The Dramatic Works.* 1874; reprint New York: Russell & Russell, 1964.

Hill, Christopher. *The World Turned Upside Down.* New York: Viking, 1972.

Hitchcock, Robert. *A Politic Plat for the honour of the Prince, the great profit of the public State, relief of the poor, preservation of the rich, reformation of rogues and idle persons, and the wealth of thousands that know not how to live* (London, 1580). In *An English Garner*, ed. Edward Arber. London, 1879.

Holinshed, Raphael. *Holinshed's Chronicles*. 1807; reprint New York: AMS Press, 1965.

Holme, Randle. *The Academy of Armory*. Chester, 1688.

Howard, Jean. "Crossdressing, the Theatre, and Gender Struggle in Early Modern England." *SQ* 39 (1988): 418–40.

——. "The New Historicism in Renaissance Studies." *ELR* 16 (1986): 13–43.

——. *The Stage and Social Struggle in Early Modern England*. London: Routledge, 1994.

Howes, John. *John Howes' MS., 1582*, intro. William Lempriere. London, 1904.

Hume, Robert. *Early Child Immigrants to Virginia 1618–1642*. Baltimore: Magna Carta Book Co., 1986.

Hyperius, Andreas. *The Regiment of the Povertie. Compiled by a learned divine of our time D. Andreas Hyperius. And now serving very fitly for the present state of this realm. Translated into Englishe by H[enry]. T[ripp]. minister.* London, 1572.

Innes, Joanna. "Prisons for the Poor: English Bridewells, 1555–1800." In *Labour, Law, and Crime: An Historical Perspective*, ed. Francis Snyder and Douglas Hay. London: Tavistock, 1987.

Ives, E. W. "Shakespeare and History: Divergencies and Agreements." *ShS* 38 (1985): 19–35.

Jardine, Lisa. *Still Harping on Daughters*. 2d ed. New York: Columbia University Press, 1989.

Jeayes, I. H., ed. *Letters of Philip Gawdy*. London, 1906.

Johnson, D. J. *Southwark and the City*. Oxford: Oxford University Press, 1969.

Johnson, Robert C. "The Transportation of Vagrant Children from London to Virginia, 1618–1622." In *Early Stuart Studies: Essays in Honor of David Harris Wilson*, ed. Howard S. Reinmuth, Jr. Minneapolis: University of Minnesota Press, 1970.

Jonson, Ben. *Ben Jonson*, ed. C. H. Herford and Percy and Evelyn Simpson. Oxford University Press, 1925–52.

Jordan, W. K. *The Charities of London 1480–1660*. New York: Russell Sage, 1960.

Judges, A. V. *The Elizabethan Underworld*. 1930; reprint New York: Octagon, 1965.

Kaula, David. "Autolycus' Trumpery." *SEL* 16 (1976): 287–303.

Kelly, J. Thomas. *Thorns on the Tudor Rose*. Jackson: University Press of Mississippi, 1977.

Kernan, Alvin. "Formalism and Realism in Elizabethan Drama: The Miracles of *King Lear*." *RenD* 9 (1966): 59–66.

Kingsbury, Susan M., ed. *The Records of the Virginia Company of London*, 4 vols. Washington, D.C.: U.S. Government Printing Office, 1933.

Kinney, Arthur, ed. *Rogues, Vagabonds, & Sturdy Beggars*. Amherst: University of Massachusetts Press, 1990.

Kirschbaum, Leo. "Banquo and Edgar: Character or Function." *EIC* 7 (1957): 1–21.

Knack To Know A Knave, A, in *Old English Plays*, vol. 7, ed. W. Carew Hazlitt. London, 1874.

Knappen, M. M., ed. *Two Elizabethan Puritan Diaries, by Richard Rogers and Samuel Ward*. Chicago, 1933.

Knight, G. Wilson. *The Crown of Life*. 1958; reprint New York: Barnes & Noble, 1966.

Knights, L. C. *Drama and Society in the Age of Jonson*. 1937; reprint New York: Norton, 1968.

Koch, Mark. "The Desanctification of the Beggar in Rogue Pamphlets of the English Renaissance." In *The Work of Dissimilitude*, ed. David G. Allen and Robert A. White. Newark: University of Delaware Press, 1992.

Kozlenko, William, ed. *Disputed Plays of William Shakespeare.* New York: Hawthorn Books, 1974.

Kronenfeld, Judy. " 'So Distribution Should Undo Excess, and Each Man Have Enough': Shakespeare's *King Lear*—Anabaptist Egalitarianism, Anglican Charity, Both, Neither?" *ELH* 59 (1992): 755–84.

Langbein, John H. *Torture and the Law of Proof: Europe and England in the Ancien Regime.* Chicago: University of Chicago Press, 1977.

Laqueur, Thomas. "Crowds, Carnival and the State in English Executions, 1604–1868." In *The First Modern Society*, ed. A. L. Beier, David Cannadine, and James Rosenheim. Cambridge: Cambridge University Press, 1989.

Leinwand, Theodore B. "Negotiation and New Historicism." *PMLA* 105 (1990): 477–90.

——. "Shakespeare and the Middling Sort." *SQ* 44 (1993): 284–303.

Leonard, E. M. *The Early History of English Poor Relief.* 1900; reprint New York: Barnes & Noble, 1965.

Levin, Harry. "The Heights and the Depths: A Scene from *King Lear*." In *More Talking of Shakespeare*, ed. John Garrett. New York, 1959.

Lewis, C. S. *English Literature in the Sixteenth Century, Excluding Drama.* Oxford: Oxford University Press, 1954.

Life and Death of Jack Straw (1594), The. Oxford: Oxford University Press, 1957.

Lindsay, David. "Ane Satire of the Thrie Estaitis." In *Four Morality Plays*, ed. Peter Happe. New York: Penguin, 1979.

Lodge, Thomas. *The Complete Works of Thomas Lodge.* 1883; reprint New York: Russell & Russell, 1963.

Logan, W. H., ed. *A Pedlar's Pack of Ballads and Songs.* 1869; reprint Detroit: Singing Tree Press, 1968.

Long, William B. "The Occasion of *The Book of Sir Thomas More*." In *Shakespeare and "Sir Thomas More*," ed. T. H. Howard-Hill. Cambridge: Cambridge University Press, 1989.

Loving Mad Tom: Bedlamite Verses of the XVI and XVII Centuries, ed. Jack Lindsay. 1927; reprint New York: Augustus M. Kelley, 1970.

Lupton, Donald. *London and the Countrey Carbonadoed and Quartred into Severall Characters.* London, 1632.

——. *Objectorum Reductio; or Daily Imployment for the Soule.* London: 1634.

Luther, Martin. *The Book of Vagabonds and Beggars with a Vocabulary of Their Language and a Preface*, ed. D. B. Thomas. London: Penguin, 1932.

M., R. *Micrologia. Characters, or Essayes, of Persons, Trades, and Places, offered to the City and Country.* London, 1629.

MacDonald, Michael. *Mystical Bedlam: Madness, Anxiety, and Healing in Seventeenth-Century England.* New York: Cambridge University Press, 1983.

Macfarlane, Alan. *Witchcraft in Tudor and Stuart England.* London: Routledge, 1970.

Mack, Maynard. *"King Lear" in Our Time.* Berkeley and Los Angeles: University of California Press, 1965.

Manley, Lawrence, ed. *London in the Age of Shakespeare.* University Park: Pennsylvania State University Press, 1986.

Manning, Roger B. "The Origins of the Doctrine of Sedition." *Albion* 12 (1980): 99–121.

———. *Village Revolts: Social Protest and Popular Disturbances in England, 1509–1640* Oxford: Oxford University Press, 1988.

Manningham, John. *The Diary of John Manningham of the Middle Temple 1602–1603,* ed. Robert P. Sorlien. Hanover, N.H.: University Press of New England, 1976.

Marlowe, Christopher. *The Complete Plays of Christopher Marlowe,* ed. Irving Ribner. New York: Odyssey, 1963.

Marx, Karl. *Capital: A Critique of Political Economy,* ed. Frederick Engels. New York: Modern Library, 1906.

Massinger, Philip. *The Plays and Poems of Philip Massinger,* ed. Philip Edwards and Colin Gibson. Oxford: Clarendon, 1976.

Masters, Anthony. *Bedlam.* London: Michael Joseph, 1977.

McClure, N. E., ed. *The Letters of John Chamberlain.* Philadelphia: American Philosophical Society, 1939.

McMillin, Scott. *The Elizabethan Theatre and "The Book of Sir Thomas More."* Ithaca: Cornell University Press, 1987.

McMullan, John L. *The Canting Crew: London's Criminal Underworld.* New Brunswick: Rutgers University Press, 1984.

McPeek, James A. S. *The Black Book of Knaves and Unthrifts in Shakespeare and Other Renaissance Authors.* Storrs: University of Connecticut, 1969.

Melchiori, Giorgio. "*The Booke of Sir Thomas More.* A Chronology of Revision." *SQ* (1986): 291–308.

Merbury, Francis. *The Marriage between Wit and Wisdom,* ed. Trevor N. S. Lennam. Oxford: Oxford University Press, 1971.

Metz, G. Harold. "The Master of the Revels and *The Booke of Sir Thomas More.*" *SQ* 33 (1982): 493–95.

Middleton, Thomas. *The Works of Thomas Middleton,* ed. A. H. Bullen. London, 1885–86.

Mikalachki, Jodi. "The Female Vagrant in Early Seventeenth-Century England." Paper presented to the Modern Language Association meeting, Washington, D.C., 1989.

Mirror for Magistrates, The, ed. Lily B. Campbell. Cambridge: Cambridge University Press, 1938.

Montaigne. *Montaigne's Essays,* trans. John Florio. London: Dent, 1965.

More, Thomas. *The Complete Works of St. Thomas More.* New Haven: Yale University Press, 1965.

———. *The Four Last Things,* ed. D. O'Connor. London, 1903.

———. *Utopia,* ed. Robert M. Adams. New York: Norton, 1975.

Morison, Richard. *A Remedy for Sedition.* London, 1536.

Mowat, Barbara. "Rogues, Shepherds, and the Counterfeit Distressed: Texts and Infracontexts of *The Winter's Tale* 4.3." *ShakS* 22 (1994): 58–76.

Muir, Kenneth, ed. *Shakespeare; "The Winter's Tale": A Casebook.* London: Macmillan, 1969.

Mullaney, Steven. *The Place of the Stage: License, Play, and Power in Renaissance England.* Chicago: University of Chicago Press, 1988.

Nashe, Thomas. *Works,* ed. R. B. McKerrow, rev. F. P. Wilson. Oxford: Blackwell, 1958.

Neely, Carol Thomas. " 'Documents in Madness': Reading Madness and Gender in Shakespeare's Tragedies and Early Modern Culture." *SQ* 42 (1991): 315–38.

Notestein, Wallace, Frances Helen Relf, and Hartley Simpson, eds. *Commons Debates 1621.* 7 vols. New Haven: Yale University Press, 1935.

O'Donoghue, Edward G. *Bridewell Hospital: Palace, Prison, Schools from the Death of Elizabeth to Modern Times.* London: Bodley Head, 1929.

——. *Bridewell Hospital: Palace, Prison, Schools from the Earliest Times to the End of the Reign of Elizabeth.* London: Bodley Head, 1923.

Orders Appointed to be executed in the Cittie of London, for setting roges and idle persons to worke, and for releefe of the poore. London, 1582(6?).

Overburian Characters, The, ed. W. J. Taylor. Oxford: Blackwell, 1936.

Palliser, D. M. *The Age of Elizabeth: England under the Later Tudors 1547–1603.* London: Longman, 1983.

Parey, Ambrose. *The Workes of that famous Chirurgion, Ambrose Parey,* trans. Thomas Johnson. London, 1634.

Patterson, Annabel. *Shakespeare and the Popular Voice.* Oxford: Blackwell, 1989.

Pearl, Valerie. "Puritans and Poor Relief: The London Workhouse, 1649–1660." In *Puritans and Revolutionaries,* ed. Donald Pennington and Keith Thomas. Oxford: Clarendon, 1978.

Peat, Derek. " 'And That's True Too': 'King Lear' and the Tension of Uncertainty." *ShS* 22 (1980): 43–53.

Peck, Russell A. "Edgar's Pilgrimage: High Comedy in *King Lear.*" *SEL* 7 (1967): 219–37.

Pedler's Prophecy, The, ed. John S. Farmer. 1911; reprint New York: AMS Press, 1970.

Peers, Edgar A. *Elizabethan Drama and Its Mad Folk.* Cambridge: Heffer, 1914.

Pendry, E. D. *Elizabethan Prisons and Prison Scenes,* 2 vols. Salzburg: Institut für Englische Sprache und Literatur, 1974.

——, ed. *Thomas Dekker.* Cambridge: Harvard University Press, 1968.

Pettet, E. C. "*Coriolanus* and the Midlands Insurrection of 1607." *ShS* 3 (1950): 34–42.

Pettit, Thomas. " 'Here Comes I, Jack Straw': English Folk Drama and Social Revolt." *Folklore* 95 (1984): 3–20.

Platter, Thomas. *Thomas Platter's Travels in England 1599,* trans. Clare Williams. London: Jonathan Cape, 1937.

Pound, John. *Poverty and Vagrancy in Tudor England.* London: Longman, 1971.

Power, M. J. "London and the Control of the 'Crisis' of the 1590s." *History* 70 (1985): 371–85.

Pugliatti, Paola. " 'More Than History Can Pattern': The Jack Cade Rebellion in Shakespeare's *Henry VI, 2.*" *JMRS* 22 (1992): 451–78.

Puttenham, George. *The Arte of English Poesie,* ed. Gladys D. Willcock and Alice Walker. Cambridge: Cambridge University Press, 1936.

Quaife, G. R. *Wanton Wenches and Wayward Wives: Peasants and Illicit Sex in Early Seventeenth Century England.* New Brunswick: Rutgers University Press, 1979.

Rackin, Phyllis. *Stages of History: Shakespeare's English Chronicles.* Ithaca: Cornell University Press, 1990.

Raigne of King Edward the Third, The, ed. Fred Lapides. New York: Garland, 1980.

Ramsey, Peter. *Tudor Economic Problems.* London: Gollancz, 1963.

Rappaport, Steve. *Worlds within Worlds: Structures of Life in Sixteenth-Century London.* Cambridge: Cambridge University Press, 1989.

Read, Conyers, ed. *William Lambarde and Local Government.* Ithaca: Cornell University Press, 1962.

Reed, Robert R., Jr. *Bedlam on the Jacobean Stage.* 1952; reprint New York: Octagon Books, 1970.

Ribner, Irving. *The English History Play in the Age of Shakespeare.* 1957; reprint New York: Barnes & Noble, 1965.

Rickey, Mary Ellen, and Thomas B. Stroup, eds. *Certaine Sermons or Homilies Appointed to be Read in Churches In the Time of Queen Elizabeth I (1547–1571).* Gainesville, Fla.: Scholars' Facsimiles, 1968.

Rid, Samuel. *The Art of Juggling or Legerdemaine.* London, 1612.

Rollins, Hyder E., ed. *A Pepsyian Garland.* Cambridge: Harvard University Press, 1971.

Rosenberg, Marvin D. *The Masks of King Lear.* Berkeley and Los Angeles: University of California Press, 1972.

Rowlands, Samuel. *The Complete Works of Samuel Rowlands.* 1880; reprint New York: Johnson Reprint, 1966.

Rowley, William. *A New Wonder, A Woman Never Vext.* In *A Select Collection of Old English Plays,* vol. 12, ed. W. Carew Hazlitt. London, 1875.

Run-awayes Answer, To a Booke called, A Rodde for Runne-awayes, The. London, 1625.

Salgado, Gamini, ed. *Cony-Catchers and Bawdy Baskets: An Anthology of Elizabethan Low Life.* Harmondsworth: Penguin, 1972.

———. *The Elizabethan Underworld.* London: J. M. Dent & Sons, 1977.

Salkeld, Duncan. *Madness and Drama in the Age of Shakespeare.* Manchester: Manchester University Press, 1993.

Saltonstall, Wye. *Picturae Loquentes* (1631). Oxford: Blackwell, 1946.

Schoenbaum, S. *William Shakespeare: A Compact Documentary Life.* Oxford: Oxford University Press, 1977.

Seaver, Paul. "The Puritan Work Ethic Revisited." *Journal of British Studies* 19 (1980): 35–53.

Seventeenth-Century Economic Documents, ed. Joan Thirsk and J. P. Cooper. Oxford: Clarendon, 1972.

Shakespeare, William. *The Complete Works of Shakespeare,* ed. David Bevington. New York: HarperCollins, 1992.

———. *Love's Labour's Lost,* ed. Richard David. London: Methuen, 1956 (Arden edition).

———. *The Second Part of King Henry VI,* ed. Michael Hattaway. Cambridge: Cambridge University Press, 1991 (New Cambridge edition).

———. *Shakespeare's Plays in Quarto,* ed. Michael J. B. Allen and Kenneth Muir. Berkeley and Los Angeles: University of California Press, 1981.

———. *The Winter's Tale,* ed. J. H. P. Pafford. London: Methuen, 1966 (Arden edition).

Sharp, Buchanan. *In Contempt of All Authority.* Berkeley and Los Angeles: University of California Press, 1980.

Sharpe, J. A. *Crime in Early Modern England 1550–1750.* New York: Longman, 1984.

Siemon, James R. "Landlord Not King: Agrarian Change and Interarticulation." In Burt and Archer (1994).

———. *Shakespearean Iconoclasm.* Berkeley and Los Angeles: University of California Press, 1985.

Sirluck, Katherine A. "Patriarchy, Pedagogy, and the Divided Self in *The Taming of the Shrew*." *UTQ* 60 (1991): 417–34.

Skelton, John. *The Complete English Poems,* ed. John Scattergood. New Haven: Yale University Press, 1983.

Skura, Meredith Anne. *Shakespeare the Actor and the Purposes of Playing.* Chicago: University of Chicago Press, 1993.

Slack, Paul. *The Impact of Plague in Tudor and Stuart England.* Boston: Routledge & Kegal Paul, 1985.

——. *Poverty and Policy in Tudor and Stuart England.* London: Longman, 1988.

——. "Poverty and Politics in Salisbury 1597–1666." In Clark and Slack (1972).

——. "Poverty and Social Regulation in Elizabethan England." In *The Reign of Elizabeth I,* ed. Christopher Haigh. London: Macmillan, 1984.

——. "Vagrants and Vagrancy in England, 1598–1664." *EcHR* 27 (1974): 360–79.

Smith, Abbot E. *Colonists in Bondage: White Servitude and Convict Labor in America 1607–1776.* Chapel Hill: University of North Carolina Press, 1947.

Spenser, Edmund. *Spenser's Faerie Queene,* ed. J. C. Smith. Oxford: Clarendon P, 1909.

Spivack, Bernard. *Shakespeare and the Allegory of Evil.* New York: Columbia University Press, 1958.

Spurgeon, Caroline F. E. *Shakespeare's Imagery and What It Tells Us.* 1935; reprint Cambridge: Cambridge University Press, 1968.

Stallybrass, Peter. "Patriarchal Territories: The Body Enclosed." In *Rewriting the Renaissance: The Discourses of Sexual Difference in Early Modern Europe,* ed. Margaret W. Ferguson, Maureen Quilligan, and Nancy J. Vickers. Chicago: University of Chicago Press, 1986.

Stallybrass, Peter, and Allon White. *The Politics and Poetics of Transgression.* Ithaca: Cornell University Press, 1986.

Stanley, Thomas. *Stanleyes Remedy: Or, the Way how to reform wandring Beggers, Theeves, high-way Robbers and Pick-pockets. Or, An Abstract of his Discoverie: Wherein is shewed, that Sodomes Sin of Idlenesse is the Poverty and Misery of this Kingdome.* London, 1646.

Starkey, Thomas. "A Dialogue Between Cardinal Pole and Thomas Lupset." In *England in the Reign of King Henry the Eighth,* ed. Sidney J. Herrtage. London: EETS, 1878.

Stevenson, J. "The 'Moral Economy' of the English Crowd: Myth and Reality." In *Order and Disorder in Early Modern England,* ed. Anthony Fletcher and John Stevenson. Cambridge: Cambridge University Press, 1985.

Stone, Lawrence. *The Crisis of the Aristocracy 1558–1641.* Oxford: Oxford University Press, 1967.

——. "State Control in Sixteenth-Century England." *EcHR* 17 (1947): 103–20.

Stow, John. *A Survey of London,* ed. C. L. Kingsford. Oxford: Clarendon, 1908.

Stubbes, Phillip. *Anatomy of the Abuses in England,* ed. F. J. Furnivall. London, 1877–79.

Students Lamentation . . . for the rebellious tumults lately in the Citie hapning. London, 1596.

Supple, Barry. *Commercial Crisis and Change in England, 1600–1642.* Cambridge: Cambridge University Press, 1959.

Tawney, R. H. *The Agrarian Problem in the Sixteenth Century.* London: Longmans, 1912.

Taylor, Barry. *Vagrant Writing: Social and Semiotic Disorders in the English Renaissance.* Toronto: University of Toronto Press, 1991.

Taylor, Gary, and Michael Warren, eds. *The Division of the Kingdoms.* Oxford: Clarendon, 1983.

Taylor, John. *The Praise and Vertue of a Jayle and Jaylers: With the Most Excellent Mysterie, and necessary use of all sorts of Hanging. Also A Touch At Tyburne For A Period.* London, 1623.

———. *The Praise, Antiquity, and commodity, of Beggery, Beggers, and Begging.* London, 1621.

———. *A Swarme of Sectaries, and Schismatiques.* London, 1641.

Thirsk, Joan. "Tudor Enclosures." In *The Tudors*, ed. Joel Hurstfield. New York: St. Martin's, 1973.

Thomas, David, ed. *Shakespeare in the Public Records.* London: Her Majesty's Stationery Office, 1985.

Thomas, J. E. *House of Care: Prisons & Prisoners in England 1500–1800.* Nottingham: University of Nottingham, 1988.

Thompson, E. P. "The Moral Economy of the English Crowd in the Eighteenth Century." *P&P* 50 (1971): 76–136.

Timpane, John P. "The Romance of the Rogue: The History of a Character in English Literature, 1497–1632." Ph.D. diss., Stanford University, 1980.

Todd, Margo. *Christian Humanism and the Puritan Social Order.* Cambridge: Cambridge University Press, 1987.

Tudor Economic Documents, ed. R. H. Tawney and Eileen Power. London: Longmans, 1924.

Tudor Royal Proclamations, ed. Paul L. Hughes and James F. Larkin. New Haven: Yale University Press, 1969.

Vickers, Brian. *The Artistry of Shakespeare's Prose.* London: Methuen, 1968.

Walter, John. "A 'Rising of the People'? The Oxfordshire Rising of 1596." *P&P* 107 (1985): 90–143.

Warren, Michael. "Quarto and Folio *King Lear* and the Interpretation of Albany and Edgar." In *Shakespeare: Pattern of Excelling Nature*, ed. David Bevington and Jay L. Halio. Newark: University of Delaware Press, 1978.

Webster, John. *The Complete Works of John Webster*, ed. F. L. Lucas. London: Chatto & Windus, 1927.

Weimann, Robert. *Shakespeare and the Popular Tradition in the Theater.* Baltimore: Johns Hopkins University Press, 1978.

West, Richard. *The Court of Conscience or Dick Whippers Sessions.* London, 1607.

Wheatley, H. B. *London Past and Present.* London: John Murray, 1891.

Wiener, Carol Z. "Sex Roles and Crime in Late Elizabethan Hertfordshire." *Journal of Social History* 8 (1975): 38–60.

Willen, Diane. "Women in the Public Sphere in Early Modern England: The Case of the Urban Working Poor." *SixCJ* 19 (1988): 559–75.

Williams, C. H., ed. *English Historical Documents*, vol. 5. London: Eyre & Spottiswoode, 1967.

Williams, Penry. *The Tudor Regime.* Oxford: Clarendon, 1979.

Wilson, Richard. " 'A Mingled Yarn': Shakespeare and the Cloth Workers." *L&H* 12 (1986): 164–80.

——. *Will Power: Essays on Shakespearean Authority.* Detroit: Wayne State University Press, 1993.

Wilson, Robert. *The Three Ladies of London.* In *Old English Plays*, vol. 6, ed. W. Carew Hazlitt. London, 1874.

Woodstock: A Moral History, ed. A. P. Rossiter. London: Chatto & Windus, 1946.

Wrightson, Keith. *English Society 1580–1680.* New Brunswick: Rutgers University Press, 1982.

Wrigley, E. A., and R. S. Schofield. *The Population History of England, 1541–1871.* Cambridge: Harvard University Press, 1981.

Youings, Joyce. *Sixteenth-Century England.* Harmondsworth: Penguin, 1984.

INDEX